98

C. STEIN NEB

DATE DUE

OCT. 13.1998		
OCT. 30.1998		
OCT. 09.1999		
6·13·06		

Demco, Inc. 38-293

D1563797

TRAINING STRATEGIES FROM START TO FINISH

TRAINING STRATEGIES FROM START TO FINISH

Paul G. Friedman, Ph.D.
University of Kansas
Lawrence, Kansas

Elaine A. Yarbrough, Ph.D.
Yarbrough & Associates, Communication Consultants
Boulder, Colorado

Prentice-Hall, Inc., Englewood Cliffs, New Jersey 07632

Library of Congress Cataloging in Publication Data

Friedman, Paul G.
  Training strategies from start to finish.

  Bibliography: p.
  Includes index.
  1. Employees, Training of.   I. Yarbrough, Elaine.
II. Title.
HF5549.5.T7F69   1985   658.3'124   84-26486
ISBN 0-13-926908-8

Cover design: Ben Santora
Manufacturing buyer: Ed O'Dougherty

Printed in the United States of America

10 9 8 7 6 5 4 3 2 1

ISBN   0-13-926908-8   01

Prentice-Hall International, Inc., *London*
Prentice-Hall of Australia Pty. Limited, *Sydney*
Editora Prentice-Hall do Brasil, Ltda., *Rio de Janeiro*
Prentice-Hall Canada Inc., *Toronto*
Prentice-Hall Hispanoamericana, S. A., *Mexico*
Prentice-Hall of India Private Limited, *New Delhi*
Prentice-Hall of Japan, Inc., *Tokyo*
Prentice-Hall of Southeast Asia Pte. Ltd., *Singapore*
Whitehall Books Limited, *Wellington, New Zealand*

To Michael and Reva

CONTENTS

PREFACE

Training is done in countless situations. Whenever someone wants to do something new or different, a learning process is required. At work learning occurs when someone joins the organization, a promotion or job switch occurs, new equipment is installed, when new procedures are introduced, or someone wants to do familiar work even better. Training creates a bridge from the status quo to the desired state of affairs by providing appropriate learning experiences.

Training takes innumerable forms. Sometimes it occurs during informal spontaneous interaction, in much the way that a mentor might converse with a protégé over lunch. Sometimes it is formal and structured: a teacher addressing an auditorium of students. Training is not a uniform process to which a single formula applies. Its function and form vary enormously from situation to situation.

It is tempting, nevertheless, to simplify it. Like the fable of the six blind men grasping the elephant, people tend to view the training process at one point and then assume that their discoveries there apply to all instances—no matter what the trainer's or the trainees' position may be. Oversimplifiers know or value a single approach, and then seek to apply it to whatever situation they encounter. Too often a mismatch exists and a feeble or even damaging training experience results. Denying the temptation of simplification, we have taken on, instead, the ambitious task of describing the elephantine training process as a *whole*.

In other words, we take a comprehensive view of training. We do this in several ways: (1) We integrate theory and methodology to give the college student, the working manager, the educator, the in-house trainer, and the free-lance consultant both the conceptual framework and innumerable "how-to's" of training. (2) We address both the content level (what is being taught) and the process level of training (how the instruction is carried out). (3) We discuss how to match training methods and learner needs appropriately. (4) We follow the trainer's efforts from the moment that he/she is first contacted about a possible training program through every step in such a project, to the point at which the final report is turned in. (5) We provide sufficient detail so that novice trainers can use this book as a guide through their first endeavors in this realm *and* seasoned experts can use it both for checking out how thoroughly they are doing their work, and for troubleshooting particular problems that arise in their most challenging projects. (6) We address training as a combination of science and art, to which contributions are continually being made by researchers and creative practitioners (and we attempt to be up to date in what we include here), rather than taking a cookbook, closed system, technician-oriented approach. (7) Finally, we take an ethical approach which assumes that the best outcomes of training emerge from a trainer-participant relationship that is mutually respectful and honest.

This book is organized into three sections. In Part I (Chapters 1 to 4) we provide, for the most part, the theoretical orientations from which we work. Specifically, in Chapter 1 is a comprehensive model of the learning process involved in training. The concepts of holism and "hard" and "soft" approaches to training are introduced. These concepts are applied to the phases of any learning sequence and to the skills needed by trainers in each phase. In Chapter 2 we extend this systems perspective to the process of diagnosing the problems which training is intended to solve. In Chapter 3 we provide specific steps for assessing trainees' needs. Finally, in Chapter 4 we explain our perspective on how change occurs and demonstrate its applicability to a comprehensive view of training.

Part II (Chapters 5 to 10) deals in detail with each phase of training described in our comprehensive model. These chapters review the methods most appropriate to each kind of training program.

Part III (Chapters 11 to 14) includes chapters that explain the training process itself and addresses special skills and problems likely to arise during that process. Specifically, Chapter 11 explains how to develop an overall training plan: how trainers can design and put together from start to finish an entire learning program. Chapter 12 discusses the "skills of facilitation" in depth. These are interventions introduced spontaneously in the midst of more structured training sessions to handle problems that arise and to improve the training as it goes along. Chapter 13 covers special problems related to trainer credibility and conflicts between people that often occur during training, and it suggests productive responses to those problems. Finally, Chapter 14 deals with efficient and effective approaches to evaluating training programs.

Training is conducted by many kinds of people—educators, technical

specialists, communication consultants, personnel directors, volunteer coordinators, religious educational directors, and others. To prepare students for these
roles, colleges and universities offer courses on the rationale and methods of
conducting training, usually in departments of communication, psychology,
business, or public administration. This book might be used in those courses. Or it
might be consulted by people already in specialized work roles who are asked to
do training and consulting but have little or no prior knowledge and experience to
call upon. We intend this book to be useful to people at every point in their
careers.

ACKNOWLEDGMENTS

We realize, like many other authors, after a project is completed that there are so many people from past and present to acknowledge that this task seems the most difficult. We first wish to thank each other for providing mutual support, hanging in there through what proved to be a long project, and helping each other understand that writing a book is both important and not important at all. Keeping perspective helps.

We also wish to acknowledge our editor, Dennis Hogan at Prentice-Hall for his support; Bob Walters, production editor, for efficient and friendly service in producing the book; and our reviewers: Mr. George Porchelli, Massachusetts Mutual Life Insurance Co., Prof. George S. Odiorne, University of Massachusetts, and Dr. Eileen Aranda, Arizona State University, who provided helpful, specific comments that led to important revisions.

The heart and soul of the book, however, are made up of two sets of people. First, our training and consulting clients over the past 33 years (collectively) who have allowed us to be a part of their learning and thus our learning. And our students at the University of Kansas and the University of Colorado who have taken in, given back, and challenged our thinking about training, facilitation, and change.

The second part of the heart of this book is made up of all those people who have influenced us in our own development. As of this writing, Paul is on a ship going round the world on the Semester at Sea program, doing what he is so superb at—teaching and inspiring. I know he would wish to acknowledge his former colleagues at Penn State and Queens College and now the University of Kansas for their support and encouragement. And also his family—Reva, Glen, Joy, and Jeremy—for helping him understand, as he has so often said, the real meaning of work and love.

I want to thank Jon Blubaugh who launched me into the field of training and consulting, taught me the ropes, furnished a wonderful role model as a person and trainer, and supplied support and confidence at any early stage of my development as well as a good duet partner on long drives across Kansas. To Richard Nadeau, a wonderful "brother" whose insights into human nature and whose sense of humor have given me the most basic *and* most developed ingredients of effective training, teaching, and being human. To Joyce Hocker and Bill Wilmot, two of the best teachers, trainers, and thinkers I have had the pleasure to know and the best soul-mates a person can have. For their persistent, unconditional support, and wonderful times at TeePee, I feel a deep sense of gratitude. To Sandy and Bill Sell-Lee for long-lasting friendship and many hours of discussion of "what's it all about." Their continuing growth and caring are an inspiration. To my dear friend, Vicki Hamer, without whose support, deeply felt faith in me and us, and baby-sitting, this book may not have been finished. To Sam Keltner for his unequaled skill in group facilitation and his untiring search for ways in which our strengths can be unleashed. To two former students, turned colleagues and friends, Jane Elvins and Mary Bendelow, for helping me through rough times with their presence and counseling. I also want to acknowledge Jane for helping proof-read the manuscript. To my parents, Homer and Drue Yarbrough, who ingrained in me the values that lead me to be concerned about human growth and development. To my colleagues in Certified Consultants International, North Central Region, whose competence and caring have infused me with continual hope.

And finally, to the two most important people in my life, Lindsay and Michael. To Lindsay, who waited 4 extra days to be born so that I could finish the book revisions and who has since provided me unbounded joy that enhances my work and life. And to Michael, my best friend and spouse, whose exquisite combination of gentleness and strength has furnished me a new vision toward which to aim in developing human potential.

CHAPTER ONE
COMPREHENSIVE TRAINING:
AN INTRODUCTION

A COMPREHENSIVE
APPROACH

The director of training and development for a growing company had just resigned. That unit had been quite effective, so the executive vice-president decided to promote a replacement from within. He called in for an interview each member of their generally young, bright, ambitious staff to determine who would be best for the job. During those interviews he inserted what to him were two key questions, which he phrased something like this:

"I am going to describe two approaches to training, and I want to ask two things about them: Which do you think we should emphasize in this department? and What are your qualifications for implementing it? The first approach is: finding out and then providing for our employees the training topics and formats which *they* prefer. The second is: preparing programs based on what *we* think our business requires—what our upper management group wants those folks to learn."

Each candidate thought for a moment and then made a case for one approach or the other and for their own ability to manage it. The V.P. generally was very impressed by their overall responses and by their expertise. His choice for the directorship, however, turned out to be a woman (Karen Wallace) whose answer to those key questions differed from the others. Karen argued that making

1

such a choice in the first place is unwise, that *both* approaches are essential, and that she had the skills needed to *integrate* the two.

Her response served to distinguish her from the other applicants. She did so in much the same way that this book is distinct from other books dealing with training. In the literature on human resources development many people and publications advocate the first approach (a bottom-up or "adaptive" philosophy), while others prefer the second (a top-down or "directive") approach. Proponents of each maintain that their particular style is more motivating, more efficient, or more readily transferred to the work setting than the other. However, neither claim to superiority is valid. Although the adaptive and directive approaches may appear contradictory, *both* can be effective when used appropriately. In fact, both are necessary.

Each is useful in different training situations, and each calls upon different, but complementary, capacities of the trainer. When being adaptive, the trainer must be sensitive and receptive to others. When being directive, the trainer must plan ahead carefully and execute those plans precisely. Knowing *when* and *how* to do both is neither simple nor easy—but being a well-balanced trainer is the only way to work successfully with whatever kind of training situation one encounters.

The traditional Oriental philosophy of Taoism provides a parallel set of ideas and a diagram we will adopt to illustrate this comprehensive approach (see Figure 1–1). Taoist writing describes the forces of yin and yang as the two qualities inherent in *all* human action. Yin is adaptive, and yang is directive. Neither is preeminent, nor are they mutually exclusive. Instead, "they are like the different, but inseparable, sides of a coin, the poles of a magnet, or pulse and

FIGURE 1–1   The Two Primary Dimensions of Training.

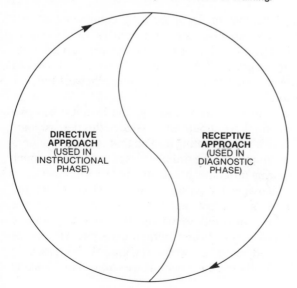

DIRECTIVE
APPROACH
(USED IN
INSTRUCTIONAL
PHASE)

RECEPTIVE
APPROACH
(USED IN
DIAGNOSTIC
PHASE)

interval of any vibration. There is never the ultimate possibility that either will win over the other, for they are more like lovers wrestling than enemies fighting" (Watts, 1975, p. 23). The process of balancing adaptive and directive approaches to training has two essential elements: the first is knowing in what *situation* to use each mode; the second is knowing how to *implement* each mode effectively. In each training project both modes play an essential role.

The initial stage of every training assignment involves *diagnosing the situation* with which one is confronted. The basic questions to be posed include: What is the status quo? What discrepancy exists between the current behavior of the trainees and what is desired? What are realistic goals for training? What method is needed to achieve the instructional objectives? To gather the information needed to answer such questions, the trainer must use an adaptive approach.

The next stage begins when a decision has been made as to what *instructional* plan seems best suited to that particular situation. As the trainer shifts from diagnosing to acting, a directive approach becomes appropriate. In this phase, the training program must be formulated and put into practice. It is time to have impact, to be proactive rather than reactive. This sequence of adaptive and directive modes is cyclical and can recur at several points throughout the course of a training project as its progress is assessed and shifts in procedure seem advisable.

Later in this chapter, the two major divisions of a training project (the diagnostic and instructional phases) are broken down further into the subcategories that lie within each.

THE TIMING AND TECHNIQUES OF BALANCED TRAINING

To stand before a group of trainees and require their attention, time, and energy is a hefty responsibility. Trainers strive to create a useful and enjoyable experience, one that will satisfy the trainees, the program's sponsor, and themselves. Under such pressure it is tempting to go with an approach that has proven its value. To find an assured winner, trainers tend to look first to their own past experiences. They are likely to employ methods that have had a personally beneficial impact on themselves, that have worked with past groups of trainees, or that they have been taught to use and feel they know well.

Drawing upon these sources for a methodology makes sense. The trainer needs to feel confident and comfortable about the approach being used. However, using only familiar methods adds up to a strictly trainer-centered approach to instruction. It ignores the learners and the situation they are in. When trainers do not focus upon the people they are to address and design procedures without reference to trainees' points of view, their program is in danger of being inappropriate and unsuccessful.

Training operates at the juncture where the interests of three parties intersect. They are the *trainer*, who acts as an intermediary between the *supervisor* or sponsor of the training (usually an administrator in an organization), and the *trainees*. Often, each sees differently the situation and the kind of training needed. It becomes the trainer's responsibility to synthesize their viewpoints.

Training is a process used by organizations to meet their goals. It is called into operation when a discrepancy is perceived between the current situation and a preferred state of affairs. The trainer's role is to facilitate trainees' movement from the status quo toward the ideal.

This movement occurs in a series of stages (see Figure 1–2). At each stage in the process a distinct form of training is most appropriate. In order to conduct a training program well suited to the situation they face, trainers must first identify at which point in the sequence the learners are. Below is a description and examples of the six major stages of the training process.

Awareness of Need

Usually, trainers first contact the system when told that a discrepancy exists between the current state of affairs and a more desirable one. This gap can occur as a result of two qualities inherent in all human functioning: *change* and

FIGURE 1–2   Six Stages of the Training Process.

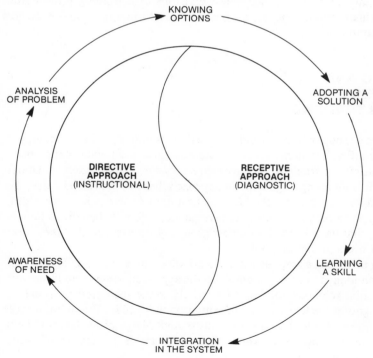

aspiration. Change is the "push," and aspiration is the "pull," that engender the need for training.

Changing creates problems that must be solved. Individuals move into or out of jobs; technology advances; companies merge; market demands shift; government regulations are introduced; and countless other changes regularly alter the circumstances within an organization. Each change imposes fresh demands upon the organization's personnel. Often they are unprepared to meet those demands. Such a situation requires remediation. The trainer can operate as a fixer or healer of the wounds caused by change.

Aspiration is the human tendency to dream, to grow, to want more. Even if things are running smoothly, an organization's leaders rarely are content. They envision methods of operating that will improve efficiency or productivity; they develop plans for expansion; they conceive new services, products, or markets. There is a pull toward new challenges. This higher level of aspiration calls for additional skills. Training in this case is creative, opening new doors for the organization and its personnel.

Whether pushed by changes or pulled by aspirations, the training process must start with the trainees' sensing a *need* for altered behavior.

Example: We were asked to present a workshop on supervisory skills at the national headquarters of a large supermarket chain. Several new managers had requested this session. However, to beef up enrollment, the personnel director also required a number of experienced regional managers to attend. He said, "It will be good for them." That older group began the workshop with their arms folded and a "what a waste of my time" attitude written across their faces. The spirits of the younger people were dampened by this know-it-all approach. Sensing this obstacle, we realized that we had to begin by developing that group's "Awareness of Need." Consequently, we spent a large portion of that morning evoking from the group examples of recent changes in their supervisory responsibilities that they had difficulty handling or wanted to handle more effectively, so that they would sense a need for what was to come. Then throughout the workshop we made a point of relating our material to the concerns that had been raised.

Analyzing the Problem

The second stage in training is assessing how best to deal with a need that has been identified. If a need is phrased in general terms (for example, "I want to become a better supervisor," or "Train that group to be better supervisors"), it next must be carefully analyzed. Otherwise, a broadside attack on that topic could result in much wasted effort. Points that already are familiar could be repeated. New dimensions could be skimmed over too lightly.

Robert Mager and Peter Pipe (1970) suggest a series of general questions to pose when analyzing any performance problem. These are briefly paraphrased below.

1. What is the performance discrepancy (or the difference between what is being done and what is preferred)?
2. Does it seem worthwhile and necessary to do something about this difference?
3. Would improving the use of a skill help?
4. If the answer to question 3 is "yes," consider:
   a. Has the skill been used before and forgotten?
   b. Can more adequate feedback be provided about how well the skill is used?
   c. Is there a simple, informal way to improve use of the skill?
   d. Can the skill be learned at all?
5. If the answer to question 3 is "no," ask:
   a. Is performing well penalized?
   b. Is poor performance rewarded?
   c. Is performing well satisfying and rewarded?
   d. Are there obstacles to performing well?

Exploring questions like these provides the analysis or understanding of the problem that permits meaningful progression to the next phase of the training process.

Example: We were asked to help the staff members in a dentist's office to work better as a team. We were told that several interpersonal problems had arisen among them recently and that at their last staff meeting, the whole group had agreed that a workshop on teamwork would be worthwhile. Clearly, that workshop need not begin with awareness of need. The danger with this group was providing training that might be irrelevant to the particular kinds of problems they face or that might inadvertently give the impression that we were taking sides in their dispute, thereby exascerbating their problems. To be appropriate and on target, their training needed to start at the second stage, "Analysis of the Problem."

Knowing Options

Trainers often deal with audiences composed of people in "open-ended" positions—jobs which include the freedom to use one's judgment or to choose an approach for handling problems. There is no one obvious, best way to operate. Individuals who work primarily with people, such as managers or salespeople, almost universally fit this description. They usually already know a way, or several ways, to carry out their roles. But they often seek training, nevertheless, in order to widen the range of alternatives they have available. They acknowledge a need, understand the problems that face them, and upon entering training, are at the point of wanting to learn more about the choices they have and how to pick from among them. It could be wasteful, even insulting, to dwell on motivational issues or problem analysis when training, for example, experienced salespersons, line foremen, or nursing home administrators in the use of communication skills. They know why and for what reason they want to learn such ways of dealing with the situations they face.

When providing options, it is helpful to include a means for choosing from among them. This usually involves two elements: (1) an objective explanation (a lecture) on how each optional procedure works and the rewards and costs likely to accompany use of each option, and/or (2) an experience that helps trainees develop a "contingency" theory (that is, guidelines regarding the circumstances for which each option is the most appropriate choice). For example, both a "productivity-oriented" and a "satisfaction-oriented" managerial style have predictable advantages and disadvantages, as well as situations in which one is recommended over the other (Fiedler, 1977).

This chapter itself provides an example of both the problem-analysis and option-building phases of training. It assumes awareness of a need. Hence, it moves quickly to the next stages: offering a way to analyze the trainer's role, options for carrying it out, and a contingency approach for choosing from among those options.

Example: We were asked to speak to a group of managers about "motivation." These were knowledgeable people; most had college (or advanced) degrees and years of experience in administrative roles. They had volunteered to attend and so felt a need, but had no problems in common to analyze. To meet them appropriately, we needed to present a useful option for motivating employees, one with which they were not familiar. Motivation is a topic that lends itself to a "Knowing Options" approach, since employees' effort can be heightened in several ways. Consequently, we informed that group of a new theory and methods for motivating employees; we suggested the kinds of situations in which it would work best; and we provided an opportunity for them to apply that motivational strategy in a simulated work situation. They each left armed with a new option to apply when needed in their own base of operations.

Adopting a Solution

Sometimes, trainers do not want to give learners increased choice-making power. A training program can be called for at a time when a single procedure is to be adopted, and the trainer is viewed as the expert hired to explain (or demonstrate) and advocate it. Examples of such instances are the orientation of new employees to an established work system, informing employees after a decision has been made to change from one way of operating to another, introducing a reorganization plan or a new technology to an organization, or when advice is being sought about how to proceed in a confusing situation.

The first stage in adopting a solution is explanatory. The procedure must be made clear and understandable to those who are to use it. The second is advocacy. The procedure must be recommended, its advantages touted to its users. The trainer's role here is to narrow trainees' choices, to channel their efforts down a particular path. The path can be one an administrator has determined, one the trainer is proposing (as an invited expert), or one which the trainees have volunteered to learn. In this role, the trainer is being highly directive (that is, shifting completely from an adaptive to a directive approach).

Example: We served in a consultant role to a state government seeking to change how social services were being provided to its handicapped citizens. This change was necessitated by funding cutbacks and was being done to coordinate more efficiently the help being provided by agencies concerned with health care, transportation, job training, education, and so on. The changes to be introduced would require the professionals involved to deal with their clients and each other differently than they were accustomed to. These new procedures could not be closely monitored and required more cooperation among that group than ever before. Hence, their genuine commitment was needed. At a general meeting, our role was to explain and advocate the new approach as one that would be better than what had been done previously, as one they all should adopt willingly and conscientiously. We were clearly in an "Adopting a Solution" training situation.

Teaching a Skill

Thus far, the emphasis has been on training as a way of affecting trainees' thinking—their attitudes about or knowledge of the work they are, or will be, doing. Often, trainers are called upon at a further step—to aid them in learning a skill (that is, how to carry out a specific sequence of behaviors).

To do so, trainees need to see each task performed correctly, to be told the steps involved in that task, to try out each step in a practice session, to receive feedback on the adequacy of their performance, and then to carry out those tasks on the job or in a situation as much like their job as possible.

Example: We were asked at one time to develop a training program for college professors to use newly acquired microcomputers. One might think that such a group would pick up these new skills quickly and comfortably. No so! They had become quite set (and relatively successful) in their use of typewriters and calculators and were hesitant to try something new (and perhaps feared losing face in the process). The manuals that came from the company that manufactured the equipment were lengthy and hard to follow. We had to devise our own step-by-step instruction, demonstration, and practice sessions on the use of the computers. We were in a "Learning a Skill" training situation.

Integration in the System

Even after new skills are mastered, they often must be employed back in a work setting where the trainees interact with many other people. If the training involves learning procedures which affect coworkers not present in the learning situation, some follow-up may be necessary to help the trainees incorporate those new procedures into the system where they must be used.

Most often people work as part of a team, in a network of coworkers, which must interact harmoniously to be effective. If one part of the team changes, the others may have to make some adjustments, as well. Sometimes the effects of training programs are dissipated because the system to which the trainees return is not supportive of what has been learned.

As a result, a final phase of training often deals with problems trainees may face in integrating new learnings into their back-home work contexts. This approach is needed when training occurs away from the work setting, or when the trainee group is drawn from a variety of organizations.

Another variation of "Integration in the System" focuses on developing better "team" interaction within an intact work group. In this case, *all* the members of a work unit meet together to clarify their goals, individuals' responsibilities in achieving those goals, and more cooperative or mutually helpful ways of dealing with each other on the job. Learning new skills may not be needed at all. Rather, the major emphasis here is on identifying when, where, and with whom people will use the skills they already know. The goal is weaving the input of capable people into well-integrated patterns so that the team's output is optimal.

Example: We led a "retreat" (a week-long session at a rural resort) for a group of managers, each of whom wanted to build a more productive and harmonious "culture" within their home organizations. One method we used to enhance their ability to do so was creating an optimal culture among ourselves at the retreat site. Since they all came from varied backgrounds and had their own well-developed management philosophies, culture building among them was a challenging task requiring much patient, frank negotiation. Toward the end of the retreat a substantial period of time was given to "Integration in the System"— anticipating problems likely to arise when integrating what they had learned back into their own work setting.

MISMATCHED TRAINING: A CASE STUDY

In this section you will have a chance to apply this scheme for analyzing training situations. We will use the hypothetical case of a well-intentioned, but inept trainer, Dr. Edgar Smart. After each episode in this account you are asked which of the six approaches he used and which approach would have been more appropriate for each program. The approaches we have discussed thus far are:

1. Awareness of Need
2. Analyzing the Problem
3. Knowing Options

4. Adopting a Solution
5. Learning a Skill
6. Integration in the System

Immediately following this case, on page 12, each episode is reviewed briefly, so you can check your answers.

East Heights is a rapidly growing suburb of an expanding metropolitan area. The new superintendent of schools, Charles Roy, wanted his staff to satisfy the expectations of a vocal, education-oriented constituency. He hired Dr. Edgar Smart as his new director of training and development. Dr. Smart was a congenial professor at a nearby university and recently had conducted some well-received workshops for the school district. He was excited about his new post, and he plunged into his work enthusiastically.

(1)   Dr. Smart's first assignment was conducting a workshop for the junior high school principals. They were a group made up mostly of men with long seniority in the district. Parents had complained to Superintendent Roy that several principals were unduly strict and rigid in disciplining their children. The principals' disciplinary actions were in response to student violations of school rules regarding orderly classroom, recess, and lunchroom behavior.

Dr. Smart decided that it would be best to establish student-teacher judiciary boards in each of the schools. Such a board would hear cases of student misconduct and decide how to handle them. The board would take much pressure off the principals and help the students and their parents feel that they were being fairly treated. At the workshop the principals were cordial, but they gave his proposal a cool reception. One month later none of the boards had been organized.

When Dr. Smart shared his disappointment about their poor response with others in the district, he learned that those principals did not see their discipline policies as needing revision. They believed that it was the parents and their children who needed to change their ways, not themselves.

What training approach did Dr. Smart use? _____

What training approach would have been more appropriate? _____

(2)   From this experience, Smart recognized that trainees' views need to be aired. He vowed not to omit that diagnostic process in the future. Consequently, when his next assignment came up—to help the district's school board prepare to work with the architects of a new building—he spent a major portion of that time asking the school board members what they thought should be done. He assured them that he understood and valued their views, and he tried to get them to agree on what their priorities were.

The board members left feeling disappointed that Dr. Smart had offered them no new ideas from his reputed knowledge of recent trends in school programs and architecture.

What training approach did Dr. Smart use? _____

What training approach would have been more appropriate? _____

(3)   At their weekly meeting, Superintendent Roy told Dr. Smart of the school board members' reactions. Smart also was given his next responsibility: to work with district guidance counselors concerned about reducing absenteeism in the schools. Wanting to heed his recent feedback, Dr. Smart this time presented many creative alternatives for dealing with this perplexing problem.

But the counselors remained confused about which of the proposed methods to implement, since the causes of the absences still were unknown.

What training approach did Dr. Smart use? _____

What training approach would have been more appropriate? _____

(4)   Realizing, too late, that in this instance the source of the problem needed more exploration, Dr. Smart spent the bulk of his next workshop—training part-time paraprofessional aides in the reading program—discussing why reading instruction was so important and what kinds of problems students were likely to have with it.

The reading teachers complained, however, that after the training their new aides still didn't know how to do their assignments, tutoring students in specific reading skills, without additional time-consuming coaching on their part.

What training approach did Dr. Smart use? _____

What training approach would have been more appropriate? _____

(5)   Since he was ever willing to learn, when Dr. Smart worked with his next group—the conflict-ridden food services staff—he emphasized practicing several concrete skills of tactful communication, and they mastered these techniques.

However, the fuzzy lines of responsibility in their area were ignored, so the essence of their problem remained unchanged. These new skills went unused and were quickly forgotten.

What training approach did Dr. Smart use? _____

What training approach would have been more appropriate? _____

(6)   Not wanting to repeat his mistake, Dr. Smart worked on role clarification and team development with the math teachers he saw next. They were about to use new texts and a new system that Superintendent Roy favored, but which they did not yet believe would be an improvement over their old way of operating.

When they continued to feel resistant and left the books unused, Superintendent Roy finally acted on his growing frustration with our conscientious Dr. Smart and fired him. Thank goodness, Smart had only taken a leave of absence from the state university, and he returned to the familiar classroom where his efforts were appreciated.

What training approach did Dr. Smart use? _____

What training approach would have been more appropriate? _____

This account is exaggerated, of course, to emphasize the consequences of *inappropriate* training. In each instance, Dr. Smart applied to the new group he faced insights gleaned from the last one. Since each group presented a different need, he consistently was off base and ineffectual.

Instead of being past-centered or self-centered, trainers must address each new situation freshly. They investigate the context in which training is to be applied and seek to identify what need is to be met before deciding how to proceed. Dr. Smart was so eager to be directive, to put across a potent training program, that he ignored the adaptive phase of training—*diagnosing the kind of training each situation called for.*

Let us review each of his actions:

(1)   The veteran junior high principals Dr. Smart encountered did not believe that they needed to change, so they rejected his "Adopt a Solution" proposal. To be appropriate, their training process should have begun at "Awareness of Need." A training program cannot proceed successfully until trainee motivation to learn is achieved.

(2)   The school board in Dr. Smart's district was to meet with an architectural team to develop plans for a new building. They knew that the building was needed and what services it should house. However, they were hesitant to propose a plan for its design before informing themselves about the available options from which they could choose. Instead of "Analyzing the Problem," they wanted to enlarge their repertoire of choices for making that decision: "Knowing Options."

(3)   The counselors Dr. Smart faced, who wanted to deal with absenteeism more effectively, were at the second point in the change process. They were aware of a symptom that concerned them and were willing to do something about it, but they had only a hazy understanding of the nature of the problem that lay behind it. Hence, they had as yet no basis for judging what solution would work best.

Their training should not begin as he did, with "Knowing Options." To be appropriate for this group, their session had to commence back at the second stage, "Analyzing the Problem." The counselors needed to explore questions such as, "Who are the absentees?", "What causes their absences?", and "What causes are within our power to change?" In other words, they needed to learn more about the problem they faced before they could decide whether, or how, they would deal with it and before they could make use of training directed at options for solving that problem.

(4) Dr. Smart was asked to help a group of aides in the district's reading program "Learn a Skill." They were hired to relieve teachers assisting individual students with reading difficulties. Their work involved specific tasks or programmed procedures that they had to learn. Knowing them would not be enough; they had to master their performance. Instead, he spent his time with them "Analyzing the Problem."

(5) The food services staff in Dr. Smart's district often fought among themselves and obstructed each other's performance of their jobs. Their problems were due chiefly to a lack of specificity about what each person was to do and resentments that arose when people did not do what was needed for each of them to carry out their work. They needed to develop clear job descriptions and agreements about how they could be mutually helpful. They had to learn how to "Integrate into the System" their own work. Teaching them communication skills ("Learning a Skill") was inappropriate because the norms in their work environment at the time did not as yet support that mode of interaction. For such skills to prove useful, they would have to agree as a team to adopt them, their supervisor would have to support the use of the new skills, a time for staff meetings might have to be provided, and subsequent training sessions in which their use was reinforced and problems were reviewed might have to be scheduled. In this, and in comparable instances, the training process must include (1) helping trainees integrate innovations into the larger system in which they are to use them, and/or (2) working with everyone in that unit to facilitate better team interaction.

(6) The math teachers were ready to "Adopt a Solution" when Dr. Smart was asked to explain their new system and new materials. They were not being asked to choose a method; they were to be told what to do. Instead, he used an "Integrate in the System" approach.

THE FLEXIBLE TRAINER

Once trainers discern the stage at which learners need to be addressed, they must then provide a program well suited to the identified need. Each point in this comprehensive sequence calls for a somewhat different set of training abilities. For trainers to facilitate change effectively at every point, they must approach their roles in a *flexible* way—being prepared to call upon the roles, skills, techniques, and personal qualities most appropriate for each kind of training.

The different hats a trainer must wear are summarized in Figure 1–3. The flexible trainer is someone who can take any of six basic "roles" vis-à-vis the trainees.

When speaking of roles, the image of the trainer as a "phony" or a "manipulator" may come to mind. That is not our intention. Being flexible is malevolent only when one is deceptive and shifts roles for surreptitious reasons.

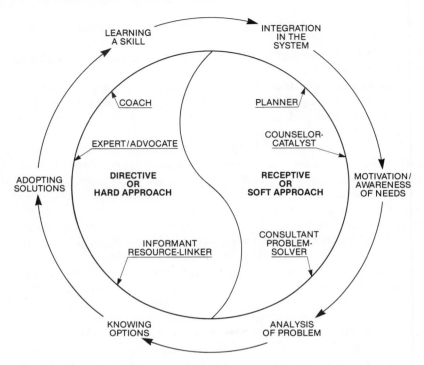

FIGURE 1–3   Roles of the Flexible Trainer.

Ethical trainers always are fully straightforward about how they view the training situation and what they hope will result from it. They communicate honestly and openly about what they are trying to do and why. Their flexibility is intended to accommodate rather than manipulate trainees. For example:

1. *Awareness of Need Stage.* When trainees are anchored in old, dysfunctional habits, the trainer will operate as a *counselor* or *catalyst* to encourage them to take a positive attitude and become more open to learning.
2. *Analyzing the Problem Stage.* When trainees are ineffectively jumping to conclusions about courses of action before thoroughly understanding the problem that confronts them, the trainer acts as a *consultant* facilitating their use of a step-by-step problem-solving process.
3. *Knowing Options Stage.* When trainees use a limited range of methods to handle situations for which (under certain circumstances) other alternatives would be more effective, the trainer becomes an *informant*, one who introduces them to resources or options they can add to their repertoires.
4. *Adopting a Solution Stage.* When trainees need to be set upon a course of action that is prescribed for them or they need advice about the best way to proceed in a perplexing situation, the trainer is looked to as an *expert* or *advocate* for a plan that will provide advice, structure, direction, or purpose to the trainees' behavior.
5. *Learning a Skill Stage.* When trainees must be taught a skill that is to be used in a predictable, consistent fashion, the trainer acts as a *coach* until they can perform that skill competently.

6. *Integration in the System Stage.* When trainees are not working harmoniously with the people with whom they must collaborate, or when they are to learn a skill that might violate the norms of their work group, the trainer is a *planner* helping them to develop ways to remove obstructions to integrating their efforts with others'.

For each role there are instructional *methods* commonly used to achieve the intended goal. To implement each of these methods effectively, specific *skills* are required of the trainer. These skills are not simply memorized behaviors; they must be based upon, or have at their source, related *personal qualities* which characterize how the trainer carries them out. These dimensions of each training role are summarized in Figure 1–4.

The flexible trainer is one who can call into play at appropriate points in the training process the methods, skills, and personal qualities needed at the time. For example:

1. *Awareness of Need Stage.* When assessing and heightening trainees' motivation to learn, trainers often use self-report *diagnostic instruments* and *include learners in the planning* of the instructional program. During their interaction, trainers respond *empathically* to learners' viewpoints and also provide constructive *confrontations* to focus their attention on data suggesting that change is needed. Trainers in this counselor or catalyst role balance *sensitivity* (to learners' frame of reference) and

FIGURE 1–4   Roles, Personal Qualities, Skills, and Methods of Trainers.

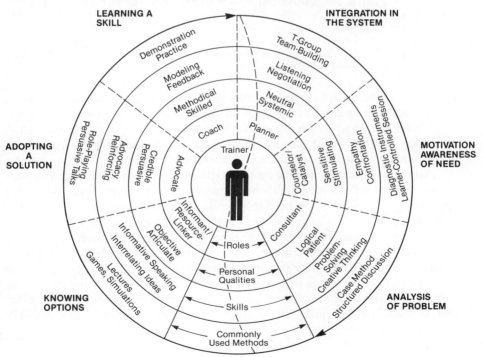

stimulation (to enhance their enthusiasm about the potential benefits of participation in the training session).

2. *Analysis of Problem Stage.* When exploring the nature of the work situation being dealt with in training, *case studies* and *critical incidents* often are used in a *structured discussion format* to experience using a thorough *problem-solving* or creative-thinking approach to analyzing problems and generating solutions. The trainer acts as a consultant who *patiently* and *logically* helps trainees to think through those situations by themselves, rather than directing them to predetermined answers.

3. *Knowing Options Stage.* When introducing trainees to new options in their work, *lectures* and *simulations,* including management games, often are used for explaining and trying out the techniques being taught. The trainer must be *articulate* in describing the requisite knowledge, as well as *objective* in presenting its potential utility in the context of the full range of options available.

4. *Adopting a Solution Stage.* When a solution must be adopted, the trainer usually describes it as vividly as possible, using *persuasive* techniques for gaining commitment to its use, and provides opportunities to *role-play* the technique(s) being advocated. To fill the role of advocate effectively, the trainer must be *credible* to the learners, *persuasive* in arguing for that system's benefits, and *supportive* or *reinforcing* of their efforts to adopt it.

5. *Learning a Skill Stage.* When teaching a skill, the trainer must provide a *demonstration* and *practice* in its use. Acting as a coach, the trainer ideally is *competent in the skill* being taught and can *model* it, then *methodically* takes the learners through a series of trials until they, too, have mastered it.

6. *Integration in the System Stage.* When a system-wide change is sought, the personnel often need to meet together as a *group* to air their assumptions, expectations, and grievances. To mold disparate viewpoints into a coordinated team, the trainer must be a *neutral, aware* listener, who, acting as a planner, has the concerns of the *whole system* in mind (as well as individuals' vested interests) and can help *negotiate* conflicting views.

One of these roles can predominate in a training program, or, in many cases, the trainer has to move through all of them during the course of a single project. The latter occurs when dealing with a heterogenous group in which individual members are at different stages in this sequence. The trainer may have to shift from one role or method to another, from moment to moment in the course of a workshop, as questions are raised and activities are carried out that touch on each phase. Hence, a flexible comprehensive trainer has all these methods, skills, and personal qualities in reserve available for use. Trainers whose range is limited to only a portion of the circle are handicapped in their adaptability.

In the remainder of this book we develop in detail how trainers can operate effectively in each of these six roles. Clearly, we have set very high standards for trainers to attain. The trainer's position inherently requires being an extraordinary performer, being someone who sets an example and maps the route for others to follow. Becoming a thoroughly competent trainer is an unending task. However, the fact that there is infinite room for growth makes this profession infinitely stimulating and rewarding.

CHAPTER TWO
THE DIAGNOSTIC
FRAMEWORK

Chapter 1 addressed the two general dimensions of comprehensive training: diagnosis and instruction. Diagnosis was defined as being aware of and analyzing problems or needs. The training program itself *may* involve diagnostic activities, but diagnosis of the clients' problems *prior* to the training *must* always occur.[1] Dr. Smart's difficulties highlight the importance of accurate diagnosis for successful training and the devastating effects of inaccurate (or the absence of) diagnosis. Before explaining more fully the phases of the comprehensive training model, in Chapters 2 and 3 we deal with problem diagnosis and analysis *before* the training.

WHY IS A DIAGNOSTIC FRAMEWORK NEEDED?

Diagnosis carries with it the assumption that a problem or deficiency exists. Trainers must have a *framework* that guides them in identifying those problems. They must know *what* to look for and *how* to look at it.

---

[1]Instructional methods to use for diagnostic work in the actual training are discussed in Chapters 5 and 6.

Specifically, a framework serves several functions. First, it allows the trainer to sort problems from nonproblems. That is, until attitudes or actions are defined as problems, there need be no solutions. For example, until racism was defined as a problem, vigilantes requiring blacks to "get out of town by sundown" were not a problem. Until Abraham Maslow described and documented the potential that people have, the dissatisfaction many people felt with conformity and adaptation (or the Psychopathology of the Normal) was not legitimized as a "problem." Until corporations were defined as institutions that should consider individual as well as organizational needs, employee complaints about the tedium of their jobs were ignored.

Second, a framework simplifies the complexity of human interaction. For example, a lack of trust in an organization is indicated by many different symptoms—increasingly rigid rules, covert decision making, and decreased flow of information. Talking about trust in training is more efficient than dealing with each individual symptom of distrust as if it were not connected to a more generic problem.

Third, a framework increases the chance that the processes of diagnosis, instruction, and training evaluation will be congruent. For example, a trainer may diagnose the problems of an organization as due to mistrust originating from guarded information and autocratic managerial styles. Without a clear and integrated framework, trainers may proceed to conduct the training in an autocratic style—telling managers what must be done to solve their problems—which is inconsistent with their objectives. Since we believe that the way in which the training is conducted and evaluated has a strong impact on what trainees learn, trainers in this situation may accentuate the problem they were hired to help alleviate.

Finally, having a clear framework for diagnosis provides guidelines for designing actual diagnostic tools—questions to ask, processes to observe, questionnaires to use and/or construct. (Specific examples of these tools are provided in Chapter 3.)

WHAT IS A COMPREHENSIVE DIAGNOSTIC FRAMEWORK?

Our framework is based on viewing people and organizations as systems.[2] We see people as complex wholes, interdependent with others through the process of communication. We also see them as constantly changing, with each part of a system affecting all others whether that system is an individual person, an interpersonal relationship, a group, an organization, or a group of organizations.

[2]For more technical discussions of the systems approach, see Monge (1977); Ruben (1972, 1978); Watzlawick et al. (1967); Capelle (1979); and French and Bell (1973).

As George Leonard says when describing the relationships among people and their environment: "We all share the same breath." We need each other to accomplish goals and to change in more productive ways. When we understand the *characteristics* of systems and, more particularly, *effective* systems, we have a standard of comparison for diagnosing problem situations.

HOW IS A SYSTEMS FRAMEWORK USED IN DIAGNOSIS?

We must first understand the characteristics of systems before we demonstrate how these concepts can be used in training and consultation (see Table 2–1).

TABLE 2–1   Diagnostic Questions About Systems

KEY QUESTIONS	SYSTEM CHARACTERISTICS
1. What are the *important parts of the system* that influence its outcomes? In an organization, for example, the following could be key elements:	1. Elements
• Key purposes of the system—overt and covert?	
• Key people—formal and informal?	
• Leadership—formal and informal; styles?	
• Rewards—for what and how distributed?	
• Culture—shared values? Norms? Formal and informal rules?	
• Developed and undeveloped skills?	
• Structure—in place to accomplish what purposes?	
• Means of handling conflict?	
2. At what *level* are you intervening?	2. Environment
• What other levels (other people, groups, organizations) have an impact on the operation of the level at which you are intervening?	
• If you intervene in a certain way, how will that affect other levels? Positively? Negatively?	
• What skills need to be developed or other preparations made to help make changes in one part of the system compatible with other parts? And vice versa?	
• Can you work with one level of a system and have a productive impact without working directly with other parts?	
• Who has the power to define the problem being addressed? At what level in the system is that person(s)? Is he/she willing to consider multiple levels of the system as being potentially responsible for the problem?	

TABLE 2-1   Diagnostic Questions About Systems (*continued*)

KEY QUESTIONS	SYSTEM CHARACTERISTICS
3. *What is* being *conveyed* to whom in the system? <ul><li>How is it being conveyed?</li><li>Does the content and style of communication match the purpose of the job? The relationship?</li><li>Do people in the system perceive that they have choices in how they communicate information?</li></ul>	3. Communication
4. What is the *stage of development* of the system? Autocratic? Participative? etc. <ul><li>Are different parts of the system at different stages of development?</li><li>How rapidly is the system changing? Does it need to change?</li><li>How does the stage of development need to affect the trainer's behaviors and planned interventions?</li><li>To what stage of development does the system aspire? To match its goals? To further its development?</li><li>Is the system willing to commit the time and resources to move to that stage of development?</li><li>Can it move to that stage of development given its resources—personnel? structure? product? mission? etc.</li></ul>	4. Time and change

Elements

Certain *elements* are common to all systems. For example, within an organizational system, Weisbord (1976) identifies six key elements that are crucial to its operation. They are the Purposes of the organization (what business are we in?), the Structure (how do we divide up the work?), the Rewards (do all needed tasks have incentives?), Helpful Mechanisms (have we adequate coordinating technologies for our purposes?), Relationships (how do we manage conflict among people? with technologies?), and Leadership (how do people keep all the other elements going and coordinated?).

Whether trainers are doing technical or interpersonal relations training, they must know the elements within a system that make a difference in how it functions. When key elements are not considered, the training is less likely to have an impact on the system. For example, if a trainer focused only on leadership, and that organization did not have a clear statement of, or agreement on, its purpose, the "trained" leaders would not know in what direction to lead and the system likely would be just as ineffective as before the training (see Egan, 1978).

Environment

Second, human systems exist within levels of ever-higher complexity. The intrapersonal level (within the individual) is not as complex as the interpersonal level (between two people); and the interpersonal is not as complex as the group level; and so on. That is, each level of a system has an *environment*; it is embedded in a context made up of higher levels of complexity. The individual is embedded in an interpersonal context such as marriage, friendship, manager/ subordinate. Interpersonal systems are embedded in groups such as work teams, families, and so on. Groups exist within a set of groups—the finance department, the marketing division. Several groups make up an organization; and an organization is part of an industry made up of other organizations which are embedded in a society.

Identification of system levels and their environments is important for several reasons. First, a systemic approach implies that the levels are related and that a change in one affects others. Conversely, if there is attempted change at one level without consideration for how that change affects other levels in the environment, the change is likely to be ineffective. For example, we were asked to conduct a training program for supervisors of the janitorial staff at a major university. The symptoms described by the supervisors included high turnover rate, high absenteeism, and "sabotage" of the cleaning efforts, such as long breaks. The supervisors wanted to know how to reduce "the problems created by the janitors." Beginning from the assumption that levels of systems affect each other, we first asked the supervisors to list the incentives that brought the janitors to work on time, helped them do a good job, and kept them on the job; and what incentives reinforced the undesired symptoms. We discovered that the janitors in question got equal "merit" raises regardless of their work; they worked at night and so had little human contact either with members of the university or their own families; they frequently were moved to new work teams so that group cohesion and teamwork were prevented; and they were feeling threatened by the university administration, which wanted to contract with a cleaning company and do away with the janitors' jobs. In short, there was little support from contiguous systems (their supervisors and the university) for the custodians to correct the "symptoms." The training intervention, therefore, could not be successful if it focused only on the intrapersonal and group levels. Instead, it had to focus on the inter-group level between the janitorial staff and their supervisors, and between the supervisors and the management group that set policy about merit increases, working hours, and work teams. An even higher level intervention would eventually have to include the university administration, which set hourly wages and had ultimate responsibility for the cleaning contracts.

Second, without considering systems and their levels, training may have a negative effect. Assertiveness training, in which a woman becomes aware of repressed feelings and needs and learns new ways of behaving, can be an example. Because of her changes, the woman might encounter conflict when she returns to her interpersonal system—marriage, for instance—if the marriage had been based on the husband's dominance and her nonassertiveness. If conflicts are not anticipated, and the woman is not given skills for dealing constructively with conflict, her new assertive skills may be eroded and/or she may feel little choice about remaining in the relationship.

Finally, a diagnosis of systems levels and their interaction is important because the meanings of behavior are difficult to assess if they are not considered in relation to other behaviors. One company wanted a training program for secretaries, who, among other things, had a tendency to guard information and not pass it on to their supervisors. During the diagnostic phase, the trainers discovered that the secretaries were withholding negative feedback about their supervisors, who then blamed the secretaries for their failures. On the other hand, the secretaries saw their own behavior as a response to their superiors. From their viewpoint, the superiors were the ones the trainers should "fix." From a systems perspective, however, the *relationship* between the secretaries and their superiors was the issue. If, as originally diagnosed by the management, the secretaries' behavior had remained the focus of the training, the problem conceivably could have increased. After relaying more information, the secretaries would most likely get increased negative responses, in the form of less responsibility and lower evaluations. In turn, the secretaries could have several responses— toleration of the situation, lowered self-esteem, pay, and consequently, lowered productivity—resulting in renewed censorship of the information, or termination.

If contexts are not considered, therefore, meanings of behaviors are often misconstrued; inappropriate interventions are planned; and people in training programs potentially are discounted and harmed. It should be remembered that many people are not aware of and/or are not willing to own their part in relationship patterns. In fact, in both the diagnostic and training phases, people often will tell the trainer how others' behaviors are causing a problem and ask for ways of making "them" change so that the situation can be improved. One of the advantages of being outside a group or organization is that the trainer has the opportunity to assess the overall pattern and seek solutions that someone embedded in any one piece of the pattern cannot see.

It would be ideal, of course, if interventions that took the whole system into account could consistently be planned and carried out. Those interventions often are major ones that call for far-ranging change. And although clients want a problem remedied, they may balk at sponsoring major interventions. Time and money are two obvious barriers. So, more likely than not, trainers will work only with parts of a system (decision making), or people at one level of a system (secretaries). Therefore, the trainer must decide to what degree the whole system will support the training to be done and what potential problems may occur in the whole system as a result of the training. Expectations of impacts from (and on) every level should be discussed when the trainer is diagnosing the system.

A common barrier to systems interventions occurs in dealing with the people in a relationship, group, or organization who have the power to define the problem and decide who is creating it. If people in higher positions of power are not willing to consider their part in the problem, trainers must be clear about what problem they are contracting to address. If trainers are not aware of these issues, they too can easily become part of the dysfunctional system. In the case of the secretaries, for example, if the trainer had "bought" the diagnosis of management and the problem had worsened, the trainer could next be blamed for not "solving the problem." The trainer has put him/herself in a no-win position.

Another reason systems issues may not be addressed directly is that trainers often work with groups made up of people from several organizations who are gathered to address a certain topic, such as effective management. In this context trainers are not in a position to deal directly with systems issues. In such cases, it is critical to help trainees understand and deal with "back-home" systems and problems themselves. Part of the instructional program should include re-entry: identification of problems likely to occur and the skills needed to address those problems. Reentry is discussed thoroughly in the following chapter and in Chapter 10.

Communication

We emphasize that a key focus of inquiry at the diagnosis stage is the relationship among elements of a system or systems levels. *Communication* is the process that connects and defines the elements and levels. It is the third characteristic of systems that must be considered in a diagnosis.

Communication has two levels inherent in its process: content and relational. The former refers to *what* is being communicated and the latter to *how* it is being communicated (Watzlawick et al., 1967). From a systems perspective, how something is communicated guides the interpretation of, and therefore the response to, the content. The same content spoken with a judgmental voice tone will be interpreted and responded to differently than if it is said with a nurturing tone.

It is imperative that trainers understand both levels of communication, whether or not the primary focus of training is technical (content) or interpersonal (relational). The nature of the work task affects how something should be communicated. For example, the manner in which an airline pilot communicates information to the control tower is effective in that context but not in the development of an intimate relationship. Conversely, we would not want the pilot, after having been to an interpersonal communication program and having learned the importance of expressing feelings, to transfer that way of talking indiscriminately on the job. In the same way, it seems that policemen in the 1960s often were mistrained by people who were caught in the rise of the "openness and honesty" ethic. Without considering the contexts of their jobs, many trainers, with good intentions, were helping police put themselves in dangerous positions. With increasing specialization of many relationships, professions, and organizations, training must involve knowledge of the jobs and roles people fill as well as how they do them, so the communication process can more accurately reflect the purpose of the work or relationship.

An important point about the communication process needs to be made here. The essence of human communication is that it is symbolic: people communicate through language, metaphorical symbols, and nonverbal signals that can take on various meanings (see Ruben, 1978). The implication, of course, is that people can perceive events in many different ways and, therefore, have *choices* about how to act.

One of the reasons systems become dysfunctional is that people act as if communication were *not* symbolic—that they have only one choice and one way to react to others. Effective management of conflict, for example, calls for flexibility of choice and behavior in order for people to reach mutual agreements. When people believe that their perception is the right and only one, and that their reaction to the situation is the only way they *can* react, there also is only one avenue for managing the conflict—one party has to win and the other lose. The effects of locked-in competition are apparent in marriages as well as international politics. One of the functions of the trainer, then, is to assist trainees in perceiving their problems in a variety of ways. Sometimes alternative perceptions lead to more efficient (or possible) solutions.

Time and Change

Finally, we come to the fourth characteristic of human systems: *time and change*. It is assumed that people, in their multiple relationships, are in constant change over time. To understand and plan for change, trainers should therefore, know the phases of development of human systems and how they progress from lower- to higher-quality forms of organizations.

There are several schema for analyzing developmental phases. Jack Gibb (1978) proposes 10 phases of development, with each stage assumed to be at a higher level of maturity and integration. The phases are (I) Punitive, (II) Autocratic, (III) Benevolent, (IV) Advisory, (V) Participative, (VI) Emergent, (VII) Organic, (VIII) Holistic, (IX) Transcendent, and (X) Cosmic. Tables 2–2, 2–3, and 2–4 list the phases and indicate the human needs and energy each utilizes and the limitations of each of the phases.

In the punitive phase, for example, people try to create order, reduce chaos, and establish security by punishing self and others. The main motivation is fear. Intrapersonally, there are feelings of blame and guilt; organizationally, employees are motivated through moralistic sanction and negative recognition. The autocratic phase has some of the same concerns, but controls the disorder through "linear relationships, hierarchy of power and responsibility, span of control and rational relationships" (Gibb, 1978, p. 52). Conformity often is a result, but it is preferred by some to being "out of control," defined as dealing with "irrational" feelings. Intrapersonally, autocracy is represented by control over feelings, rationalizations as a defense mechanism, low tolerance for ambiguity, and authoritarianism. Organizationally, the power structure is highly defined and differentiated; the information flow and evaluations are unidirectional (from top to bottom); and there is no outlet (formally) for attitudes, feelings, and expression of discomfort with organizational policy.

Each phase can be applied to all levels of systems. It is assumed that the higher the phase of development, the higher the quality of the human environment;

TABLE 2–2   The Development of Environmental Quality

PHASE THEME	DEFINITIVE NATURE OF PHASE	KEY FUNCTION BEST NURTURED
I Punitive	Punishment as a form of control and socialization	Reduces frightening chaos and apparent danger
II Autocratic	Power and authority used to maintain control and order	Provides order and structure
III Benevolent	Parental nurturing and caring as a primary theme	Provides security and affection
IV Advisory	Focus on consultative help and data collection	Expands the data base and enriches communication
V Participative	Focus upon participation, consensual decision-making, and choice	Increases involvement, loyalty, and group strength
VI Emergent	Rise of group and community as new and leaderless level of reality and interaction	Reduces dependency, adds vitality and functional resources
VII Organic	Rise of major role of emphatic and intuitive modes of being and communicating	Taps intuitive and sublingual sources of creativity and being
VII Holistic	Integration of unconscious, archetypical and latent processes into enriched living	Releases wellsprings of energy and creativity
IX Transcendent	Integration of altered and extra-sensory states into being and consciousness	Taps non-sensory sources of being and energy
X Cosmic	Focus on cosmic, universal, and nirvanic states of community and being	Taps into as-yet-little-known universal energy and being

Source: Jack Gibb, *Trust: A New View of Personal and Organizational Development* (Los Angeles: The Guild of Tutors Press, 1978).

and the higher the quality, the greater the chance for people to use all their human resources. However, this is not to say that all training programs should be focused on Phase X, especially since the highest development of many people and organizations is Phase V. It is important for trainers to remember that the level of development which they have reached and at which the training is focused must be considered in light of the stage of development of the trainees. It is difficult to facilitate productive change if trainers operate more than two stages removed from the training group. It may be that the trainers have advanced to higher levels, but they must be able and willing to facilitate movement at lower levels in order to bridge the gap between their knowledge and skills and those of the trainees.

TABLE 2-3 Dynamics of the Environmental-Quality States

PHASE THEME	KEY LIMITATION OF THE PHASE	PRIMARY FEAR-REDUCING EXPANDED FLOW	FOCUS OF THE ENERGY
I Punitive	Produces guilt and residual hostility	Fear of rebellion and loss of control	Survival, retribution
II Autocratic	Creates passivity and dependency	Fear of ambiguity, disorder, anarchy	Power, control, obedience
III Benevolent	Fosters multiple emotional disorders and apathy	Fear of emotional weaning	Reward and punishment
IV Advisory	Failure to tap energy and action and to distribute responsibility	Fear of conflict, diversity, and action	Communication, validity of data processing
V Participative	Ambiguity of leader role	Fear of leaderlessness and responsibility	Influence, choosing, resolving conflict
VI Emergent	Overreliance upon rational and verbal processes	Fear of being into non-rational and non-verbal states	Being, freedom, searching
VII Organic	Overreliance upon conscious processes	Fear of mysteries of unconscious and primal	Expression, integration, sensing
VIII Holistic	Overreliance upon sensory data and experience	Fear of loss of conscious and voluntary control	Creativity, spontaneity
IX Transcendent	Overreliance upon mind and body	Fear of leaving security of bodily and sensory base	Transcending sensory and body states
X Cosmic	Little or no data available	Fears may be transcended	Cosmic being

Source: Jack Gibb, *Trust: A New View of Personal and Organizational Development* (Los Angeles: The Guild of Tutors Press, 1978).

TABLE 2-4 The Wants Hierarchy and the Environmental-Quality Phases

PHASE THEME	ASCENDENT WANT, SUSTAINING THE PHASE	SECONDARY WANTS THAT ENRICH THE BASIC AND ASCENDENT WANT DURING THE PHASE STATE
I Punitive	To survive	To be secure, to punish and be punished, to be moral and to impose morality, to fight, to withdraw
II Autocratic	To give and gain power	To control, to be controlled, to maintain order, to get status, to obey, to rebel, to have authority, to evaluate
III Benevolent	To protect and to be protected	To help, to teach, to parent, to be cared for, to rescue, to be dependent, to give and receive warmth
IV Advisory	To understand and to be understood	To consult, to give and get advice, to be rational, to be aware of order, to gain wisdom
V Participative	To join and to be joined	To collaborate, to encourage involvement, to persuade, to influence, to be a member, to be included, to include others
VI Emergent	To be in community	To be part of a whole, to touch, to be aware, to be self-determining, to be close
VII Organic	To feel and to express feelings	To get sensory gratification, to create self, to get new experience, to be impulsive and spontaneous
VIII Holistic	To be whole	To find my roots, to create a free will, to have voluntary control over all bodily functions, to expand self
IX Transcendent	To transcend	To be egoless, to be need-free, to be born anew, to move into new areas of being and awareness
X Cosmic	To join the universal all	To transcend self, to be want-free, to transcend need for separateness

Source: Jack Gibb, *Trust: A New View of Personal and Organizational Development* (Los Angeles: The Guild of Tutors Press, 1978).

For example, we have worked with engineers who have been promoted to managerial positions. By nature of their background and profession, many tend to interact with people as they do with engineering designs, wanting the same predictability and expecting obedience to their one-way communication to subordinates. The trainer needs to accept the newly promoted engineers' initial preference for the punitive and autocratic approach before expecting them to envision the benefits and skills of participative management.

We advocate recognizing and accepting where trainees *are* and beginning at that point. Results of not following this principle are, at best, a lack of understanding and comprehension by trainees, and at worst, wholesale resistance and waste of time. People often feel put down by trainers who begin at phases too far removed from them. That feeling, in turn, fosters fear and defensiveness, which in terms of Gibb's phases, push people back to Phases I and II. The training style has thus created the problem it was trying to solve.

It has been assumed that the trainers are more advanced than the trainees. That may not be so, in which case the training is equally dysfunctional.

Finally, the values and skills useful in lower phases often become dysfunctional at higher levels. For example, power control may be helpful in the autocratic phase, but is not helpful when trying to move to a participative style in which skills of shared power are important. In the same vein, trainers cannot facilitate movement to higher levels with lower-level training strategies: they cannot facilitate movement to the participative phase with autocratic strategies. The strategy must match the movement. This issue is addressed in the next chapter.

WHAT ARE PRODUCTIVE SYSTEMS?

We are assuming that all human systems have the characteristics just described. Some systems, however, are more effective than others. In order to diagnose the deficiencies of human systems, it is important to specify the characteristics that distinguish effective or productive systems (see Table 2–5).

We believe that productive systems are *open, flexible, congruent,* and *affirming.* Since human systems are continuously changing and, in large part, dependent on their immediate environments for information, it follows that they must be open to receiving information and flexible in responding to it. When systems become rigid and closed, they cannot obtain the information needed to make appropriate decisions.

For example, some people wall themselves off from or distort comments about their impact on others. If the problem is slight, they come to be viewed as slightly rigid or ineffective interpersonally. The more they resist change and do not adapt to environmental and interpersonal feedback, the less their needs are met; they cannot develop effective interpersonal relationships; and they continue

TABLE 2-5   Diagnostic Questions About Productive Systems

KEY QUESTIONS	PRODUCTIVE SYSTEM CHARACTERISTICS
1. Does the person, group, or organization have the information needed to perform the task and accomplish the goal?	1. Openness
• Is there too much information being sent and received?	
• How and when does the system sort out needed from extraneous information?	
2. Does the person, group, or organization perceive choices in response to information? How do present choices block articulated goals?	2. Flexibility
• How do personal and organizational structures promote or block flexibility?	
• Is action taken in a timely manner to fulfill the system's goals?	
3. Does how the system operate to match its stated goals and purposes?	3. Congruency
• Does the system's culture match its structure? Purpose? Demands for leadership? Demands from the external environment?	
• Is the system aware of its multiple resources? Can it coordinate those resources?	
4. Do people and groups in the system have an opportunity to be recognized for strengths?	4. Affirmation
• Do they perceive they contribute their best talents?	
• How are the system rewards set up to reinforce contributions? To thwart them?	
• Do the people in the system perceive its purposes and means of operating to be meaningful? To contribute to a sense of purpose in their lives?	
• What is the atmosphere of trust? Of mistrust? How are trust and mistrust communicated?	

repeating their mistakes. When this problem is exaggerated, they are likely to be diagnosed as having some kind of mental disorder.

By the same token, if organizations are not open and flexible to their environments, they lose resources, markets, and employees. Many organizations have failed because of their unwillingness or inability to change and adapt. The latter is often true, for example, of businesses that began as family-owned enterprises and do not change their management styles when they grow into large companies. There are no job descriptions for employees (whom the owners no longer know personally); the accounting system does not reflect the complexity of the financial flow and the owners therefore cannot keep track of or invest their resources wisely; and the reward system for employees is based on personal commitments and loyalty to the owners which does not work when employees do not have personal relationships with the owners.

Openness and flexibility do not mean that a person or organization should respond to all incoming information and change erratically. Rather, part of the characteristics of an effective system is that it has the ability to choose information important to its functioning. For example, if a person is undergoing several important life changes (geographical move, divorce, change of job), it may not be functional for that person to be open to a great deal of new information. On the other hand, if people have a work setup that offers little outside stimulation and change, they may need to provide inlets for more and different information to flow toward them. Similarly, in some organizations, employees are given information not relevant to their tasks. They are sometimes overwhelmed and cannot do their work efficiently. On the other hand, in some organizations, employees are not given enough information to do their assigned jobs. Information is hoarded and handled strategically. They also cannot do their work efficiently.

Choice making is guided, in part, by the third characteristic of effective systems: congruency. Congruency involves a fit, a matching, of all parts of the system in relation to its purposes and actions. To be congruent, then, the system has to be *aware of* and *able to* coordinate its multiple resources, purposes, and actions. On the intrapersonal level, for example, people can be congruent to the extent that they are aware of a full range of thoughts and feelings in relation to a certain purpose and are able to express that awareness to others. When people are not aware of, or must stifle, some important feelings, their expressions are often incongruent. That is, they may be feeling angry, yet have to keep smiling because there is no permission for conflict to surface.

On the organizational level, Weisbord (1976) contends that diagnosis of an organization turns around three issues, all of which have to do with congruency. First is the congruency or "fit" between the organization and its environment. (Is the organization doing what it needs to do in order to survive and prosper?) Second is the fit between the organizational structure and its purposes. (Does a hierarchical system match the purpose of developing creative products, or would matrix management be more productive?) Third is the fit between individuals and the organization. (Does the informal network of contacts among personnel enhance or detract from the stated purpose of the organization?)

The final characteristic of effective systems is that they are affirming. Argyris (1970) lists three qualities that we believe lead people in a system to a feeling of affirmation of themselves and others. The three qualities are self-acceptance, confirmation, and essentiality. Argyris says:

> The higher the self acceptance, the more the individual values himself. The more he values himself, the more he will tend to value others because he knows that only by

interacting with human beings who value themselves will he tend to receive valid information and experience minimally defensive relationships. [Pp. 38–39]

In a similar fashion, Argyris says that when people are confirmed—receive feedback from others which indicates that they are worthwhile—the greater will be their self-acceptance and the more they will confirm others. Finally, the more essential a person feels, "is able to utilize his central abilities and express his needs . . . the more committed he will tend to be to the system and its effectiveness" (p. 39). Peters and Waterman in their best-seller, *In Search of Excellence*, emphasize that outstanding companies motivate through positive and not negative reinforcement. (1982, Chap. 3).

Let us sum up the characteristics of effective systems by examining the intrapersonal system in some detail. Transactional Analysis conceptualized the *elements* of the intrapersonal system as the Parent, Adult, and Child ego states, which are defined as consistent patterns of thinking, feeling, and behaving. The quality of the *communication relationships* among these three, and consequently the relationship of the system to its interpersonal *environment*, define the health of the system. When the channels of communication are relatively open among the three ego states, the intrapersonal system has *flexibility, openness, congruency*, and the possibility of being *affirmed*. Conversely, when any of the ego states overlap (contamination), are underdeveloped, or are cut off from the communication network, the intrapersonal system is not fully functioning and some predictable disorders, characteristic of ineffective systems, occur. *Flexibility* is decreased and the skills needed for certain situations are not forthcoming; interpersonal relationships are relatively rigid and closed; and interpersonal communication is *congruent*. Incongruency is the basis for games, which, in turn, are the basis for negative recognition and lowered self-esteem (affirmation) (see James and Jongeward, 1971). *Developmentally*, a person may be stuck in the Autocratic Phase (II), in which feelings are blocked. The person therefore has a low tolerance for ambiguity and probably controls by authoritarian means. Hence, the person's *environment* is affected. He/she probably is limited to relationships and professions that match the intrapersonal pattern. However, if placed in a job that does not match (that is, is incongruent with), the intrapersonal system (for example, a person is promoted to a management position that calls for tolerance of more ambiguity), the person will have to change inwardly or be unable to handle the job.

Even though trainers may not be working directly with the intrapersonal system, as in counseling, they need to know how that system works and how it interacts with interpersonal and group levels if they are to comprehend the communication patterns they will observe in training.

For example, when training fairly rigid people, trainers need to begin the program in a structured way and then move to less structure. Specific and less ambiguous information can be presented initially, with more abstract information presented later. In the same way, highly structured simulations may be used in the first part of training, both to provide guidance to the trainees and to evoke feelings which begin the transition to higher levels of development. A sense of humor also will help lighten the training and may facilitate movement to the Benevolent Stage of development.

In diagnosing an organization, the same kind of system characteristics as were used for diagnosing someone interpersonally, need to be considered. A diagnosis we did of a planning and development (P & D) division within a human resource department of a large company provides an example of the use of system characteristics and their effective (and ineffective) use.

The manager and each of his staff were interviewed to discover what system *elements* were key in contributing to the overall feelings of mistrust in the division. It was discovered that the style of leadership, kinds and means of rewards, and the inability and unwillingness of staff to confront conflict directly were key elements to the problems.

In terms of *communication*, not enough information was being shared among the staff and even confirmation of minor decisions was being routed through the manager, making decision making extremely slow and burdensome. Communication between the manager and his staff and among the staff was also characterized by double messages. For example, the manager would say verbally that he wanted his staff to make risky decisions and not always have to check the decisions with him. However, on several occasions when they had done so, and upper management had not approved, the P & D manager had not supported his staff to upper management.

Furthermore, the P & D division was embedded in a larger human resources (HR) department (the *environment*), the norms of which did not coincide with those of the division. For example, within the division, the manager encouraged his staff to discuss openly their disagreements about major policy decisions. On the other hand, the HR manager preferred (insisted) that people come to him with firm opinions and be ready to argue for their point of view. When part of the P & D staff met with the HR manager, there was confusion about how to present information and make decisions. The consultants did decide that it was possible to intervene in the P & D division to improve its internal functioning without intervention in the larger system; but ideally, for the efficient functioning of the entire HR staff, decisions needed to be made in the future about how the whole HR department would run.

Finally, the purposes of the P & D division, which housed the training and organizational development functions of the company, did not match its speed of decision making and stage of development. The division needed to respond promptly to requests for training and for intervention into other company units; and the staff could not do so given the kind of communication they had and the style of management used (autocratic). Thus, in terms of a system, the *time and change* of the division thwarted, rather than enhanced, its functioning.

Effectiveness of a system is implied in the discussion above, but the specific characteristics of a productive system need also to be considered. In terms of *openness*, the P & D staff did not have the kind of information or enough information to perform their tasks efficiently. Further, they did not perceive *flexibility*—that they had other choices in how to respond to problems that emerged. For example, the more they encountered conflicts with each other, the more they withdrew, making the conflicts worse rather than trying new strategies to manage their disagreements.

As was implied earlier, the structure of the division was not *congruent* with its purposes and needed increased speed of decision making. Finally, work that was accomplished was not verbally rewarded (*affirmed*). Performance appraisals were infrequent, and the staff viewed them as a one-way process of evaluation rather than as a chance to be affirmed for work well done.

In summary, the characteristics of effective systems assume that people operate best when they feel good about themselves, have information relevant to particular relationships or tasks, and have some flexibility or choice in their response. By using some basic guidelines of system characteristics and their effective implementation, trainers and consultants have a framework for diagnosing problems and making recommendations for interventions.

CHAPTER THREE
ARRANGING TRAINING PROGRAMS

The systems framework just described serves as a guide to trainers as they go through the practical steps necessary for a thorough diagnosis of an organization or group and arrangement of the training program. In this chapter we discuss those steps: (1) initial contact with the client, (2) contracting for the training, and (3) in-depth diagnosis and analysis of the problems and aspirations of the client group.[1] (See Table 3–1 for an overview of these steps.)

HOW ARE INITIAL CONTACTS HANDLED?

The training and consulting process usually begins when a potential client and trainer make contact by phone or at an informal meeting.[2] There are at least five areas of information the trainer needs to request during this time—information about (1) the contact person, (2) the client group and the problems they are having, (3) the type of training desired, (4) an initial assessment of time and fees,

---

[1] See also Lippitt and Lippitt (1978) and Schein (1969a) for additional insight into these steps of consulting and training.

[2] This chapter is written from the perspective of the external consultant. However, most of the questions and concerns in this chapter can be helpful to the internal or in-house trainer/consultant.

TABLE 3–1   Arranging Training Programs: An Overview

PHASE	KEY QUESTIONS ABOUT:
1. Initial contact	• Contact person • Client group • Type of training desired • Initial assessment of time and fees • Procedures for contractual step
2. Contracting	• Client's expectations of the training and trainer • Trainer's expectations of the client • Definition of the problem • Phases of the project • Fees • Conditions for the training
3. Further diagnosis	• Synthesis of information from initial contact and contracting • Proposal and acceptance of the initial contract • In-depth diagnosis: interviews, questionnaires, observation of work groups • Synthesis of diagnostic data • Feedback to client systems • Contracting for further intervention

and (5) procedures for the contractual step. (See Table 3–2 for a summary of these steps.)

The general purpose of this stage of diagnosis is to get an overall view of the system, the relationships of the people involved, their view of identified problems, and their desired relationship with the trainer.

Area 1: Information About the Contact Person

After introductions, the trainer should ask the following:

1. How did the contact person happen to call this trainer?
   Was there a referral?
   Has someone in the client group worked previously with the trainer?
   What qualities is the client group looking for?

There should be a clear picture of the process by which the trainer was contacted and what expectations led to taking this step. Sometimes, a person in a group or organization has worked with the trainer before, probably under different circumstances, and it may be helpful to explore how appropriate it is to transfer those expectations about the trainer's performance to this new situation.

TABLE 3–2   Phase 1: Initial Contact

AREAS OF INFORMATION NEEDED	KEY QUESTIONS
1. Contact person	• How did the contact person happen to call this trainer? • What is the contacting person's connection to the client in terms of position and decision-making power?
2. Type of group and problems	• What type of group are we dealing with? (see Figure 3–1 for types) • What are the preexisting relationships of the people to be involved in the training? • What is the initial diagnosis of problems? — Observable data? — Who agrees? Disagrees? — To what is the problem attributed? — Have there been previous attempts to remedy the problem?
3. Type of training desired	• Specific outcome desired? • Best and worse that can happen?
4. Assessment of time and fees	• Joint assessment of time for training • Initial negotiation of range of fees
5. Planning for the contract	• Time of decision on actual contract • Time of next contact with trainer • Additional planning time and fees • Contact person for the trainer in the next stage

2.   What is the contacting person's connection to the client in terms of:

Position: Director? President? Chief executive officer? Personnel or training director? Program planner? Secretary?

Decision-making power: Does this person, after speaking with you, have the authority to contract with you? If so, for whom is the person making the agreement, and what is the indication of support for the training effort? If not, who or what group makes the decision? On what will they base their decision? For whom will they be making the decision, and what evidence is there of support for the training?

These are basic questions which often are asked later in the interview. Sometimes people in an organization decide what problems they think others have, get nominal support for the training, and contact the trainer to make arrangements. In reality, there may be little support for the effort, and this time and money will be wasted and hard feelings created.

A couple of examples will make the point. The executive director and the regional directors of an international health organization were having a great deal of conflict. After losing some highly trained personnel, the regional directors decided to confront the executive with the need for conflict management training.

The executive did not object, and one of the directors assumed the task of setting up the training. In discussing the proposed training, it became obvious that the major problem, as diagnosed by most of the staff, involved the management style of the executive. That should have been the trainer's first clue to involve the executive and get his consent before spending additional time on the planning. That did not occur, however, and after a great deal of time was spent planning, setting dates, and making travel arrangements, the executive vetoed the training.

Another example involved the city council members of a local government, who wanted a team-building session. The personnel director made the contact and assured the trainer that the council had agreed that it needed the session because of its difficulty in reaching decisions and setting priorities. Again, after scheduling the diagnostic interviews with the council members and planning a trip to the city, the trainer was called 15 minutes prior to departure and told that the council had voted the previous night to "postpone the training indefinitely."

In both cases, the trainers lost time and money and were victimized in the process. Both of these mistakes could have been circumvented in several ways. For one, the trainer could have pushed for more and clearer information about the agreement to conduct the training. When large organizations are involved or when there are multiple decision-making steps for acceptance of the training, a written request or confirmation of the training is needed. Another way to circumvent the problem is to make clear, from the beginning, that if the training is not "okayed," the organization will be charged for planning time. Finally, some trainers do not schedule events for organizations or groups until after they receive payments. The latter solution is not possible with some institutions because of their payment policies. It is, however, possible for many businesses in the private sector.

At this early stage of the contact, there are three potential problems to listen for and ask about. They relate to the previous examples. First is the "I smell a rat syndrome," which is the "technical" name for responding to requests for training to straighten out a particular person or group. Several people may want to hire a trainer to "fix" a person or group, so that they will not have to confront a problem themselves. Several results are possible, none of which are very productive. If the person to be "fixed" is the chief executive officer, the training probably will not get accepted as proposed. Another result is that the training will be conducted with minimal commitment and be unsuccessful. The trainer may then be blamed for the failure.

Blaming the trainer is part of the second potential problem: victimage. Often, when groups are not willing to confront their problems openly, they look for an outside person to do "magic" for them and make their problems painlessly disappear. So when the trainer is not clear about expectations and the training does not solve the problem, the group has an outside person to victimize for not doing the job; and they prove that there is little reason to address their problems since even an outside expert was unsuccessful.

A third kind of problem arises if the contact person is a personal friend or acquaintance. In such a case there is a temptation to omit some of the diagnostic steps. However, trainers risk making errors and misdiagnosing if they do. Boss and McConkie (1979) make a full report of an ineffective organization development effort because they let their friendship with a company vice-president replace careful analysis and diagnosis.

Area 2: Type of Group and Problems

Figure 3–1 categorizes the types of groups and training with which trainers may be asked to deal. Questions about the group and its problems should vary according to its type. Group I, heterogeneous, refers to a group composed of people from multiple backgrounds and with multiple needs. Training for this type of group usually centers around a topic. For example, a division of adult education wants to have a workshop on conflict management that is open to the public. Since further diagnosis of the actual participants is not possible, the trainer can ask the contact person about kinds of people who usually attend and about some of their interests. In addition, at the beginning of the workshop, the trainer can have participants introduce themselves by saying what brings them to

FIGURE 3–1   Types of Groups and Training.

| | | TYPES OF GROUPS | | | |
	I	II	III	IV	V
	Heterogeneous	Homogeneous but not Intact Work Groups	Natural Work Groups	Homogeneous Organiza-tional Levels	Multiple Organiza-tional Levels
A *Content:* —task skills —technical skills —goal clarity					
B *Relationship:* —quality (climate; trust; con-flict; etc.) —skills (communica-tion; leader-ship; etc.) —structure (management organization; evaluation procedures; etc.)					

TRAINING FOCUS

the workshop (specific problems) and what they hope to gain. During the workshop, the trainer can create small groups of people who have similar interests and have them develop role plays of problem situations which can be analyzed with the material to be presented.

If the group to be addressed is of type II (homogeneous but not from the same work group or organization, such as lawyers, clergy, or teachers), more questions can be asked about typical problems of the group. The contact person also can be asked for names of people to contact who can furnish background on special problems and interests of the group. We have followed this procedure a great deal and found it helpful for fitting material to the needs of the group—using appropriate examples to illustrate topics, constructing role plays and case studies in advance, and so on. For example, similar conflict management strategies may well apply to a number of professions, but law enforcement officials, advertising professionals, and managers of volunteers have their own special problems that require different emphases in the training of these strategies.

Group III is an intact work group—members of one industrial division, or a university department, or of a special project team—and often includes supervisors *and* subordinates. Group IV includes people in similar positions in an organization but in different departments, areas, and so on. For example, the trainees could be first-level managers in various divisions in a company or executives from subsidiaries in various geographical locations. Finally, Group V involves intact work groups or people who are interdependent with each other and span hierarchical and/or horizontal levels in an organization.

When the types of training groups are III, IV, or V, the trainer needs information about the preexisting relationships of the people to be involved in the training. This will help in planning the training and in being aware of any special problems likely to emerge among participants. Two general questions to be asked are:

1. What are the formal relationships of the proposed participants?
    Superior/subordinate?
    Peers in the same department?
    Across multiple levels?
2. What are the informal relationships?
    Past history of problems?
    Flow of information?
    Liking of each other?
    Competition—personal and/or departmental?
    Leadership styles?
    Reward systems?
    Communication patterns?
    Trust?

Even if the training is technically oriented, relational issues between people in the training can facilitate or block learning. If the training is focused on relational learning and there are problems among participants which are not being addressed, the training goals probably will not be reached. For example, the problem for which the trainer is hired may be ineffective decision making. The trainer proceeds to teach decision-making skills without understanding the relationships of the participants, who, it turns out, do not give each other information because of low trust. Unless the issue of trust is explored, decision making probably will remain ineffective.

Not only do trainers need to know the type of group, they also need to make an initial diagnosis of problems. Specific questions to ask at this stage include:

1. What is the problem or aspiration to be addressed in the training?

   What are the presenting symptoms; that is, what is *actually happening* in the group or organization?

2. How does the person know it is a problem?

   What is happening that should not be, or not happening that should be?

   What is the specific, observable data? For example, if the caller says that the group has a lack of trust, ask what behaviors are happening that indicate a lack of trust—rumors, increasing control of employees, and so on.

3. Who, at this point, agrees that there is a problem?

   Do they agree with the diagnosis of the problem?

   Will these people be involved in the training?

4. To what does the person attribute the problem?

   Certain personnel?

   Structure of the organization?

   Lack of technical skills?

   Lack of relational skills?

   Reward system in the organization?

   Demands of the particular role of the job?

5. Has similar or other training been conducted previously?

   With the same or different people?

   With what result?

Many of these questions will be explored in more depth during step 3 (discussed later in this chapter)—further diagnosis—but they need to be explored to some degree during the initial contact so that the trainer can decide whether or not to consider conducting the training, declining it, or referring it to someone else.

Area 3:
Type of Training Desired

Figure 3–1 also distinguishes two types of training: content and relationship. Often, of course, the two types overlap. The content may be about the relationships, as in team building, or the success of a program on new accounting systems (content) may turn on the kinds of relational problems that exist among participants.

The trainer needs to get an idea of the client's content *and* relationship goals to assess whether or not they are reasonable expectations for the kind of training requested. Some people, for example, wait a long time to hire a trainer/consultant and then want the person to work miracles in a day-long workshop. Questions to ask at this point include:

1.   If this training were optimally successful, what would be the outcome?
     Specifically and behaviorally?
     What content will be mastered?
     How will relationships among the participants change?
2.   What are the best things that could happen?
     What are the worst?
     (The responses to these questions also will help the trainer assess relational issues among participants.)

Area 4: Initial Assessment of Time and Fees

In order to make a decision about continuing the relationship with the client, trainers must also get an idea of the time involved and the amount of money the client has committed to the project. They need to let the client know their fees for the type of training requested and the possible range for negotiation around time and fees. Some trainers have sliding scales for different groups and need to make the client aware of this fact when applicable.

Area 5: Planning for the Contract

Sometimes the information exchanged in this area is simple, especially if the group is of type I or II. There often is one contact person who has been authorized to contract with the trainer and negotiate for time and money, and the agreements are settled during the initial contact. Even with this kind of contact, however, elements of a contract, discussed in the next section, should be understood. At least, the trainer should request a letter of confirmation about the goals, time, and fees of the training.

If the training involves groups III, IV, or V, additional questions need to be asked:

1.   When will the decision be made about the training?
2.   When will the trainer be contacted again?
3.   Are there expectations for additional planning with others before the agreement? (If so, the trainer should communicate the expectation of planning fees, if any.)
4.   With whom will the trainer be in contact in the future? Where?

Sometimes information is passed back and forth through the contact person by people in a group or organization who have the power to make decisions. If this is discerned, the trainer may request a meeting directly with those people to have an unfiltered line of communication and potentially less distortion of information and expectations.

HOW IS THE TRAINING CONTRACT NEGOTIATED?

Much training has been less than successful because of a lack of clear psychological and working contract between trainer and client. Novice trainers sometimes confuse getting a clear contract with demonstrating a lack of trust. On the contrary, trust is enhanced when expectations from both trainer and client are clearly understood.

This step needs to be accomplished with the person or people directly responsible for negotiating the training. Table 3–3 includes the areas of information needed for contract negotiation and the specific items that the trainer should consider including. Table 3–4 provides a sample contract form.

These agreements may be written or agreed to verbally. If the training project is lengthy and involves a large sum of money, most trainers prefer to have an explicit contract written and signed.

HOW IS FURTHER DIAGNOSIS INTRODUCED?

We have explained, in general, the first two steps of the diagnostic phase of training: initial contact and contracting. To demonstrate these two steps, we will describe the planning of a training experience with a type III group, natural and intact. In this example we also will move ahead one more step and illustrate step 3, further diagnosis.

The initial contact with the organization was with the president of the board of a local human service organization. Recently, a new executive director and several new board members had been appointed. The board members were volunteers, and the executive director held a paid position. Ostensibly, they all were peers. The board met once a month in an open meeting, usually with newspaper reporters in attendance. The president had been directed by the board to find "some kind of workshop that might help us with our problems." During the initial interview, the trainers discovered that the organization had a history of internal conflict, and as a result, there now was a possibility of losing funding from the local government. Until there was a crisis (losing funds), the president believed that meeting individual goals had taken precedence over the group goal of keeping the organization alive and effective.

TABLE 3–3   Phase II: Contract Negotiation

AREAS OF INFORMATION	SPECIFICS TO INCLUDE:
1. Client's expectations of the training and trainer	• Desired outcomes of the training • Time involved for planning and training • Budget expectations • Materials to be produced (films, manuals, handouts, etc.)
2. Trainer's expectations of the client	• Types of support needed: logistics, time, contacts with specific people paving the way for pretraining diagnosis and interviews • Type of relationship before, during, and after the training: availability, collaboration in determining goals and details of the training, and expectations of revising goals during and after diagnosis
3. Definition of the problem	• Agreements and disagreements about the actual problem to be addressed • Arrangements for and phases of the diagnostic step • Agreements on the kind of diagnosis to be done and the people to be involved (including, potentially, the contracting agent) • At this point, agreements about the potential congruency among type of problem, type of training requested, possible outcomes, and time and money allotted
4. Phases of the project	• Possible trial period to test for trainer/client compatibility • Review points during the length of the project (e.g., after the diagnostic step to determine whether or not there is enough agreement on the problem to proceed with the training)
5. Money	• Matching the fees and type of training • Fees for particular phases of the training (e.g., for diagnostic activities, after which the contract may be terminated if there is little agreement on ways to proceed) • Time of payment
6. Conditions of training (known at this point)	• Whether or not people, extraneous to the training, will be allowed to attend (*Note:* Sometimes people who are part of a problem but do not want to risk the training will request to observe the training process and the trainer. Often the climate created thereby is one of suspicion and distrust. Trainers need to say explicitly whether or not the conditions can bear observers.) • Termination of the contract: How? When? • Any payment if there is cancellation of training and consultation?

TABLE 3–4 Sample Consultation Agreement

The purpose of this document is to confirm the terms of agreement on

_____ between _____ and
Yarbrough & Associates for the consultation detailed below.

Name of consultant:

Dates of consultation:

Times of consultation:

Fee:

Place:

Payment:

Materials:

Follow-up:

Cancellation agreement:

Statement of disclosure:

The consultant of Yarbrough & Associates agrees to receive

_____ information and information relating to

_____ rights in confidence, not to disclose
same to any person or entity not a party to this agreement, and not to use same
for the benefit of the consultant or any third party.

_____ agrees not to use materials furnished by
Yarbrough & Associates for any future purposes without the consent of
Yarbrough & Associates.

Yarbrough & Associates

By _____   By _____

Title _____   Title _____

We asked how the group actually operated and what symptoms of ineffectiveness were apparent. The president said there were informal cliques or subgroups that met outside the board meetings to form coalitions about certain matters. The subgroups tended to be composed of people from similar political persuasions, from more to less radical. Their prior interaction, she believed, left little room for negotiation and actual decision making in the meetings. As a result, in board meetings, members and the director discussed trivial matters at length, and some decisions, such as drafting their funding proposal, were made too late. When decisions were proposed by one subgroup, other groups usually blocked or vetoed them.

The role of the board, as formally described, was to make policy decisions and offer guidelines for the organization. The role of the executive director was to implement policy by establishing programs for the community. However, the board and director spent a great deal of time discussing particular programs and activities and arguing about what should and should not be done. There also were many arguments between the subgroups about what programs were worthwhile. The conflicts, reported the president, tended to repeat themselves, "like tape recordings."

In the discussion with the trainers, two themes continually emerged: (1) a lack of clarity about the purpose of the organization, and (2) conflicts that were not openly addressed. The ritualized nature of the conflicts suggested that there were more basic issues involved than the ones being discussed.

The president requested a one-day workshop on conflict and had the authority to contract for the training. However, it did not seem to the trainers that there was consensus among the group members about the kind of training needed or the goals it was intended to accomplish. In addition, the president did not have authority to contract for the fees to be paid. The trainers therefore constructed a tentative contract with the president and requested that she present it to the board and director for approval. The contract included the following elements:

1. General area of training: conflict management
2. Goals
   a. Clarification of issues and goals: short and long term.
   b. Clarification of organizational purpose.
   c. Clarification of roles of the board and the director.
   d. Clarification of power relationships within the board and between the board and the director.
   e. Development of alternatives to their present method of conducting conflict.
3. Diagnostic steps
   a. Interview each board member and the director.
   b. Observe at least one board meeting with a focus on the communication dynamics of the group.
   c. Discuss with the board and director (as a group) the information gathered from the interviews and the meeting. Prioritize the issues uncovered within the group and decide upon a proposal for training, if that was still desired.
4. Submission of training proposal to the group for approval

5. Contractural conditions
    a. Fee for the diagnostic steps, with an agreement to renegotiate for the training after the diagnosis.
    b. All board members must agree to be involved and interviewed.
    c. After the diagnosis, either side could agree to terminate the contract.

The proposal was submitted and approved.

As was suggested by the tentative contract, *observation* and *interviews* were the two means of further diagnosis used in this case. (*Questionnaires* distributed to organizational members are another common diagnostic method.)

The content of interview questions, observation forms, or questionnaires should address the characteristics of systems suggested in Chapter 2. To clarify the process of diagnosis we first review the areas examined in our illustrative context. Then we provide the sample questions and observation forms actually used when diagnosing this organization.

Level of Complexity of the System.   For this training, the group and intergroup were the target levels of the system. Those levels included all the lower levels of complexity—intrapersonal and interpersonal.

Environment.   The initial diagnosis indicated that the system under consideration also was having difficulty with its immediate environment—its funding agencies. That level also had to be taken into consideration in the diagnosis.

Elements.   The trainer must know the important elements of the system being observed. We suggested earlier that relevant elements in an organization are purposes, structure, rewards, relationships, helpful mechanisms, and leadership. A special focus, at least as indicated in the early diagnosis, was conflict. Questions and observations, then, also should be based on the conceptual elements and dynamics of the conflicts process.

Communication.   Communication is the process that defined *how* the system operates. In this case, communication was one of the major elements to be diagnosed.

Stage of Development.   To plan training at the appropriate level, trainers must know the approximate stage of development of the organization and its members. The 10 phases proposed by Gibb provide guidelines for asking questions about stages of development (see Tables 2–2, 2–3, and 2–4).

Effective Systems Characteristics.   Trainers need to assess how open, congruent, flexible, and affirming the system is to its members. When there are problems such as the ones described, many of the conflict issues involve personal feelings of self-worth, which often are not considered "legitimate" to discuss in organizational settings, although they may be at the heart of the conflicts. Again, we wish to emphasize that even during diagnosis trainers themselves become part of the system and develop relationships with the people in the organization, and these interactions should be reflective of effective systems. In other words, trainers need to model the qualities they hope to instill in the client system. Since conflict and mistrust appear to be high in the case we are examining, trainers may want to attend a board meeting (or request a special meeting) before the interviews, where they can be introduced and answer questions about their background, interests in this particular project, commitment to its success, and so on. It should be remembered that *how* trainers communicate this information is equal in importance to *what* is conveyed.

At this time and/or during the individual interviews, trainers also need to ask clients about their expectations of the training. In turn, trainers need to share with the clients their perceptions of what are realistic (and unrealistic) expectations, given the history and extent of their problem(s) and the time allotted for training.

Based on the considerations noted above, the following questions could form the bases for the interviews:

1. How would you describe the *purposes* of the *organization*? How would you know when they are reached; that is, what programs would be consistent with those purposes? Which are not?

2. What are *your purposes* for being here? (*Note*: This was especially important since the board members were volunteers.) What has to happen to make your service worthwhile? Be specific.

3. What *differences* do you think exist among board members and between the board and director as to purpose? What specifically has happened that would lead you to that conclusion?

4. What special talents do you bring to this position? Do others recognize those talents? How do you know when you are appreciated? When you are not?

5. What is the *function* of the board (and that of the director)? How do you know when that function has been carried out successfully?

6. What information do you need to carry out your function? From whom? How often? Do you get it? If not, what is your assumption about why you do not?

7. Does the *structure* (board and director) and the scheduled meeting time help you fulfill your function? If not, what is missing? Do you need to see each other more often? In different contexts?

8. How would you assess the *relationships* of the people involved in terms of the following?

Interdependence and power

   a. What does the board need from the director (and vice versa) to accomplish its tasks? What do you request or get now that you do not need for accomplishing your tasks?

   b. What person(s) is recognized for being most expert in the group? What kind of expertise is needed? Does someone in the group possess needed areas of expertise?

   c. Whose opinions are listened to in the group?

d. What people are linked together (in subgroups) in the organization? Is there a subgroup that is recognized as most powerful? How do you know?

e. Are there values shared by the group in common? Who most typifies those values? Are there values shared by the members of certain subgroups? Who typifies those values?

f. In your perception, who has the most power in the group? Based on what?

g. What power do you have in the group? Based on what?

h. How are you (or the group you identify with) seen by other groups? How would you like to be seen? How do you know how you are seen?

Trust

a. To whom would you be willing to express your feelings, both positive and negative? To whom do you talk outside regular meetings?

b. Is conversation in regular meetings polite? Controlled? Candid? Do people listen to each other? How or how not?

c. How can you tell if people value each other?

d. To whom do you feel most similar? Dissimilar? In what ways? How do you know?

e. What are some additional words you would use to describe the atmosphere (climate) in the organization?

Self-esteem

a. How do you feel about yourself in this group?

b. How and by whom do you get positive or negative recognition?

c. What would your ideal role be in this group? How would others respond to you?

Conflict strategies

a. How do you know when there is a conflict? What do people do? What do you do?

b. When and how are feelings and perceptions expressed in this group? Openly? Covertly? After the meeting?

c. Do people avoid conflicts? How?

d. Do they compete? How?

e. Do they accommodate? Who accommodates whom?

f. Is there compromise? Around what kinds of issues?

g. Is conflict acceptable to this group? To you? What is your response when there is a conflict?

Leadership

a. Who are the leaders in the group? Formal? Informal?

b. How would you describe the leadership style of those people? Authoritarian? Democratic? Nondirective? What do leaders actually do that leads you to that conclusion?

c. In what areas do you need more or less leadership? What kind?

Environment

a. From whom outside the organization is support needed to accomplish its purposes? What kind of support? Recognition? Political? Financial? Media?

b. What is the constitutents' evaluation of the services being offered? How do you know?

9. Finally, to make the organization and your participation in it ideal, what resources, people, mechanisms, or changes would the organization need?

Some of these questions call for high self-disclosure. If they are not being responded to, the interviewer has several options. He/she may ask more general, "safe" questions. Or, the trainer may ask the clients to complete questionnaires (anonymously) that obtain information on similar topics. Included at the end of the chapter are sample questionnaires on trust (Form 3–1) and on assessing the major elements in an organization (Form 3–2).[3] These are all instruments that have been widely used. Trainers also can construct their own, in much the same way as the questions in this chapter were constructed, when they know the elements and processes that are considered central to the phenomena or the organization they are diagnosing.

Trainers are likely to obtain a great deal of information from the interview. They must then look at all the data and synthesize what they have. They can do so by noticing patterns in the responses: (1) themes that were most common; (2) topics that were conspicuously absent or that people "ignored" vehemently, such as refusal to discuss issues of power; (3) similarities and differences among responses; and (4) questions that received the most intense answers in terms of length of responses, loudness of voice tone, emotion demonstrated, and behaviors that were most denied. The guidelines for effective observation offered in Chapter 12 also will help the trainer in interviewing, observing groups in the diagnostic phase, and sorting the data that are received.

In addition, how interviews are conducted affects what and how much information is obtained. Trainers must remember that the purpose of the interview is to enter the world of others, to perceive it as they do, and not to be judgmental of their perspective, either verbally or nonverbally. In other words, the trainer is to listen empathically.

Interviewees are likely to perceive trainers as empathic if they keep in mind some of the following guidelines:

1. Listen for the kinds of words the clients use so that you can use them. For example, if they use the word "input" rather than "information," you should also. If trainers use humanistic words such as "group energy" or "life space" when they are interviewing technically oriented people, the respondents and the information they give may be confused.
2. Match the way in which clients process information. For example, if they use such words and phrases as "I *see* that . . . ," "The overall *picture* is . . . ," the interviewer should also (initially) use visually oriented words. If they use auditory words—

[3]There are several sources from which trainers can obtain diagnostic questionnaires and observation forms on interpersonal and organizational topics. One source is *Instrumentation in Human Relations Training*, by J. William Pfeiffer and Richard Heslin (San Diego, Calif.: University Associates, Inc., 1973). Another source is the annual yearbooks published by University Associates. A third source is Teleometrics, an organization in Austin, Texas, that has a primary goal of constructing and validating diagnostic instruments. Trainers also can find measuring instruments by researching a particular topic in the social sciences indices (for example, *Psychological Abstracts, Sociological Abstracts, Communication Abstracts*).

"that I *hear* around here is . . .," "it *sounds* like . . .," or "It does not *ring a bell* . . ."—so should you. [See Bandler and Grinder(1979) for a full explanation of this system.]

3. Be aware of nonverbal cues that indicate you are listening. Egan (1978) suggests the following effective listening cues:

    S: face the other *squarely*, not at an angle
    O: maintain an *open* posture
    L: *lean* toward, instead of away from, the other to signal availability
    E: maintain steady *eye* contact with the person (neither staring nor looking away)
    R: maintain a *relaxed* pose, which can be facilitated if you breathe deeply and focus your awareness on the other rather than being self conscious, fantasizing what the other is "really" thinking, or rehearsing what you will say next [P. 97]

4. Ask questions that move from low to high risk so that the relationship between you and the clients has a chance to develop before they are asked to entrust controversial information to you.

5. Ask open-ended questions and then follow up with questions that require specific information, so you will know how to use the information you get. For example, if the interviewees say there is low trust, but do not say how they have made that assessment, you will not know how to intervene to address the issue.

6. Do not discuss information obtained in interviews with other interviewees. Inappropriate disclosure of information (directly or indirectly) will harm your credibility.

After the interviews in our extended example the most intense issues that surfaced were (1) differences of opinion about the purpose of the organization and, therefore, who it should be serving, and (2) the use of power in the organization. Consequently, there was low trust and guarding of information necessary to complete tasks. The trainers therefore focused on several areas in the board meeting they agreed to observe. These included:

1. Who talked to whom and how often.

2. The topics that carried the most intensity and whether the intensity was expressed directly or indirectly. For example, if topics such as programs to offer in the following year created the most tension, this interaction could imply disagreement over organizational goals.

3. Interruption patterns: who interrupted, and who was interrupted, on what topics. (If every time someone made a decision, another person or subgroup blocked the decision, the character of power struggles may be indicated.)

4. Openness of expression (see Form 3–3).

5. Communication styles (see Form 3–4).

6. Conflict strategies (see Form 3–5).

After the meeting, trainers may ask the group members themselves to complete forms that elicit information about their own group processes. This opportunity often lowers the defensiveness of the people involved. In addition, group members learn *what* to look for in effective and ineffective groups and begin learning *how* to give feedback about their own group interaction. Simple forms can be created that take only a little time for participants to fill out. Examples of conflict, communication, and group participation checklists are given in Forms 3–6 to 3–9. Again, trainers can easily create their own forms when they identify the problems of their particular client system.

After the meeting (and the completion of any forms) trainers should give the group feedback on their observations. Trainers should talk about general patterns and be careful not to identify any "culprits" in the group, blaming certain people for the group's problems. Trainers also should practice good feedback skills, which include reporting feedback in terms of the observable data, clearly identifying any interpretations, and suggesting consequences of the particular patterns of interaction. Trainers should let the group know about their effective as well as dysfunctional communication patterns, but they should be careful not to overload the group members with more information than they can use during this initial feedback session. At this point, trainers also can report to the participants the information obtained during the interviews. Finally, they should openly discuss the training phase of the contract.

After these steps are completed, the diagnostic phase is brought to a close and the trainer must recontract with the organization for specific training events. In the case just cited, the training may consist of a weekend workshop on clarifying the goals of the organization and managing conflict productively. The emphases would be on identifying subconflicts within the group and using power productively. The two issues seem to fit together for this group since much of the conflict originated from the lack of agreement on general *and* specific goals of the organization. In addition, there may be a need for the trainer to attend additional meetings of the group to help the members develop skills and mechanisms for processing their group meetings effectively. In the long run, the group may need assistance with rebuilding their public image and strategizing to obtain needed funding. That training, however, probably would not be effective until *after* the group clarifies its purposes and learns to manage its internal conflict with some degrees of success. Just as in the first tentative contract, the trainer, in conjunction with the group, should specify the exact terms of the second or "training contract," in regard to number of training days, goals, fees, expectations of the training group, and so on.

In summary, then, we have described a framework within which to diagnose the needs of a potential training client. We also discussed three steps of the diagnostic phase: initial contact, contracting for training, and in-depth diagnosis. The systems framework guides our thinking and planning in each of those steps, in terms of assessing both the client groups and our relationship with the people in those groups. To plan the actual training, we next discuss a perspective of change consistent with the framework presented in this chapter.

FORM 3–1 *DIAGNOSING YOUR TEAM: A TORI SCALE**

Instructions: In front of each of the following items, place the letter that corresponds to your degree of agreement or disagreement with that statement.

SD = strongly disagree   D = disagree   A = agree   SA = strongly agree

_____ 1. I think this team will accept me as a full member no matter what unusual thing I might do.
_____ 2. There are lots of things I don't tell the team, and they are just as well left private.
_____ 3. I assert myself on this team.
_____ 4. I seldom seek help from other members on tasks.
_____ 5. Members of this team trust each other very much.
_____ 6. Members are not really interested in what other members have to say.
_____ 7. The team exerts little pressure on members to do what they should be doing.
_____ 8. Everyone on this team does his or her own thing with little thought for other members.
_____ 9. I see myself as a very cautious member of this team.
_____ 10. I don't think that I have to cover up things with this group.
_____ 11. On this team I do only the things that I am supposed to do.
_____ 12. I think that everyone on this team is willing to help me when I ask for help.
_____ 13. The team is more interested in accomplishing tasks than in helping members on personal problems.
_____ 14. Members tell it like it is.
_____ 15. Members do what they ought to do, out of a strong sense of responsibility to the team.
_____ 16. This team really "has it together" in many ways.
_____ 17. I trust members of this team.
_____ 18. I am afraid that if I told this team my innermost thoughts they would be shocked and have negative feelings about me.
_____ 19. When I am with this team I think I am free to do what I want.
_____ 20. I often think that I am in a minority on this team.
_____ 21. Members of this team know who they are; they have a real sense of being individuals.
_____ 22. When at work, members are very careful to express only relevant ideas about the task.
_____ 23. The goals of this team are clear.
_____ 24. The team finds it difficult to go ahead and do something it has decided to do.
_____ 25. If I left this team they would miss me very much.
_____ 26. I can trust this team with my most private and significant ideas and opinions.
_____ 27. I often find that my goals are different from those of the team and of other members.
_____ 28. I look forward to getting together with this team.
_____ 29. Members of this team are often not being themselves and are playing roles.
_____ 30. We know each other very well.
_____ 31. This team puts work pressure on each member.
_____ 32. This team will be able to handle an emergency very well.
_____ 33. When I am with this team I feel very good about myself.
_____ 34. If I have negative feelings when I am with this team, I don't express them very easily.
_____ 35. It is easy for me to take risks when I am working with this team.
_____ 36. I often go along with the others simply because I have a sense of obligation.
_____ 37. Members seem to care very much for each other.
_____ 38. Members often express different feelings and opinions outside meetings than they do when members are present.
_____ 39. We really let members be who they are as individuals.
_____ 40. Members of this team like to either lead or be led, rather than to work together as equals.
_____ 41. My relationship to this team is a very impersonal one.
_____ 42. Whenever I feel something strongly I feel easy about expressing it to the team members.
_____ 43. I think that I have to keep myself under wraps in here.
_____ 44. I enjoy working with members of this team.
_____ 45. Each member has a definite and clear role to play and is respected on the basis of how well he or she performs it.

_____ 46. Whenever there are negative feelings they are likely to be expressed at some point.
_____ 47. At times members seem very apathetic and passive.
_____ 48. We are well integrated and coordinated at many levels.
_____ 49. I feel like a unique person when I am on this team.
_____ 50. I would feel very vulnerable if I told members my most secret and private feelings and opinions.
_____ 51. The team thinks that my personal growth and learnings are very important.
_____ 52. I don't feel like cooperating with others on this team.
_____ 53. Team members have a high opinion of my contributions.
_____ 54. Members are afraid to be open and honest with each other.
_____ 55. When decisions are being made, members quickly express what they want.
_____ 56. Members are very much individuals and do not work together as members of a team.
_____ 57. When with this team I don't feel very good about myself.
_____ 58. When with this team I am free to be exactly who I am and never have to pretend I am something else.
_____ 59. It is very important to me to meet the expectations of other members.
_____ 60. I would miss anyone who left because each of the members is important in what the team is trying to do.
_____ 61. It is easy to tell who the "in" members are.
_____ 62. Members listen to others with understanding and empathy.
_____ 63. The team spends a lot of energy trying to get members to do things they don't really want to do.
_____ 64. Members enjoy being with each other.
_____ 65. I am an important member of the team.
_____ 66. My ideas and opinions are often distorted by the team.
_____ 67. My goals are similar to the goals of the total team.
_____ 68. Members seldom give me help on things that really matter to me.
_____ 69. Members listen to the things I have to say.
_____ 70. On this team, if members feel negative they keep it to themselves.
_____ 71. We have a lot of energy that gets directed into whatever we do as a team.
_____ 72. You really have to have some power if you want to get anything done on this team.
_____ 73. I sometimes don't feel very genuine when I'm with this team.
_____ 74. There is hardly anything I don't know about the other members.
_____ 75. If I did what I wanted to do on this team, I'd be doing different things.
_____ 76. Members often help me in things I am trying to do.
_____ 77. Some members are afraid of the team and of its members.
_____ 78. Members are very spontaneous and uninhibited when they are around each other.
_____ 79. The goals are often not really clear.
_____ 80. We really work together as a smoothly functioning unit.
_____ 81. I care very much for the members of this team.
_____ 82. Members misunderstand me and how I feel and think.
_____ 83. When we reach a decision I am usually in agreement.
_____ 84. I have no real sense of belonging to this team.
_____ 85. We treat each person as an important member.
_____ 86. It is easy to express feelings and opinions in here if they are positive, but not if they are negative.
_____ 87. Members of this team are growing and changing all the time.
_____ 88. We need a lot of controls in order to keep on the track.
_____ 89. I often feel defensive when I'm with this team.
_____ 90. I keep very few secrets from other members.
_____ 91. It is not OK for me to be myself with this team.
_____ 92. I feel a strong sense of belonging.
_____ 93. It is easy to tell who the important members are.
_____ 94. Members don't keep secrets from each other.
_____ 95. A lot of our team energy goes into irrelevant and unimportant things.
_____ 96. We have little destructive competition with each other.

*From Jack Gibb, _Trust: A New View of Personal and Organizational Development_ (Los Angeles: The Guild of Tutors, 1978).

TORI DIAGNOSING YOUR TEAM SCALE: SCORE SHEET

Instructions: The TORI Diagnosing Your Team scale yields eight scores: four depicting how you see yourself on this team in terms of the four core team processes (Trusting-being; Opening; Realizing-growing; and Interdependence-teaming), and four capturing your sense of what your team is like. Look back at the items for one of the eight scales on the instrument to see how you responded. On the Score Sheet, circle your response for each item according to whether you marked "Strongly Disagree," "Disagree," etc. Then sum the item scores for the scale. Do the same for each scale.

Trusting-Being

Item	SD	D	A	SA
1.	0	1	2	3
9.	3	2	1	0
17.	0	1	2	3
25.	3	2	1	0
33.	0	1	2	3
41.	3	2	1	0
49.	0	1	2	3
57.	3	2	1	0
65.	0	1	2	3
73.	3	2	1	0
81.	0	1	2	3
89.	3	2	1	0

Opening-Showing

Item	SD	D	A	SA
2.	3	2	1	0
10.	0	1	2	3
18.	3	2	1	0
26.	0	1	2	3
34.	3	2	1	0
42.	0	1	2	3
50.	3	2	1	0
58.	0	1	2	3
66.	3	2	1	0
74.	0	1	2	3
82.	3	2	1	0
90.	0	1	2	3

Realizing-Growing

Item	SD	D	A	SA
3.	0	1	2	3
11.	3	2	1	0
19.	0	1	2	3
27.	3	2	1	0
35.	0	1	2	3
43.	3	2	1	0
51.	0	1	2	3
59.	3	2	1	0
67.	0	1	2	3
75.	3	2	1	0
83.	0	1	2	3
91.	3	2	1	0

Interdependence-Teaming

Item	SD	D	A	SA
4.	3	2	1	0
12.	0	1	2	3
20.	3	2	1	0
28.	0	1	2	3
36.	3	2	1	0
44.	0	1	2	3
52.	3	2	1	0
60.	0	1	2	3
68.	3	2	1	0
76.	0	1	2	3
84.	3	2	1	0
92.	0	1	2	3

How I see *Myself* on the team:

T □ O □ R □ I □

Trusting-Being

Item	*Item Score*			
	SD	D	A	SA
5.	0	1	2	3
13.	3	2	1	0
21.	0	1	2	3
29.	3	2	1	0
37.	0	1	2	3
45.	3	2	1	0
53.	0	1	2	3
61.	3	2	1	0
69.	0	1	2	3
77.	3	2	1	0
85.	0	1	2	3
93.	3	2	1	0

Opening-Showing

Item	*Item Score*			
	SD	D	A	SA
6.	3	2	1	0
14.	0	1	2	3
22.	3	2	1	0
30.	0	1	2	3
38.	3	2	1	0
46.	0	1	2	3
54.	3	2	1	0
62.	0	1	2	3
70.	3	2	1	0
78.	0	1	2	3
86.	3	2	1	0
94.	0	1	2	3

Realizing-Growing

Item	*Item Score*			
	SD	D	A	SA
7.	0	1	2	3
15.	3	2	1	0
23.	0	1	2	3
31.	3	2	1	0
39.	0	1	2	3
47.	3	2	1	0
55.	0	1	2	3
63.	3	2	1	0
71.	0	1	2	3
79.	3	2	1	0
87.	0	1	2	3
95.	3	2	1	0

Interdependence-Teaming

Item	*Item Score*			
	SD	D	A	SA
8.	3	2	1	0
16.	0	1	2	3
24.	3	2	1	0
32.	0	1	2	3
40.	3	2	1	0
48.	0	1	2	3
56.	3	2	1	0
64.	0	1	2	3
72.	3	2	1	0
80.	0	1	2	3
88.	3	2	1	0
96.	0	1	2	3

How I see the *Team:*

T ☐   O ☐   R ☐   I ☐

TORI DIAGNOSING YOUR TEAM SCALE: INTERPRETATION SHEET

Trusting-Being:

A team member who scores *high* on this set of items is saying:

View of Myself: "I trust myself, have a fairly well-formed sense of my own being and uniqueness, and feel good about myself as a person and team member."

View of the Team: "I tend to see team members as trusting, and as providing a good environment for me to work in."

A team member who scores *low* on this set of items is saying:

View of Myself: "I feel less trusting of myself, have a less well-formed sense of my own being and uniqueness, and feel less well about myself as a person and team member."

View of the Team: "I tend to see team members as un-trusting, as impersonal and in role, and as providing a somewhat negative and defensive environment for me and for other team members."

Opening-Showing:

A team member who scores *high* on this set of items is saying:

View of Myself: "I feel free to show myself to others on the team, show who I am, and express my feelings and attitudes with little pretense to cover-up."

View of the Team: "I tend to see people as open and spontaneous and as willing to show themselves to other team members."

A team member who scores *low* on this set of items is saying:

View of Myself: "I feel un-free to be open, feel vulnerable and not safe, and I think it is necessary to keep large areas of myself private and unshared with the team."

View of the Team: "I tend to see team members as fearful, cautious, and unwilling to show feelings and opinions, particularly those feelings and opinions that are negative or non-supportive of other team members."

Realizing-Growing:

A team member who scores *high* on this set of items is saying:

View of Myself: "I feel free to take risks, assert myself, do anything that I really want to do, and follow my own motivations. I have a sense of self-realization."

View of the Team: "I tend to see team members as allowing others their freedom, and as providing an environment for me and other team members that makes it possible for us to reach our goals. Team members allow others to be who they are."

A person who scores *low* on this set of items is saying:

View of Myself: "I am aware of the pressure of extrinsic motivations. I feel that I must try to do what I am supposed to do and that I must attempt to meet the expectations of other team members."

View of the Team: "I tend to see other team members as exerting pressures on me and others to conform, to do things that we may not want to do, and to work toward team goals that are not significant to me as a person or team member."

Interdependence-Teaming:

A team member who scores *high* on this set of items is saying:

View of Myself: "I have a strong sense of belonging to the groups that are important to me, and I enjoy working with, helping, or meeting with other team members."

View of the Team: "I tend to see other team members as cooperative, working effectively, and relatively well integrated into the life around them and to the teams they belong to."

A person who scores *low* on this set of items is saying:

View of Myself: "I do not have a strong sense of belonging to the groups of which I am a member and do not especially enjoy working with this team or with others in a team way. I have competitive, dependent, or other feelings that get in the way of my working with other members of the team."

View of the Team: "I tend to see other team members as not being cooperative and not working well with others. I see team members in general as not easy to work with or team with, and as having feelings that get in their way."

FORM 3–2 *ORGANIZATIONAL DIAGNOSIS QUESTIONNAIRE** Robert C. Preziosi

From time to time organizations consider it important to analyze themselves. It is necessary to find out from the people who work in the organization what they think if the analysis is going to be of value. This questionnaire will help the organization that you work for analyze itself.

Directions: Do not put your name anywhere on this questionnaire. Please answer all thirty-five questions. *Be open and honest.* For each of the thirty-five statements circle only *one (1)* number to indicate your thinking.

1—Agree Strongly
2—Agree
3—Agree Slightly
4—Neutral
5—Disagree Slightly
6—Disagree
7—Disagree Strongly

	Agree Strongly	Agree	Agree Slightly	Neutral	Disagree Slightly	Disagree	Disagree Strongly
1. The goals of this organization are clearly stated.	1	2	3	4	5	6	7
2. The division of labor of this organization is flexible.	1	2	3	4	5	6	7
3. My immediate supervisor is supportive of my efforts.	1	2	3	4	5	6	7
4. My relationship with my supervisor is a harmonious one.	1	2	3	4	5	6	7
5. My job offers me the opportunity to grow as a person.	1	2	3	4	5	6	7
6. My immediate supervisor has ideas that are helpful to me and my work group.	1	2	3	4	5	6	7
7. This organization is not resistant to change.	1	2	3	4	5	6	7
8. I am personally in agreement with the stated goals of my work unit.	1	2	3	4	5	6	7
9. The division of labor of this organization is conducive to reaching its goals.	1	2	3	4	5	6	7
10. The leadership norms of this organization help its progress.	1	2	3	4	5	6	7
11. I can always talk with someone at work if I have a work-related problem.	1	2	3	4	5	6	7
12. The pay scale and benefits of this organization treat each employee equitably.	1	2	3	4	5	6	7
13. I have the information that I need to do a good job.	1	2	3	4	5	6	7
14. This organization is not introducing enough new policies and procedures.	1	2	3	4	5	6	7
15. I understand the purpose of this organization.	1	2	3	4	5	6	7
16. The manner in which work tasks are divided is a logical one.	1	2	3	4	5	6	7

	1—Agree Strongly 2—Agree 3—Agree Slightly 4—Neutral 5—Disagree Slightly 6—Disagree 7—Disagree Strongly	Agree Strongly	Agree	Agree Slightly	Neutral	Disagree Slightly	Disagree	Disagree Strongly
17.	This organization's leadership efforts result in the organization's fulfillment of its purposes.	1	2	3	4	5	6	7
18.	My relationships with members of my work group are friendly as well as professional.	1	2	3	4	5	6	7
19.	The opportunity for promotion exists in this organization.	1	2	3	4	5	6	7
20.	This organization has adequate mechanisms for binding itself together.	1	2	3	4	5	6	7
21.	This organization favors change.	1	2	3	4	5	6	7
22.	The priorities of this organization are understood by its employees.	1	2	3	4	5	6	7
23.	The structure of my work unit is well designed.	1	2	3	4	5	6	7
24.	It is clear to me whenever my boss is attempting to guide my work efforts.	1	2	3	4	5	6	7
25.	I have established the relationships that I need to do my job properly.	1	2	3	4	5	6	7
26.	The salary that I receive is commensurate with the job that I perform.	1	2	3	4	5	6	7
27.	Other work units are helpful to my work unit whenever assistance is requested.	1	2	3	4	5	6	7
28.	Occasionally I like to change things about my job.	1	2	3	4	5	6	7
29.	I desire less input in deciding my work-unit goals.	1	2	3	4	5	6	7
30.	The division of labor of this organization helps its efforts to reach its goals.	1	2	3	4	5	6	7
31.	I understand my boss's efforts to influence me and the other members of the work unit.	1	2	3	4	5	6	7
32.	There is no evidence of unresolved conflict in this organization.	1	2	3	4	5	6	7
33.	All tasks to be accomplished are associated with incentives.	1	2	3	4	5	6	7
34.	This organization's planning and control efforts are helpful to its growth and development.	1	2	3	4	5	6	7
35.	This organization has the ability to change.	1	2	3	4	5	6	7

ODQ SCORING SHEET

Instructions: Transfer the numbers you circled on the questionnaire to the blanks below. Add each column, and divide each sum by 5. This will give you comparable scores for each of the seven areas.

Purposes	Structure	Leadership	Relationships
1 _____	2 _____	3 _____	4 _____
8 _____	9 _____	10 _____	11 _____
15 _____	16 _____	17 _____	18 _____
22 _____	23 _____	24 _____	25 _____
29 _____	30 _____	31 _____	32 _____
Total _____	Total _____	Total _____	Total _____
Average _____	Average _____	Average _____	Average _____

Rewards	Helpful Mechanisms	Attitude Toward Change
5 _____	6 _____	7 _____
12 _____	13 _____	14 _____
19 _____	20 _____	21 _____
26 _____	27 _____	28 _____
33 _____	34 _____	35 _____
Total _____	Total _____	Total _____
Average _____	Average _____	Average _____

ODQ PROFILE AND INTERPRETATION SHEET

Instructions: Transfer your average scores from the ODQ Scoring Sheet to the appropriate boxes in the figure below. Then study the background information and interpretation suggestions that follow.

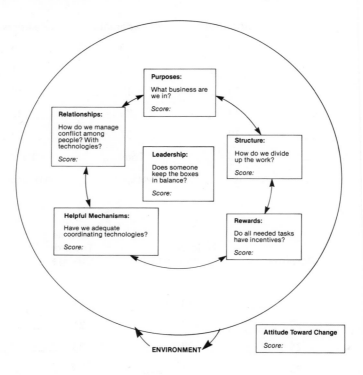

Background

The ODQ is a survey-feedback instrument designed to collect data on organizational functioning. It measures the perceptions of persons in an organization or work unit to determine areas of activity that would benefit from an organization development effort. It can be used as the sole data-collection technique or in conjunction with other techniques (interview, observation, etc.).

Weisbord's Six-Box Organizational Model (1976) is the basis for the questionnaire, which measures seven variables: purposes, structure, relationships, rewards, leadership, helpful mechanisms, and attitude toward change. The first six areas are from Weisbord's model, while the last one was added to provide the consultant/facilitator with input on readiness for change.

The instrument and the model reflect a systematic approach for analyzing relationships among variables that influence how an organization is managed. The ODQ measures the informal aspects of the system. It may be necessary for the consultant/facilitator also to gather information on the formal aspects and to examine the gaps between the two.

Using the ODQ is the first step in determining appropriate interventions for organizational change efforts. Its use as a diagnostic tool can be the first step in improving an organization's or work unit's capability to serve its clientele.

Interpretation and Diagnosis

A crucial consideration is the diagnosis based upon data interpretation. The simplest diagnosis would be to assess the amount of variance for each of the seven variables in relation to a score of 4, which is the neutral point. Scores above 4 would indicate a problem with organizational functioning. The closer the score is to 7 the more severe the problem would be. Scores below 4 indicate the lack of a problem, with a score of 1 indicating optimum functioning.

Another diagnostic approach follows the same guidelines of assessment in relation to the neutral point (score) of 4. The score of each of the thirty-five items on the questionnaire can be reviewed to produce more exacting information on problematic areas. Thus diagnosis would be more precise. For example, let us suppose that the average score on item number 8 is 6.4. This would indicate not only a problem in organizational purpose, but also a more specific problem in that there is a gap between organizational and individual goals. This more precise diagnostic effort is likely to lead to a more appropriate intervention in the organization than the generalized diagnostic approach described in the preceding paragraph.

Appropriate diagnosis must address the relationships between the boxes to determine the interconnectedness of problems. For example, if there is a problem with relationships, could it be that the reward system does not reward relationship behavior? This might be the case if the average score on item 33 was well above 4 (5.5 or higher) and all the items on relationships (4, 11, 18, 25, 32) averaged above 5.5.

*Reprinted from the *1980 Annual Handbook for Group Facilitators,* John E. Jones and J. William Pfeiffer, eds. (San Diego, Calif.: University Associates, Inc., 1980). Used with permission.

FORM 3-3 OPENNESS IN PERSONAL COMMUNICATION*

	Here and now: feelings expressed are current and based on immediate interactions	Here, not now: feelings expressed relate to immediate interaction but are not current	Not here, not now: feelings expressed are not current and relate to past experience unrelated to present interaction	Not Mutually Relevant
Mutually Relevant				Not Mutually Relevant
Feeling Owned	Owned: Use of "I feel"	General ownership: "Some of us feel" — Other owned: "Some people"	General Other: "People . . ." or "Society . . ."	Not Owned Feeling
Source of Feeling Specified	Directly specified: "John, toward you I . . ."	Indirectly specified: "Some people make me feel . . ."	Generally specified: "I feel around people (in general)"	Source Not Specified
Causal Connection (Re: Feeling)	Stated: "because . . ."	Suggested: "may be because"	Alluded to: "there may be a reason"	No Causal Connection
Perception Owned	Owned: "I think . . . ."	General ownership: "Some of us think . . ." — Other owned: "Some people think . . ."	General other: "People . . ." or "Society . . ."	Perception Not Owned
Source of Perception Specified	Directly specified: "Mary, you . . ."	Indirectly specified: "Some people in the group . . ."	Generally specified: "I think people are usually . . ."	Source of Perception Not Specified
Causal Connection (Re: Perception)	Stated: "You're aggressive because you're insecure . . ."	Suggested: "The reason may be that you're insecure . . ."	Alluded to: "There may be a reason . . ."	No Causal Connection
Behavior Specified	Specific behavior cited: ". . . you're yelling at Sue . . ."	Type of behavior specified: ". . . say unkind things"	Existence of behaviors indicated not not cited: ". . . some of the things you do . . ."	No Behavior Specified

*From Joe McDoniels, Elaine Yarbrough, Clare Kuzmal, and Kim Giffin, "Openness: Personalized Expression in Interpersonal Communication," paper presented at the International Communication Association, Phoenix, Ariz., 1971.

FORM 3–4   *COMMUNICATION STYLES**

		Words	*Body*	*Insides*
1.	Blaming	Accusatory Condescending	Finger-pointing Overpowering	I am lonely, unsuccessful, afraid
2.	Placating	Agreeing constantly Accommodating	Helpless	I feel like nothing; worthless
3.	Computing	Ultrareasonable	Expressionless; rigidly calm	I am vulnerable
4.	Distracting	Irrelevant	Angular; dizzy	Nobody cares; I am scared

5. Leveling—words, body, and insides of the person are congruent; going in the same direction. Leveling does not mean that the person tells "everything" that he/she knows and feels, but that the communication responses are an accurate representation of the person at the moment.

*Adapted from Virginia Satir, *Peoplemaking* (Palo Alto, Calif.: Science and Behavior Books, Inc., 1972). Reprinted by permission of the author and publisher.

FORM 3–5   *STRATEGIES AND TACTICS IN CONFLICT**

You can move a conflict in one of four directions:

1. Avoid
2. Escalate
3. Maintain
4. Deescalate

All are useful at different times. The choice of which one(s) to use should be based on the desired outcome of the conflict. Below are some tactics (specific behaviors) that typically move conflicts in one of the four directions.

Used Well or Poorly,
Resulting in:

I. *Avoidance*

Postponement

Using formal rules

Changing the physical environment

Tacit coordination (*exp.:* agreeing on votes before a meeting)

Gunnysacking (saving up feelings until later then they become explosive)

Coercive (*exp.:* pulling rank)

Refusing to recognize the conflict

Fogging (agreeing with part of a conflict)

Linguistic manipulation (*exp.:* "There's no conflict; just a slight disagreement")

II. *Escalation*—involvement in the conflict increases; issues are more sharply defined; number of issues increase; and parties often polarize

Labeling (naming the other or the relationship)

Issue expansion (connect many other issues to the ones in the conflict)

Coalition formation (to increase power)

Threats

Constricting the other (*exps.:* allowing only a certain time for a conflict; restricting access to an important person in a conflict)

III. *Maintenance*—neither reducing nor escalating the conflict

Quid pro quo (getting something for something)

Agreement on relational rules (how to conduct the conflict)

Combine escalation and reduction tactics

IV. *Deescalation*—reducing the conflict

Fractionate (break the issues into small, manageable units)

Ask for more information about the conflict

Metacommunication (discuss the relationship)

Response to all levels of the conflict (thoughts and feelings)

Compromise

Establish outside criteria for managing the conflict (decide how decisions will be made)

*Adapted from Joyce Hocker and William Wilmot, *Interpersonal Conflict* (Dubuque, Iowa: Wm. C. Brown, 1978).

FORM 3–6 *CONFLICT CHECKLIST*

Instructions: Check A or B, whichever is closer to your perception of this group meeting. Give an example under each category if possible.

I.   People in our group were:

_____   A. Purposeful in pursuing their own goals

_____   B. Purposeful in pursuing goals held in common among group members

II.   Communication in our group was mainly:

_____   A. Secretive

_____   B. Open

III.   People in our group used strategies that were:

_____   A. Unpredictable (for surprise)

_____   B. Predictable, flexible, and not designed for surprise

IV.   Communication included:

_____   A. A great many threats and bluffs (covert or overt)

_____   B. None or few threats and bluffs

V.   The group members believe that success is enhanced by:

_____   A. Forming bad stereotypes of certain group members; by increasing hostility

_____   B. Dropping stereotypes, considering ideas no matter what the source, and positive feelings

VI.   Group members believe that in pursuing their goals:

_____   A. Some have to win and some lose

_____   B. The only way to win is for all to win

FORM 3–7   *COMMUNICATION IN AND BETWEEN GROUPS*

Communication in our group was:
A.   Judgmental _____
B.   Descriptive _____

Communication between groups was:
A.   Judgmental _____
B.   Descriptive _____

People in our group attempted to:
A.   Control others _____
B.   Share ideas to get the problem solved _____

People from other groups attempted to:
A.   Control others _____
B.   Share ideas to get the problem solved _____

Communication in our group seemed to be:
A.   Strategic _____
B.   Spontaneous _____

Communication between groups seemed to be:
A.   Strategic _____
B.   Spontaneous _____

Concern for other group members was:
A.   Neutral _____
B.   Caring, empathetic _____

Concern for people in other groups was:
A.   Neutral _____
B.   Caring, empathetic _____

The attitude of most people toward others in the group was one of:
A.   Superiority _____
B.   Equality _____

The attitude of most people toward others in other groups was one of:
A.   Superiority _____
B.   Equality _____

The climate in our group was one of:
A.   Certainty (people stated their opinions and did not change) _____
B.   Openness (people were willing to consider viewpoints other than their own) _____

The climate between groups was one of:
A.   Certainty (people stated their opinions and did not change) _____
B.   Openness (people were willing to consider viewpoints other than their own) _____

FORM 3-8　*RATING GROUP EFFECTIVENESS*

There are ways that groups operate to arrive at solutions to problems that can utilize the human resources (the group members' ideas and feelings) in the group or fail to utilize them. You have just interacted with some other people in a group problem-solving exercise. Now take time to evaluate that experience by circling the number on each scale below that best describes how the people in your group interacted with each other. Each item on the questionnaire identifies an area that needs to be considered so that the group can utilize all its resources.

A: Goals

Poor										Good
1	2	3	4	5	6	7	8	9	10	

Confused; diverse; conflicting; indifferent; little interest

Clear to all, shared by all; all care about the goals, feel involved

B: Participation

Poor										Good
1	2	3	4	5	6	7	8	9	10	

A few dominate; some passive; some not listened to; several talk at once or interrupt

All get in; all are really listened to

C: Feelings

Poor										Good
1	2	3	4	5	6	7	8	9	10	

Expected; ignored or criticized

Freely expressed; empathetic responses

D: Leadership

Poor										Good
1	2	3	4	5	6	7	8	9	10	

Group needs for leadership not met; group depends too much on single person or on a few persons

As needs for leadership arise, various members meet them ("distributed leadership"); anyone feels free to volunteer as s/he sees a group need

FORM 3-8 *RATING GROUP EFFECTIVENESS (Continued)*

E: Decisions

Poor										Good
1	2	3	4	5	6	7	8	9	10	

Needed decisions do not get made; decision made by part of group; others uncommitted

Consensus sought and tested; deviates appreciated and used to improve decision; decisions when made are fully supported

F: Trust

Poor										Good
1	2	3	4	5	6	7	8	9	10	

Members distrust one another; are polite, careful, closed, guarded; they listen superficially but inwardly reject what others say; are afraid to criticize or to be criticized

Members trust one another; they reveal to group what they would be reluctant to expose to others; they respect and use the responses they get; they can freely express negative reactions without fearing reprisal

G: Use of My Resources

Poor										Good
1	2	3	4	5	6	7	8	9	10	

What I could have contributed to the group was not offered by me or not used by the group

What I could have contributed was contributed and used by the group

H: Use of Other Members' Resources

Poor										Good
1	2	3	4	5	6	7	8	9	10	

Other people did not contribute their resources (ideas and feelings) to the group

Other people did contribute their resources and they were used

FORM 3-9   *GROUP CLIMATE INVENTORY*

Directions: Think about how your fellow group members normally behave toward you. In the parentheses in front of the items below, place the number corresponding to your perceptions of the group as a whole, using the following scale.

>5   They can *always* be counted on to behave this way.
>4   *Typically* I would expect them to behave this way.
>3   I would *usually* expect them to behave this way.
>2   They would *seldom* behave this way.
>1   They would *rarely* behave this way.
>0   I would *never* expect them to behave this way.

I would expect my fellow group members to:

1.   (____) ____ ____ ____   level with me
2.   ____ (____) ____ ____   get the drift of what I am trying to say
3.   ____ ____ (____) ____   interrupt or ignore my comments
4.   ____ ____ ____ (____)   accept me for what I am
5.   (____) ____ ____ ____   feel free to let me know when I "bug" them
6.   ____ (____) ____ ____   misconstrue things I say or do
7.   ____ ____ (____) ____   be interested in me
8.   ____ ____ ____ (____)   provide an atmosphere where I can be myself
9.   (____) ____ ____ ____   keep things to themselves to spare my feelings
10.   ____ (____) ____ ____   perceive what kind of person I really am
11.   ____ ____ (____) ____   include me in what's going on
12.   ____ ____ ____ (____)   act "judgmental" with me
13.   (____) ____ ____ ____   be completely frank with me
14.   ____ (____) ____ ____   recognize readily when something is bothering me
15.   ____ ____ (____) ____   respect me as a person, apart from my skills or status
16.   ____ ____ ____ (____)   ridicule me or disapprove if I show my peculiarities

____ ____ ____ ____

(____)   Genuineness
   (____)   Understanding
      (____)   Valuing
         (____)   Acceptance

Reprinted from J. William Pfeiffer and John E. Jones, eds., *A Handbook of Structured Experiences for Human Relations Training,* Vol. III, p. 25 (La Jolla, Calif.: University Associates, Inc., 1974). Used with permission.

CHAPTER FOUR
DYNAMICS OF CHANGE

Before delving into the specific phases of the training model, we think it is crucial for trainers to understand how they view the change process itself. Trainers may know the content they are teaching, whether it be communication, financial planning, or computer programming and they may be able to present their material using several methods of training. But more basic than content and methods are the *assumptions* which guide choices about the sequence of training activities, responses to trainees, instructional methods, and training evaluation. Indeed, it is the process of change, set in motion by how the training is conducted, that affects, and in most cases directs, *what* is learned and *how* that learning is used by people when the training is over. We therefore think it is critical that training practitioners clarify their ideas about the dynamics of change.

An example may clarify the point. Traditional classroom education is based on several assumptions regarding how change occurs. Some are that learning is an intellectual process, that people learn when they are first made to feel that they do not know enough, that the instructor is superior and should rarely be questioned, and that learning is, therefore, a one-way communication from instructor to students who are said to have learned when they have memorized what the instructor sent out.

Traditional education is based on a compliant model of change, one which has inherent consequences regardless of the content of the courses taught (see

Wight, 1970). For example, conformity and competition, dependence on and distrust of authority, and a search for "right" answers are encouraged. Diversity and cooperation, independent thinking, and creativity are less likely to develop. These consequences can be observed in relationships and organizations: distrust of superiors, a lack of risk or initiative, and competition among individuals, divisions, and departments resulting in lowered productivity and more distrust. Ironically, many organizations attempt to solve their problems by using methods of change that initially helped create the problems, such as tighter controls, more discipline, and fewer rewards. Their "solutions" can, therefore, accentuate problems.

As such, the compliant model violates assumptions of the systems perspective discussed in Chapter 3. It precludes meeting the conditions for effective systems: flexibility, congruency, openness, and affirmation. For example, trainers cannot teach flexibility if they are interested in single right answers; and they cannot affirm people if they are interested in demonstrating superiority.

The point is, then, that the trainer's approach to change affects the outcomes of training and can enhance or block development of effective systems. The change model we discuss here reflects and facilitates the characteristics of healthy systems and directs trainers' thinking regarding what to include in programs, how to conduct them, and how to assess their outcomes. We first explain the perspective of change which is the basis of this model and then discuss the phases and conditions of change necessary to operationalize the model. Specific instructional methods, program sequencing, facilitation skills, and evaluation procedures congruent with this perspective are discussed in detail in subsequent chapters.

WHAT IS THE PERSPECTIVE?

First and foremost, change is a process. (See Table 4–1 for a summary of the perspective). As such, it is always occurring for one of two general purposes: *maintaining* the system's stability, or *transforming* it for movement in new directions (see Lippitt, 1973; Palazzoli et al., 1978). Both functions are needed, but problems occur for people and organizations when they are either too stable or change too rapidly. For example, if organizations become too rigid and do not plan for change in relation to new markets and personnel, they soon begin to lose their efficiency. One common symptom of rigidity is that important activities begin to occur outside regular organizational channels. For example, many women's groups currently are being organized to furnish support and education for women who are being promoted to higher levels of management. Instead of encouraging these groups, many managers are threatened by them and either do not support or actively discourage them. By so doing, they alienate participants in such activities and push them further underground, into the informal organizational structure.

TABLE 4-1   Perspective of Change

ASSUMPTIONS	IMPLICATIONS

1. Change is a *process*
  • For maintaining and/or transforming a system
  • Indicating that problems have multiple causes
	• Trainer's goal is to influence the direction and rate of change
	• Trainer is part of the client system
	• Every situation is unique
	• Collaborative approach is essential
	• Skills and structure in the system must be built for long-term change

2. Change is *paradoxical*	• Requires full awareness and acceptance of present circumstances at multiple levels of the system (nonavoidance) • Requires speaking the unspeakable in the client group • Requires understanding that positive recognition is more powerful for enhancing change than negative recognition • Requires nondualistic thinking: opposite characteristics can coexist (strength and weakness) • Requires a distinction between *what* qualities people have and *how* they are using them
3. Both *first-order* change (change within the structure of a system) and *second-order* change (change of the structure) are possible	• Decisions need to be made about the order of change to match the client's problems and goals • Misdiagnosis of the order of change can be ineffective and detrimental to the system

On the other hand, if the rate of transformation and change is too rapid in organizations, people may experience "future shock." They do not know what to expect, and how to plan, and therefore decrease their efficiency and production. It is paradoxical, but true, that the opposite extremes of too much stability and too much change tend to produce similar consequences.

When change is thought of as a process, it becomes apparent that problems within the system have multiple causes which mutually influence each other. In other words, it is not consistent with the process view of change to figure out "who done it" or who is to blame for problems that occur. It is more productive to assess how *all* parts and people in a system contribute to the situation. For example, when most people look at two people, one dominant and one overly submissive, they tend to blame the dominant one for the problems that arise. In contrast, from a process view of change, it is important to consider how the behaviors of both people fit together and how they mutually reinforce the patterns of dominance and submission (see Watzlawick et al., 1967). A submissive person, for instance, may subtly persuade another person to be dominant, by refusing to make decisions, just as a dominant person overwhelms a submissive partner by making all the decisions.

There are several practical implications for trainers when they view change as a process. First, their task is not to create or stop change but to *influence its direction and rate*. A discussion of two kinds of conflict training should show the difference between a process and a static view of change. For a long time, conflict training was labeled "conflict resolution." As such, conflict was not seen as an inevitable process whose direction and rate needed to be controlled, but rather as an unproductive occurrence that should be avoided or squelched. In contrast, the term "conflict management" connotes the naturalness and inevitability of conflict and the need to manage it for certain purposes. When seen from these two perspectives, trainers teach conflict in different ways and respond differently to its occurrence during training. With a "resolution" view, trainers have one general goal—to get rid of the conflict, usually by avoiding it or competing to win. With a "management" view, conflict can be increased, decreased, maintained, or avoided by using any one of several styles—avoidance, accommodation, compromise, collaboration, or competition (see Kilmann and Thomas, 1975; Hocker and Wilmot, 1978). In other words, with a process view of change, trainers increase their own choices of response and are, therefore, able to provide trainees with more choices. Trainers also are able to deal with situations as they arise, and the goal changes from one of getting rid of unpleasant circumstances and participants, to using whatever comes up as material with which to work.[1] (The upcoming chapters on facilitation skills and special problems give trainers ideas of how to respond to situations and people from a process perspective.)

A second implication of a process perspective is that *trainers become part of the system* with which they are working. Therefore, they are aware of their relationships with their clients in each stage of the training process. Some trainers may see their interventions as beginning and ending with the actual training sessions. They disregard the importance of their presence in the organization from the first contracting phase of consulting. As soon as contact is established, of course, there is no possibility of noninfluence; and each time the trainer talks with the client system, he/she is making an intervention that will have impact on that system.

The third implication is that since change is continual, *every situation may be viewed as unique*. Hence, trainers must respond to each client in a fresh way. This does not mean that entirely different training programs must be constructed for each new situation. It does mean that there should be the possibility of varying training programs for each new situation so that the training fits the clients' individual circumstances.

Fourth, if we assume that mutual influence is inevitable, we are led to a *collaborative* approach to *change*, which basically means that both trainers and

---

[1]For a greater understanding of this philosophy, trainers may want to read *The Myth of Freedom* by Chogyam Trungpa (1976).

clients must participate in defining problems and creating their solutions. The role of the trainer is to work with clients to understand their system first, and then to decide collaboratively what interventions will shed new light on a problem, provide new options, or teach new skills. Thus, trainers move away from power-coercive strategies, that is, making people do things for "their own good" (see Chin and Benne, 1969).

It should be noted that collaboration does not mean trainers forfeit their influence. It means that the kind of influence exerted changes from a forceful, heavy-handed approach to a more gentle one. The latter approach begins with developing a shared, full understanding of a particular system, so that decisions made about it seem evident and worthwhile to everyone involved. When trainers do not take sole responsibility for the changes that occur or do not occur, they also are less likely to be frustrated by the actions of the client(s) and can maintain a more objective and therefore more helpful view of their system.

Finally, a process view of change implies that once a system has been redirected, there is no guarantee that it will continue in that direction. Therefore, trainers must keep in mind that one of the primary goals of training is to *teach participants skills to use after the trainers have gone.* Trainers also should keep in mind a need for building mechanisms into the system that will facilitate ongoing change. For example, the goal of stress management training is not only to help trainees reduce stress during training but also to facilitate their inclusion of stress reduction factors in their work environment (for example, scheduling alone time or occasional breaks from pressure at work and home, more effective time management, a company exercise program).

The second major assumption we are making about the change process is that it is paradoxical; at least it *seems* paradoxical when compared to traditional ways of conceptualizing change (see Beisser, 1970). Basically, a paradoxical approach means productive change occurs when there is an *awareness* and *acceptance* of where people are at the *present* as well as acknowledging where they would *prefer* to be. In using a paradoxical approach, trainers should assess the present skills of trainees, recognize and affirm what they do well, get information about problems they are having, and then suggest how present skills can be extended and new ones learned for problematic situations. For example, we have conducted a great deal of conflict training for women's groups. A typical style of conflict management for these women is avoidance, which contributes to such problems as backstabbing and poor decision making. Many trainers will attempt to convince the women that they should *stop* avoiding conflict and *change* their strategies. A paradoxical approach would be to discuss the *advantages* gained from avoiding conflict; to explore current problems and the advantages and disadvantages of avoiding them; to indicate that the group does not have to give up avoidance but simply can add other behaviors to their repertoire, if desired; and finally, to suggest additional strategies for dealing with problems. This sequence tends to affirm people and build from the present to the future. It begins with a thorough understanding and acceptance of where people are and moves from there. This approach to change is helpful with all groups and is particularly important with highly *resistant* groups. Novice trainers often violate this principle and spend their time and energy trying to convince groups how they could do things better. Trainees may then feel disconfirmed and react with apathy or rebellion when trainers imply that they have been doing things wrong and should change. These common errors are discussed in detail in Chapter 13.

As simple as the paradoxical approach sounds, it flies in the face of how we are taught to motivate and change ourselves and others. Typically, we assume several things if we want others to change. First, we must let them know what they have *not* been doing or have been doing *badly*, so they will stop the behavior and correct their errors. Second, we assume that if we let people know what they do well, they will think they are superior to us, will become conceited, and/or will be uninterested in further improvement. Finally, we tend to assume that focusing on weaknesses produces greater fear and arouses more energy and is, therefore, a greater motivator than is recognizing and accepting strengths. Operating on these assumptions occasionally produces some kinds of change, but they very often evoke defensive resistance. Also, people feel insulted and cling more rigidly to old patterns. There is a great deal of evidence to suggest that this approach to change leaves people frustrated and dissatisfied; they do not develop as quickly or as thoroughly as people who are recognized for their accomplishments; and overall, they have lower self-esteem than do people who are affirmed for what they already do well. Low self-esteem, in turn, is connected with lower regard for other people, who then are not recognized for what they do well; and the cycle continues.[2] In fact, Gibb (1978) indicates that fear strategies are lower-level ones and, therefore, keep people and organizations stuck at lower stages of human development (see Tables 2–2, 2–3, and 2–4).

If traditional views of change create such problems, why do clients cling to those views? First, when they feel threatened or judged, some clients resist defining problems. Second, they may believe that to maintain power they must define things from a good/bad perspective (usually in terms of what is wrong with other people) and have the trainer resolve the problems created by the "other guy." For similar reasons they may also resist clear definition of a problem in which conflict is inherent. They view conflict as negative and therefore as something to be avoided. Furthermore, if they recognize conflict, they assume that it will get out of hand and be uncontrollable. So instead of clearly defining the conflict, they prefer at first to ignore, avoid, or suppress it. Their myth is that conflict will disappear if ignored. Instead, it tends to emerge in covert and uncontrollable ways. Intrapersonally, it may appear in the form of bodily ailments (for example, ulcers). Interpersonally and organizationally, it may emerge in refusals to cooperate, extreme competition between people or departments, rumors in the company, or high turnover and absenteeism rates.

The point is that the consequences people fear tend to occur when they are *not aware* of or cannot accept the reality of problems, rather than when they take

---

[2]A discussion of a traditional approach to change in different areas can be found in Capra (1975); Gibb (1978); Boulding (1977); Deikman (1968); Yarbrough (1979); Wilmot (1980); and McGregor (1960).

the time and courage to recognize them.[3] From a paradoxical perspective, the role of the trainer is to enhance awareness by helping to define problems. To do so, the trainer often must be willing to "speak the unspeakable," to recognize patterns of interaction that are unacceptable to participants. An example may clarify the point. In a week-long workshop on interpersonal communication, the spoken goal was creation of a cooperative community of mutually supportive people. The unspoken assumption was that to be cooperative and loving, people must manifest no competition. Yet there was an unspoken sense of competition among them. Instead of dealing with this competition directly, participants were competing covertly over who was most cooperative and loving. This subterranean struggle precluded their goal of real cooperation. Trainers needed to "speak the unspeakable" by discussing such "taboo" dynamics as competition, which, through discussion, is legitimized and potentially used productively. In this case, the trainers introduced a paradoxical intervention. They created a game in which participants got points for cooperation. This kind of intervention is, at first, confusing to participants because they are cooperating and competing at the same time, actions they previously thought were mutually exclusive. By doing *both*, however, they begin to understand how the two can be integrated and that both are legitimate means of interacting with others.

The unspeakable in some hard-nosed businesses is that people really want to be cared for and to express their feelings. The unspeakable in many human service organizations is that people like and want power. The unspeakable in many community women's groups, in which the goal is to create sisterhood, is that some women do not like each other. Unless confronted and dealt with, the "unspeakables" control people to a much greater extent than do the things people are allowed to talk about.

In order for awareness of speakables and unspeakables to lead to productive change, however, the second condition of paradoxical change must be apparent—acceptance of present conditions. Acceptance means recognizing that certain problems exist, that no one is "wrong" or "evil" because of that, and the people involved can own responsibility for creating them and for changing them. Acceptance also means focusing on current strengths as well as deficiencies. It does, indeed, seem paradoxical that acknowledging problems and conflicts as "okay" must precede the effort to solve them, that strengths are being affirmed when deficiencies are supposed to be the target.

The paradox is less confusing when we clarify a few other assumptions. First, we are assuming that people need recognition and will get it whether it is positive or negative.[4] Some people are adept at getting negative recognition and

---

[3]This idea parallels Jung's discussion of the Shadow side of the personality. The Shadow is composed of qualities (feelings and thoughts) that are disowned and relegated to the Unconscious. They become negative and have a great deal of control over the person's behavior. The goal of many therapies is to increase the awareness and ownership of seemingly negative qualities so that they can be integrated into the conscious personality. See, for example, Polster and Polster, *Gestalt Therapy Integrated* (1973).

[4]Transactional Analysis literature has a great deal to say about needs and means of recognition. See James and Jongeward (1971).

feel more secure dwelling on what they do badly. They know that people often take care of people who seem helpless. We also are told that it is bad to "blow your own horn" or to give the appearance of "being conceited." Therefore, people will often engineer getting negative recognition for fear of getting none at all. There is, at least, a certainty in what they will get.[5]

Major change, however, emerges from a state of uncertainty. Positive recognition (for people used to negative) is more uncertain, more jarring to the self-concept, and, if accepted, is potentially more helpful for building self-esteem and productive relationships. Positive recognition also is needed to enhance the confidence people need to make attitudinal and behavioral changes. We assume that it is risky to make changes and that people need to feel good about where they are at present before they decide they can be better. Continually telling people that they do wrong does not build that confidence.

It may be easier to use the principle of acceptance when trainers realize there is a difference between *how* someone uses a quality or characteristic and *what* the quality is. For example, a group may use its creativity for destructive purposes. The trainer can affirm the creativity without accepting the destructiveness. A specific example occurred in a counseling interview. A consultant was interviewing a woman who said her marital relationship was deteriorating, that she was attempting to care for her three children and keep her career going, and that she was having multiple affairs. The therapist praised the woman for her amazing organizational skills and suggested that she could use those same skills for changing the direction of her life, if she so desired.

As was discussed previously, the tendency for both trainers and trainees is to eradicate negative behavior rather than accepting it and transforming it for positive use. In contrast, from a paradoxical perspective, the trainer may plan interventions that have trainees increase their current behavior, so that they can get a clearer picture of it, sort out the functional from the dysfunctional, and learn to transform existing patterns to productive uses. For example, trainers may be working with highly competitive departments of an organization that have the goal of enhancing their cooperation. Instead of pushing for cooperation, a first intervention may be to plan an activity that surfaces the competition. Beckhard's confrontational meeting uses this principle (1967). One format is having employees of competing departments independently generate lists of how they see themselves, how they see members of other departments, and how they think other departments see them. Dynamics between departments, both positive and

---

[5]Many psychological theories indicate that people develop life positions or orientations to self and others so that their life patterns are repeated. Transactional Analysis labels the life positions: "I'm OK—you're not OK"; "I'm not OK—you are OK"; "I'm not OK—You're not OK"; and "I'm OK—you're OK." The first three are the basis of negative life scripts, repeated dramas (see Steiner, 1974). In a similar fashion, Karen Horney (1945) labels life orientations as moving toward people, moving away from people, and moving against people. This is apparently true for organizations as well as individuals. See Jongeward, *Everybody Wins: Transactional Analysis Applied to Organizations* (1973).

negative, are brought into awareness and examined openly. The employees are thus free to check their perceptions of the situation and decide on further courses of action.

By the same token, if people in an intact work group or workshop do not respond to each other, the trainer may direct them to become even more passive and nonresponsive. For example, trainers may instruct participants not to talk with or acknowledge each other, or actually separate them into different rooms. Frustration usually builds; participants get a clear indication of their feelings and their rewards for passivity and, paradoxically, for their need for more contact.

Trainers may need to convince clients that seemingly opposite qualities are, in reality, compatible and integratable. Therefore, people and organizations do not have to choose between competition and cooperation, aggressiveness and passivity, anger and love, thinking and feeling. Rather, competency calls for an ability to use multiple characteristics depending on the situation and the people involved. Some recent thinking on leadership recognizes the need for flexibility. Hersey et al. (1978), for example, propose four leadership styles and four kinds of employees and indicate how they can be matched for highest productivity and worker satisfaction.[6] The goal for leaders and managers is to be able to use all the styles, depending on the maturity of the subordinate and the nature of the task. Hersey's conceptualization contrasts with earlier ideas about effective management which indicated that a "democratic" or collaborative style was the best to use at all times.[7]

WHAT TYPES OF CHANGE ARE POSSIBLE?

We have discussed the importance of understanding change as a process that permits paradox. It also is important to distinguish between first- and second-order changes (Watzlawick et al., 1974). First-order change is one that occurs within a given system which itself remains unchanged, and second-order change is a change of the system itself(p. 10). Examples are important for understanding the concepts and their implications.

During the 1960s, blacks were interested in making more of an impact on

---

[6]Leadership style is based on two dimensions in Hersey's formulation: task behavior (the amount of direction given by a manager) and relationship behavior (the amount of socioemotional support given by the manager). Each kind of behavior can range from low to high. The combination of low to high and the two kinds of behaviors produce four styles. Therefore, a manager could be: high task and low relationship (style 1), high task and high relationship (style 2), high relationship and low task (style 3), and low relationship and low task (style 4).

The comparable dimension for employee style is maturity, which is based on job maturity (ability to do something), and psychological maturity (willingness to do something). Each can be low or high, too. Thus, employee style 1 (low job maturity and high psychological maturity) should be matched with leadership style 1 for most productivity and satisfaction; employee style 2 with leadership style 2, and so on.

[7]See, for example, Blake and Mouton (1964).

public decision making. After much conflict in some communities, blacks were placed on local advisory boards or elected to public office. Even though these pioneers had high visibility, they remained in the minority and had little impact on the kinds of decisions made. In other communities, blacks worked to alter the structure of the system by redrawing gerrymandered districts or pushing for elections at large in communities where they were the majority. In some cases, a majority of blacks were elected to government positions and began making different kinds of decisions about money allocation and governmental appointments. The first case is an example of tokenism and of first-order change; the second, of second-order change, alteration of the structure of the system.

First- and second-order change also can be applied to training programs. For example, many people attend personal growth or human relations events because they are dissatisfied with their relationships and want new ways of being with people. Prior to the training, one of their beliefs might be: "People should not disclose their feelings because disclosure is a sign of weakness." After the training, they may believe: "People should always disclose their feelings because disclosure leads to intimacy and satisfaction."

The trainees have made a first-order change, a pendulum swing to the opposite pole, and may be surprised to discover that the *structure* of their relationships remains the same. Although the content of their choice has changed, they remain with only *one* choice of interaction: prior to training, they would not disclose; after training, they always disclose. Furthermore, they still are controlled by what they *should* do and likely will continue attempting to control others by the same means.

Many organizational development (O.D.) efforts have been criticized for focusing primarily on first-order change and, therefore, being ineffective. O.D. is designed to affect the human subsystem of organizations, which is only one of the subsystems that affects employees. Intervention to change leadership styles or decision-making abilities, for example, may temporarily have a major impact on the organization. However, the effects of the interventions may be wiped out later because other factors affecting worker satisfaction come to restore their influence on the organizational culture. An example was given in Chapter 2 of an intervention in the telephone company to improve the communication skills of the operators, whose interaction was greatly affected by the company's evaluation procedures. In that case, for long-term effectiveness, a second-order change was needed to alter the payoffs and penalties of the system as well, so that they would reinforce the desired communication behavior.

The point is: Trainers need to assess which order of change is needed and wanted by a group, decide whether training can accomplish that change, and/or determine whether first- and second-order changes can be compatible. For instance, we were conducting training for law enforcement officials. In the assessment, we discovered that the reward structure needed change to facilitate the organization's goals of crime prevention and detection. Rewards were given to officers who made arrests but not to those who conveyed information that led to the arrests. As a consequence, valuable information was, at times, not given to fellow officers. It was not possible for us to intervene in the reward structure to introduce second-order change; but we decided that a first-order change potentially could facilitate a second-order one. That is, if members of the unit increased their communication skills and sense of themselves as a team, they might share information in spite of the reward system. In the long run, officers might even initiate change of the system.

We have two final thoughts on the orders of change. At times, trainers may desire a second-order change when clients do not. We were working with a group of fairly traditional women who wanted to improve their conflict skills. However, they did not want to change the *structure* of their relationships, the dominant/submissive roles of husband and wife. It was not the role of the trainer to insist that the trainees be more assertive, but to present them with a number of conflict strategies which they could use as they chose.

Finally, it may be interpreted from the examples given that first-order change is ineffective and that second-order change is always preferable. That is not consistently true. A series of first-order changes often lead to second-order change, at which point new norms are incorporated into personal and professional relationships. This sequence of change often is necessary. Second-order change usually alters the power structure in relationships and institutions and, therefore, often is resisted if proposed too soon. For example, the push for affirmative action in many institutions can represent a second-order change; if adopted, the rules of hiring and firing are altered, as is the composition of the work force. New kinds of employees, if they exist in sufficient numbers, influence the kinds of decisions made in the institution; and those decisions are likely to affect the power bases of the people who have been protected by the institutional rules. It is not surprising, then, that the passage of affirmative action laws took a long time and that their enforcement continues to be problematic. Many affirmative action directors and supporters have learned to initiate first-order changes so that the eventual enforcement of the law may evolve. Examples of those changes are influencing the institution to include a policy statement about their support of affirmative action, collecting and publicizing concrete data on women and minority salaries and ranks, and having women and minorities appointed to key decision-making boards.

New norms are created gradually. Then, when major decisions have to be made in the institutions, there are precedents for the support for affirmative action. If trainers and consultants are dealing with potentially volatile social issues, they will be particularly interested in the distinction and sequence of first- and second-order change.

In terms of organizational development, the phases of environmental quality (see Tables 2-2 and 2-4) also can be explained using the concepts of first- and second-order change. The first five phases, from Punitive to Participative, involve a series of first-order changes. Each phase moves people to a higher quality of interaction, but each is still dependent on a hierarchical form of leadership. Gibb says that participative life "is the highest form of leadership and the most effective form of environment within the limitations of leadership as a critical dimension of social life. The crucial limitation is that action and decision-making are only as effective as the leader" (1978, p. 54).

The emergent phase, Phase VI, represents a second-order change, in that the structure and rules of the interaction shift.

> The emergent group and community grow a new and leaderless level of reality and interaction. There are vestigial remains of the dynamics of power, control, and influence. Primarily, however, concerns about power, influence, and control are replaced by concerns about interpersonal skills, being, awareness, experimentation, and empathy. [Gibb, 1978, p. 54]

However, people and organizations cannot jump from a Punitive to an Emergent phase. There must be a series of first-order changes before reaching Phase IV. In addition, trainers need to remember that second-order change not only requires awareness of new possibilities, but also requires the acquisition of new skills. For example, many teachers in the public school, trained in traditional methods of teaching, were thrust into "schools without walls" (a second-order change) without being retrained. They used familiar methods and the new structure was rendered meaningless. In the same vein, some organizations, such as the aerospace industry, because of the nature of their work, have experimented with matrix management in which work teams are formed and reformed based on their expertise on a given project. Participants in work teams, at all levels, must have sophisticated communication skills to keep needed information flowing and their trust level high. If retraining does not take place, matrix management is less efficient than a standard hierarchical organization; and the special expertise that the matrix was designed to tap is lost.

Unless trainers understand and can distinguish first- and second-order change, they may be unable to diagnose the needs of their clients accurately and, therefore, make ineffective interventions; and they are likely to be frustrated with (and to frustrate) clients whose goals do not match their own. When trainers can assess the different orders of change, they are free to accept or reject a training contract with a clear understanding of their own and the client's expectations.

WHAT ARE THE PHASES AND CONDITIONS OF CHANGE?

We have explained the perspective and orders of change that we think are important for productive training. There also are identifiable phases of change, a recognition of which can help trainers diagnose problems and plan their training programs. The phases are the ones identified by Kurt Lewin: unfreezing, changing, and refreezing (Lewin, 1951). They are broader than, but correspond with, the stages of learning enumerated in Chapter 1. Figure 4–1 indicates their relationship.

Unfreezing connotes a readiness for change, for new information and skills. It necessitates the presence of some level of uncertainty, dissatisfaction, or aspiration which must be combined with a level of trust so that the fear produced by uncertainty opens rather than closes people to experimentation and new information (see Schein, 1969b).

The importance of unfreezing is emphasized by the following examples. The first ones have to do with training groups in which the uncertainty (or motivation) was not high enough to facilitate change. A large company asked us to conduct short workshops to expose their managers to current ideas about organizational behavior. Since the program was voluntary, we assumed that the participants would be open to new ideas. We found that they were motivated only to attend, not to explore new approaches to management. Many of them were highly argumentative and resistant to the ideas presented. They were "frozen," presenting an impenetrable wall to alternative views. Had we known

FIGURE 4–1   Phases of Change.

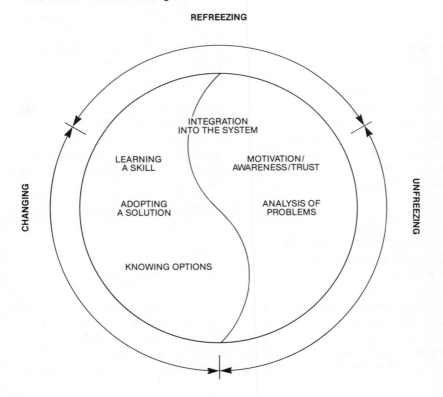

this, we would have begun the program differently, perhaps by having the participants complete self-evaluation questionnaires which may have brought to the surface some discontent with the status quo and a desire to grow. Unfreezing often is precipitated when a discrepancy is identified between the actual and the ideal.

In such instances, people attend training programs for reasons other than obtaining new information or skills. They may want a break from work or a visit to a nice part of the country. Consequently, they may be apathetic or even resentful of the time spent in training. In such cases, the initial activities need to be maximally involving, for example, the use of simulations, small-group discussion, and self-evaluation instruments to melt or unfreeze their "icy" perspective.

Finally, in some instances, trainers can facilitate the unfreezing stage *prior* to the training. A case in point involved a long-term community development project. The general goal was to organize diverse groups of people in small towns and train them in social planning for their communities. There was openness to the training from some people in the cities but not from a sufficient number to make the training successful. Therefore, the initial six months of the project were spent interviewing people, asking them about their social needs, and suggesting how the training might facilitate their goals. The interviews were conducted with opinion leaders in the communities so that at the end of the six months, the trainers had covered the power network in the small cities. Had the unfreezing phase not been included there would have been few participants at the training.

Sometimes it is necessary to *reduce* uncertainty to a workable level. If uncertainty is too high, people may cling to their existing familiar, "safe" ideas rather than being open to new ones. Trainers should remember that openness to change is risky and requires vulnerability. If people feel too vulnerable, they cannot risk being open to new information. An example of this situation involved a training program for a large group of secretaries in one company. The climate of the company was such that the secretaries did not feel supported in their work, and they were afraid the trainers were cohorts of upper management. Even though we began the program in what we thought was a supportive way, the atmosphere in the room was one of extreme caution. The participants were "frozen" by their anxiety. They did not talk, offer information, or participate actively in the experiential exercises. Finally, we stopped to talk about the interaction and to ask trainees about their responses. We had assumed that they knew each other and had been well informed about the purposes of the training. Neither was true. Therefore, to establish a safe climate, we essentially started the training again by conducting several low-risk exercises that gave them the opportunity to get to know each other and to ask the trainers questions about the training, privately and in small groups. Trust was increased and training could progress as planned.

Trainees will work with uncertainty best when they *trust* themselves, other participants, and the trainer. The foundation of trust is faith in oneself, which comes from awareness and acceptance of the self. (The process for developing self-trust is explained in Chapter 12.) The next level is interpersonal trust, which has several characteristics. First, it is *mutual*: it involves us both. If I trust you, and you do not trust me, eventually the overall trust between us will diminish. Second, trust is meaningful only when *mutual vulnerability* exists. I must have something at stake that is important to me that you can affect, and vice versa. In that state of vulnerability, we both must perceive each other as relatively supportive and nonjudgmental. Third, trust is built *gradually*. If I or you entrust *too much* of self before a relationship has been established, distrust may be the result. Finally, trust must be *communicated*. If I feel it but do not let you know directly by saying it, or indirectly by the way I relate to you, trust is not likely to be built (see Rossiter and Pearce, 1975).

With these characteristics of trust in mind, trainers can do several things to enhance a trusting environment. First, they can let participants know when they have been affected and influenced by them. When participants give their insights about the training material, trainers can say directly how participants have helped them understand a concept or become more skilled. Trainers also can demonstrate their vulnerabilities. We often tell stories about the problems and successes we have had trying to master the skills we teach. Or if we are team teaching (say, a course on communication skills), we may tell stories about each other and/or how we had to coordinate our communication styles to cotrain effectively. Riskier still is communicating during the training program about some problem we are having as a team or with the training. Engaging in conflict productively, for example, while teaching conflict management probably is the best tool trainers have for conveying their ideas. Participants often say that the stories we tell and the skills we demonstrate help them gain confidence and stop feeling like they were the only ones struggling to give up old habits and learn new skills.

Since trust building is gradual and reciprocal, trainers need to remember that the amount of self-disclosure in their stories and the intensity of the interaction between cotrainers needs to be appropriate to the stage of the training program. That is, trainers need to build from lower to higher levels of disclosure and from less to more intense conflict. For the same reasons, the participants' experiences in training programs need to be structured so that they move from low-risk subjects and activities to those that involve greater vulnerability.

Finally, trainers must know how to communicate trust. They can do so with communication that is

1. Descriptive rather than evaluative or critical
2. Oriented toward solving mutual problems rather than gaining personal power and control
3. Spontaneous and genuine, that is, said because it is felt, not because it is what should be said
4. Empathic rather than indifferent
5. Indicative of an attitude of equality rather than superiority
6. Tentative, with ownership of opinions, rather than dogmatic and certain [Gibb, 1961, 1978]

At this point, you may notice that since trust is mutual, and people must be vulnerable to establish it, the existence of trust in a training workshop relates to how the trainers exert power. Power usually is defined as influence *over* people, creating dependency so that one person can have an impact on what another does. The powerful person, therefore, would be invulnerable and the other vulnerable. If power is used in this way, trust cannot also be established. Therefore, paradoxically, trainers must give up power over people in order to gain trust and power *with* people. To do so, trainers must be willing to be vulnerable and to tolerate uncertainty themselves. Typically, they are faced with this challenge when what they thought would happen in a workshop does not occur, or vice versa. At this point, many trainers either will try to convince participants even more strongly that they, the trainers, are right and know the answers or they will begin to flounder and not know what to do next. An alternative is to accept uncertainty and welcome it as an opportunity to gain new information and to see things in a new way. In this way, trainers demonstrate that they are open to the influence of trainees, can establish equal power, and as a result, will develop a more trusting environment.

Not only must trainers be aware of their own behavior and attitudes with participants, but they must also attend to the interaction among participants in order to establish a trusting climate. To do so, trainers can do several things at the beginning of a program: minimize perceived differences, maximize interdependence, and equalize power among participants (see Walton, 1965). For example, trainers can structure introductions so that participants are giving similar information and their expertise and vulnerability are equalized; they can share their hopes and fears about the training program, the problems they have come to address, and so on. To maximize interdependence, trainers can emphasize how meeting training goals is dependent on the entire group's participants. Everyone present is a potential resource to everyone else. To equalize power, trainers can treat all people in the program similarly, regardless of their status or position; they can avoid combining people from various hierarchical positions in an organization in the same training (unless, of course, the training was designed for that purpose); and they can put more emphasis on the content of trainees' responses than on their titles or occupations.

In summary, then, unfreezing is the first essential phase in the overall change process. It requires moderate uncertainty and maximum trust to fulfill the requirements for productive change and effective systems.

The second phase of the change process is labeled "changing," which is the actual assimilation of new information and the learning of new skills. As the learning model suggests, there are three steps in this phase: recognizing options, adopting solutions, and acquiring new skills. A single training program may be concerned with one or several of these steps. Specific instructional methods and the conditions for their use are described in the following chapters. At this point, we would like to suggest some general concepts for trainers to remember when planning for change.

First, and foremost, it is preferable that trainees attribute their learning to themselves, not to the trainer or the instructional activities. That is, if there is a great deal of pressure for trainees to change, from their organization, peers, or trainers, they probably will believe they changed because of external forces and not because they chose to do so. Consequently, when the external pressure is removed—when the training ends or when there is no surveillance by supervisors— any change in attitudes or behaviors will be short-lived.[8] For example, some companies have mandatory training programs to teach participatory leadership styles. Both the inconsistency of the messages and the strong pressure for trainees to change mitigate against acceptance and use of the new information.

In a similar fashion, some trainers like to be seen as charismatic leaders who can "do magic" to transform peoples' lives. After the training, trainees may remember being awed or pressured by the trainer more than they remember the content of the training. They are likely to attribute the value of the ideas and skills advocated to the expertise or forcefulness of the trainer and not see their ideas as applicable to themselves. Hence, they will not fully internalize the workshop objectives nor use the material to which they were exposed.[9] The conditions that we specified for the unfreezing phase will help create the atmosphere needed to enhance self-attribution. For example, when a high degree of trust develops, participants feel free to make their own choices, and, therefore, attribute their changes to themselves.

The probability of long-term change is higher if trainers understand the paradoxical process of change discussed earlier and understand why people alter their attitudes and behavior. In other words, participants do not change or resist change capriciously. Their current attitudes and behaviors exist, in Lewin's terms, in a force field and reflect the best way they know to cope with their existing situations. A person's force field is made up of pressures that are internal (attitudes, feelings, beliefs, past experiences) and external (roles, institutional expectations, interpersonal relationships, and cultural norms) to the person. These forces exist in a balance that maintains that person's status quo. The balance must be altered for change to occur. Some existing forces would *support* the instructional objectives, some would *restrain* their achievement. To succeed, the training design and method must increase the supporting forces and decrease the restraining forces. For example, trainees may want to learn effective listening skills. Their supporting forces may include a desire to be a good listener, a need to hear information accurately in their jobs, and feedback from others in a workshop that they feel misunderstood. Restraining forces could include a fear that to listen is to be less in control, the impression that the only way to impress others is by talking entertainingly, or believing that people need no overt reassurance that a

---

[8]See Hastorf et al. (1970) for a theoretical explanation of how and when people make self- or environmental attributions.

[9]There are several areas of study which indicate that there are short-term effects when messages are heard from highly credible sources (see Hovland and Weiss, 1951) and possible negative effects of a charismatic style in human relations or therapeutic groups (see Lieberman, 1972).

listener is attending to them. Trainers may increase a supporting force by providing an opportunity for participants to use role playing to receive feedback on their listening ability. They may decrease restraining forces by describing and modeling active listening skills, by creating chances for success with the skills, and by helping participants understand that control and openness in listening are not mutually exclusive. The last can be done in several ways. One is to have participants imagine that people they believed were both powerful leaders *and* good listeners and describe their behaviors. Another is to have trainers create a dialogue between the parts of themselves that are in conflict, the listener and the controller. The trainer can assist the participants in managing their intrapersonal conflict and even integrating the two parts.[10]

Many times, it seems, either the supporting or restraining forces are overlooked. For example, when participants are eager, trainers forget that participants have restraining forces such as fears about changes. When participants are resistant, trainers forget that *some* internal or external forces brought them to the training or that the training can be redefined to be in greater harmony with forces that motivate the participants. Keeping both forces in mind can help trainers pace the training—slowing it down for some by checking on their unexpressed fears or speeding it up for others by eliciting from resistant participants their reasons for attending the training.

The third and final stage of change in our model is refreezing, or the stabilizing of changes that may have occurred (see Schein, 1969b, p. 102). Just as supporting and restraining forces are important to consider during training, they are just as important to consider in the refreezing or reintegration phase. People return to back-home environments that contain forces (not present in the training context) that will affect the stability of the change. Methods to help trainees reenter their home environments involve (1) dealing with trainees' anticipated problems near the end of the training session, (2) helping them plan for building the mechanisms or channels through which their goals can be reached, such as support groups or institutional channels, and (3) planning ways that trainees can publicly commit themselves to their new goals. These three, together with T-group and team-building methods, which also aid integration of changes into a system, are described thoroughly in Chapter 10.

In summary, the way in which change is conceived and planned for affects the substantive outcomes of the training programs. Our assumptions about change underlie the remainder of our discussion. We propose seeing change as a paradoxical process that has three phases: unfreezing, changing, and refreezing. Within each of these phases, specific instructional methods are recommended. These are the next subject for consideration.

[10]For a full description of this method, see Yarbrough (1983).

CHAPTER FIVE
AWARENESS OF NEED

We now return to the model presented in Chapter 1 that explained the six phases of training. For each, we answer questions of when a phase should be used, what skills are required, and what training methods are appropriate.

WHEN MUST AWARENESS OF NEED BE EMPHASIZED?

In many training situations the major challenge, or at least the first, is to develop participants' awareness of a need or a desire for learning. Often, training programs are set up by administrators, and participants are simply told to attend. Occasionally, such programs are welcomed as a pleasant relief from the usual work routine or as indications of the organization's interest. In many instances, however, participants see training events as an imposition, a waste of time, or even as insulting. Hence, they enter the classroom feeling apathetic, resistant, or hostile.

A training program is severely handicapped when learners approach it with these attitudes. If we learned from earlier diagnostic work that a genuine need for training does exist, the initial phase of training must be concerned with overcoming participants' resistance. To do so, let us first consider why it might exist.

People welcome training when they believe *that the outcomes of their work would improve if they were to operate more skillfully—and that training can provide those skills.* They are likely to resist training if any of these ingredients are missing. This can occur in several ways:

1. They cannot imagine how they could be more effective or satisfied in their work.
2. They do not believe their work could (or should) be done any differently than they are now doing it.
3. They believe others are more responsible than they are for how their work turns out.
4. They do not believe the trainer knows about the realities of their work situation or can offer anything that they can use profitably.
5. They do not believe that new skills are teachable.
6. They do not believe in their own ability to operate differently than they have been.

These characteristics often apply to people who have slipped into habit patterns over long periods of time in a job. They occur most commonly among people who are insulated from critical feedback by regulations that protect their positions. These could include, in some situations, civil service employees, workers in powerful unions, people with socially esteemed professional credentials, those who own their own businesses, and others whose tendency to settle into behavioral ruts is not counterbalanced by sufficient challenge or stimulation to maintain an open, growing, learning approach to their work.

They may have come to *identify* the job and themselves with how they have been handling it. That job *is* what they do in it; their identities as workers *are* defined by what they do. In such instances, to acknowledge a need for change could feel threatening. It would seem to imply that they have been doing something "wrong" all their years on the job or that they themselves are inadequate.

Perhaps they have been blaming any poor outcomes or unsatisfying interactions on their bosses, on their customers, on the way the system is set up, or on society in general. To be open to learning new skills might be seen as assuming total responsibility for what occurs on the job, rather than putting it off on others—although no such "either/or" choice is intended. They may resent the assumption that an "outsider" (the trainer) knows something about their jobs that they do not, or that something could be learned in the sheltered environment of the classroom that would be applicable in the midst of the hustle and bustle of their actual work settings. Finally, if they have not been in a training situation for a long time or have done badly in school heretofore, they may question their ability to do well in that context and fear imminent embarrassment or failure.

If any one, or a combination, of these circumstances seems to exist, they must be taken into account if the trainees are to see their training experience positively and optimistically.

Let us consider an example of how this problem might exist. Imagine that you have been asked by a major supermarket chain to work with the district managers of their convenience store division. This group is made up predominantly of men who rose through the ranks of the larger stores to their present positions. Thus, they are hardworking and proud of their accumulated knowledge. They supervise convenience store managers who are a new breed: They are just beginning their careers; they are not committed to remaining in the grocery business; they are underpaid; several are members of minority groups; and they are impatient about advancement. The store managers have too high a turnover rate, and some have complained about the high-handed, authoritative way they are being treated by the district managers. Your task is to devise a training program to enable the district managers to communicate more effectively with their store managers, particularly when criticizing or evaluating their work and in encouraging them to use more initiative in running the store and motivating employees.

You are an outside trainer, hired only for this project, with no experience in this industry. These district managers have never had this kind of training before. They blame turnover problems on the company's policies of low pay and little opportunity for advancement, as well as on the general lack of responsibility among contemporary youth. The workshop is to take two days, which will put these managers behind in work they will have to catch up on afterward. They have known each other for a long time, are a cohesive, mutually reinforcing group, and put newcomers to their ranks through a long but good-humored initiation period. You suspect that they do not believe they need this training, that they believe the company is scapegoating them in regard to the turnover problem and see you as a company representative, that they believe their work can be learned only through experience in it, and that they resent this imposition on their time. In sum, they will resist what you have to offer.

You, as the trainer in this case, must facilitate their envisioning that things can be better on their job than they are now, that changes in their own behavior can lead to that improvement, and that through the training experience they can be enabled to do what is necessary to move toward realizing that vision. This phase of training calls for methods that shift trainees' view of the elements in the situation they are in from a "closed" to an "open" orientation.

WHAT SKILLS ARE EMPHASIZED IN DEVELOPING AWARENESS OF NEED?

A sense of need exists when people see a discrepancy between what could (or should) be happening in their work and what they currently are able to do. They also believe in their own ability to improve or close that gap and in the capacity of the training program to help them accomplish that improvement. Participants who are in this position have the qualities of self-awareness, self-confidence, and knowledge of what is possible in their work roles.

For example, the district managers in our sample case would have to believe that the store manager turnover rate and performance ability could improve, and would somewhat, if they were to deal with them differently. They would recognize and acknowledge their own communication styles and their impact on store managers. They would believe in their own ability, with the trainer's help, to bring about change in the desired direction.

When qualities such as these are lacking, trainers must be able to develop them. To do so they must be competent in handling several skills, including:

1. The ability to devise means, and to talk with trainees in ways, that elicit how they currently perceive themselves and their work situations
2. Eliciting their fears and hopes in regard to change
3. Supporting their faith that positive change is possible and will be profitable to them
4. Collaborating with them in designing a learning program that they perceive to be useful and appealing

In other words, the trainer must be able to diagnose worker needs and self-perceptions and, moreover, to communicate this information in ways workers will understand and accept. This includes empathizing with their feelings about participating in training and changing on the job. It involves, too, developing with them a viewpoint about or explanation for the training program that places it in a positive self-enhancing perspective. Finally, it may include entering into dialogue with them about how the training will be carried out. Participant involvement in the planning of training procedures can be a vehicle for reducing their concerns and building their investment in the training process.

The basic means for implementing these skills is *empathic*, reflective communication. However, at times, what is heard and understood finds trainers and learners at an impasse; that is, points of view are uncovered that would impede effective training. At these junctures, two additional communication skills are needed. One is *reframing* or redefining their view of the situation, that is, identifying how training now is seen as an obstruction to their meeting work responsibilities and then suggesting how it can be reenvisioned as an asset in their lives. The second is confrontation. This involves *challenging* them, pointing out inconsistencies in their thinking, or reminding them of facts or elements in their situation they would prefer to ignore.

Specific techniques are available to trainers for implementing these skills as effectively as possible. We discuss them in the next section.

WHAT METHODS AID IN DEVELOPING AWARENESS OF NEED?

Awareness of need grows as trainees develop viewpoints that are conducive to learning about four key elements in the training process: (1) the trainer, (2) themselves, (3) the training experience, and (4) the job to which the training relates. We will divide our discussion of methods into these four elements.

Perceiving the Trainer

Trainees who doubt the value of learning see the trainer as irrelevant or intrusive. They do not see him/her as being on their side or seeing their positions as they do. Hence, the trainer's task is to work toward understanding their viewpoints and communicating that awareness to them.

The first step is eliciting, prior to the actual start of a workshop or during its initial phase, a detailed picture of trainees' perceptions. The danger to be avoided at this point is assuming too readily from sketchy descriptions of their work situation, embellished by interpretations based on your own past experiences, that adequate understanding has been attained. For example, in the case of our district managers a biased portrait of the situation will emerge if only the view of either the company administrator hiring the trainer, the district manager group, or the store manager group is used to understand what is needed.

The process of learning how training participants see their situations is discussed in Chapter 3. If that process cannot be done, Form 5–1 provides a quick review. In the workshop itself it is essential to indicate that awareness by talking about the training material in terms relevant to the participants' needs. The trainer must indicate by the phrases used that he/she speaks their language, by the scenes described that he knows how their world looks to them, by the feelings he refers to that he has a sense of what constitutes the highs and lows of their work experience. In this way, the trainer is building rapport through sharing participants' realities—by becoming a temporary member of their world rather than acting as an outsider imposing change on them.

The emphasis at this point is articulating their needs, putting into words the moments at which they themselves are likely to feel less productive or satisfied with their work than they would like to be. Once this has been established, the trainer indicates how the upcoming experience will relate to those needs, how it is likely to provide some of the ingredients necessary for the participants to act more effectively at those moments.

This message must not be presented as a put-down, in a way that diminishes the trainees' dignity or the quality of their previous efforts. The trainer is someone who is a specialist, someone who has invested greater attention or done something innovative in a particular aspect of work life, and who is providing the fruits of that endeavor with the group. The trainer's confidence must be based on his/her own expertise or sense of self-worth and not on a demeaning comparison of his/her own abilities with those of the trainees.

This process, in essence, is building the trainer's "credibility." Some elements that enhance credibility are *expertness* (providing evidence of the trainer's demonstrated ability or knowledge, usually when he/she is introduced), *trustworthiness* (by being honest and frank in presenting oneself to and interacting with the group, and by relieving participants' concerns about being evaluated by the trainer), and *dynamism* (by indicating genuine caring and involvement through enthusiasm, effort, eye contact, careful preparation, etc.) Conscious attention to these three elements will encourage participants to attend receptively to the trainer's message.

In our previous example, the trainer might initiate the session by reporting the indicators that led to setting up the workshop: for example, convenience store growth, management turnover, or the new breed of managers. The district managers' concerns, as they reported them, should be discussed. Distinctions should be made between what at present are the "givens" in the situation (for example, the company's pay and advancement policies, the store managers' limited backgrounds, the district managers' expertise) and where there is room for change (for example, how the district and store managers interact). The trainer's potential contribution or expertise should be identified (for example, his/her knowledge and experience in business communications and in teaching), as well as how he/she views the current workshop situation (for example, acknowledging their concerns about the value and appropriateness of using this approach to change and his own faith, forethought, and plans for making it a worthwhile experience).

If the trainer indicates empathy for the trainees' problems and goals, if the trainer includes in expressing that understanding some of the trainees' own language, and if embedded in those messages are elements that build credibility for the trainer and for the trainees, their openness to the training situation is likely to be enhanced.

Trainees

When trainees see how a program fits in their lives and see some benefits and success for themselves emerging from it, they are most likely to value and invest in it. Sometimes, these possible outcomes are clear to them, and sometimes they must be clarified as part of the training program itself. There are two ways to engender the motivation to learn: (1) extrinsically, by highlighting the rewards training can bring, and (2) intrinsically, by encouraging participants to identify values within themselves that they can satisfy through the training. We will discuss both methods here.

Extrinsic motivation grows as the outcomes of training are clear and appealing to participants. This can be enhanced by specifying the training objectives as concretely as possibly, and doing so in ways that relate to how the trainees can make immediate use of them (see Form 5–2). Vague goals can sound amorphous and idealistic. Goals couched in vivid, specific terms seem practical and achievable. The goals, therefore, should answer the questions: Who? What? Where? When? So what? How will we know?

For example, to tell the district managers "You will learn how to communicate better with the store managers" probably is less appealing than "We will discuss and practice techniques for critiquing (what?) store managers (who?) that can be used during the conferences (where?) after your weekly visits (when?), which are most likely to encourage their compliance and morale (so what?) and reduce turnover (how will we know?)." The latter goal can be more easily visualized, be seen as worthwhile, and be less threatening (by reducing uncertainty) than the former.

Intrinsic motivation grows as trainees see that improvement in their performance will meet their personal needs better than before. A person's job often fits into a general life or career plan, a sense of who they are as individuals, of what they are doing now, and where they hope to move in the future. The workshop will appeal to them more if it is personally meaningful to them in these ways. For example, the district managers could be encouraged to think about their own career paths, who helped them along the way, what those people did when they were being helpful, how being helpful to a younger person can feel, how efforts to be helpful can cause personal insult or rebelliousness as well as goodwill, how they can use their greater experience and maturity to overcome these barriers, what they see as the meaning or deeper purpose of their work roles at this point in their lives (to themselves, their company, the store managers, and society in general), what the traditional mentor-apprentice relationship is and how it can prove most satisfying to both parties involved, what the next step in their own careers might be and how improved functioning in this role can help them to achieve and do well in it, how the process of opening up an area of their work for deeper exploration can be a stimulating, gratifying process in itself, and so on. Discussing these issues can lead to reconceiving their work role and the training experience in ways more conducive to learning and personal satisfaction—thereby increasing their intrinsic motivation to participate enthusiastically in it.

Sometimes trainees have a self-image that discourages them from investing in a learning experience because they fear failing in it. What is to be taught may seem too complicated or confusing or demand changes they will not be able to make. Their self-esteem may need bolstering. The trainer may need to affirm what they *can* do well, as well as pointing out a need for change. He/she might initiate the program with brief activities in which the participants are validated and achieve early success. This can be done by asking for recall of earlier times when they did similar tasks successfully or by providing an exercise which they can handle with relative ease. For example, the trainer might ask each of the district managers to identify a store manager with whom they work particularly well and to specify what occurs in those interactions. Thus, effective procedures can be elicited from their own past successes, rather than emanating from the trainer as the expert who knows more than they do.

In all these ways, the readiness of the trainees to be receptive to what the training has to offer can be enhanced.

The Training

The way trainees view how the training program is planned and conducted affects their involvement in it. Should they be highly motivated, the trainer can offer them a preplanned, directive, straightforward workshop and feel relatively assured that it will achieve its intended effect. If they are somewhat resistant, more effort must go into planning a program that they will perceive positively. Perhaps the best way to do so appropriately is by involving the participants in making decisions about the design of their own learning experiences.

Dugan Laird (1976) uses what he calls "Learner-Controlled Instruction" (LCI) for this purpose. It is based, in part, upon Rogers' (1969) proposition that "Significant . . . learning has a quality of personal involvement—the whole person in both his feeling and cognitive aspects being *in* the learning event. It is *self*-initiated" (p. 5). Laird approaches LCI by supplying the learner with:

1. A clear statement of the objectives to be achieved.
2. An explanation (or sample) of the evaluation that will be used to demonstrate satisfactory achievement of the objective.
3. A list of the resources (materials, activities, and people) available to help the learner master the objective. This list may be referred to as a "learning map" since it describes useful "stopovers" on the route from the trainee's position at the start to his/her ultimate goal.

He qualifies this starting point by suggesting that occasionally even objectives and means for measurement can be learner initiated. In some cases, the trainer must set basic goals, but supplementary aims can be elicited from the group; or they can choose, from a list supplied by the trainer of equally appropriate objectives, those that they see as being most useful to pursue. This approach is analogous to the balance between required and elective courses inherent in most academic curricula. In many instances, too, the learners themselves are the best source for determining when and by what means to assess that they have mastered the material.

The district managers in our example can be given a detailed list of communication skills involved in supervision and can be asked to rate each regarding its importance and/or frequency of occurrence when dealing with store managers, as well as their self-perceived ability to apply each skill in that interaction. Those rated highest in importance and frequency and lowest in competence can be given greater emphasis in the workshop. Similarly, they can be asked to generate a "critical incident" which typifies those in which they might have to apply these skills. It can be role-played toward the end of the workshop to assess how well they now are able to use the skills in a simulated give-and-take situation.

Once the basic parameters of the training are established, the learners can be given opportunities to make decisions regarding several aspects of the workshop. These include:

1. *Pacing or speed of learning.* Some older adults learn more slowly than (but ultimately can do just as well as) younger adults. Also, Laird reports that when a training program was switched to LCI, the first class completed a six-month cadet program in three months, and a second group met the objectives, reported to work, and was appraised as equal or superior to conventional graduates after only two months of study. So self-pacing can improve training efficiency.
2. *Sequence.* When students are allowed to determine where to begin their work and how to proceed, they often can make more individually appropriate decisions than can an instructor who is unfamiliar with their backgrounds and interests.
3. *Materials.* When students bring in their own problem situations (see the next section of this chapter), when they are asked to report on what they found to be worthwhile in self-selected readings, when they suggest topics for the group to discuss, or when they can divide into self-selected subgroups to pursue more focused issues of particular interest to them, they are most likely to see the workshop as directly relevant to their needs.

The trainer's role in this process may best be titled "facilitator." He/she mediates between the learner and the resources available, which can include printed materials, audiovisual aids, cases, field trips, and so on, rather than acting as a mere mouthpiece for the content of the program. Thus, the instructor helps the trainees define the precise questions which are troublesome or motivating and then directs them to probable sources of information. As a rule, the trainer responds to requests for assistance, rather than lecturing, preaching, or criticizing.

LCI need not be the predominant method of instruction. It can be integrated with a more directive approach, as appropriate. For example, only one segment of a longer workshop can be set aside for learners to use as they wish. Trainees can be given an hour to use however they choose. They can be given options, such as reading, listening to a tape, dialogue with another participant who has similar interests, or just going for a walk and thinking things over. That period of time is theirs to use as they choose and is to be respected as such. In general, LCI methods involve learners in making decisions that produce more relevant, memorable, and motivating learning experiences.

In this chapter we have summarized when and how to move learners who are apathetic, reluctant, or even hostile into a state of mind from which they will be receptive and motivated to participate enthusiastically in a training program.

FORM 5–1   *PERCEPTIONS OF TRAINING*

Purpose: It will be helpful to me in planning and carrying out our training session to know your views about what we will be doing. Would you share them briefly in the space below?

1. I volunteered _____ was told _____ to attend (check one).

2. I do_____ do not_____ expect to find this program worth the time and effort I will give to it.

3. I believe _____ do not believe _____ that I need this experience.

4. I believe _____ do not believe _____ that this training is the best means for improving my work situation.

5. I expect_____ do not expect_____ to be more effective in my job as a result of this training.

6. What I would like to see happen in this training is:

7. What I would *not* like to see happen in this training is:

FORM 5–2 *SPECIFYING OBJECTIVES*

Purpose: This instrument can help trainers to specify and describe their workshop objectives to make them maximally clear and appealing to participants. To use it, think of a program you plan to offer and answer the questions about it below. Then incorporate as much of this material as possible, or as appropriate, into your description of the program.

1. By what role title do the participants identify themselves?

2. With whom will they use what they learn?

3. In what context or situation will they use it?

4. What knowledge is required to do this?

5. What attitudes on their part, on the part of the receivers of their services, are most desirable?

6. What are the skills called that they will use?

7. What behaviors must be put together to comprise that skill?

8. What happens just before to indicate that the skill is needed?

9. What happens afterward if that skill is used well?

10. What happens afterward if that skill is *not* used well?

11. What long-range benefits and losses accrue as a result of these immediate outcomes?

CHAPTER SIX
PROBLEM ANALYSIS

WHEN MUST PROBLEM ANALYSIS BE EMPHASIZED?

Training programs often are set up for people who are assuming new or expanded responsibilities. They might be moving from a position in which they had performed outstandingly and, hence, merited a promotion. One reason they may have done well is that they had developed a personal method or style of operating that "worked." In their new position, these upwardly mobile people are likely to look once again for *the* right approach to handling their new jobs. Too often they simply stick with what is familiar and superimpose their previously successful mode of behavior onto the new situations they face.

However, the broader the range of responsibility managers have, the more options or variables they have to manipulate to achieve their objectives. A line foreman rarely can transfer an employee, set production quotas, offer incentives, redesign a work area, and so on, but with an increase in status and power such alternatives become available. However, people accustomed to working within a narrow range of choices often become accustomed to a relatively rigid set of procedures. If they carry only these tried-and-true methods into their new position, they are likely to fall victim to the famous "Peter Principle"—being promoted to their level of incompetence.

Furthermore, when individuals assume a broader range of responsibilities, they often shift from working in a small area, where they are experts, to managing activities they know less about. Hence, they will be dealing with colleagues of differing abilities, backgrounds, and outlook (for example, a board of directors). The skills of persuading rather than ordering subordinates, of sizing up the important issues in an unfamiliar area, of using the expertise of others to illuminate a problem, and of formulating long-term policy need to be developed. For these purposes, the process of working through the analysis of problems or case studies among a group of peers is a very appropriate approach to training.

Training in problem analysis also may be suitable for young people moving into supervisory roles right out of school. They, too, have been conditioned by academic testing to look for a "right answer." Also, their previous education may have stressed general management theory and minimized application of knowledge in real situations. They need experience in "getting down to cases"—a process emphasized in problem analysis.

WHAT SKILLS ARE EMPHASIZED IN PROBLEM ANALYSIS?

The fundamental intent of the problem-analysis aspect of training is to help trainees slow down the process of decision making, to encourage them to think before they act, to avoid jumping to snap conclusions about the problems they face. It redirects their attention away from identifying immediate solutions and shifts it toward understanding the many facets of the situation being faced and to choosing wisely from the alternative responses available to them.

The primary skills employed in problem analysis are: using a sequenced problem-solving process and using creative thinking to generate ideas. Problem solving can include several steps:

1. Identifying the organizations basic goal(s)
2. Identifying which forces in the situation obstruct and which aid in achieving that goal
3. Disentangling interrelated difficulties into distinct issues to be addressed
4. Identifying who is involved and what their points of view and vested interests are
5. Distinguishing what information is factual and what is being inferred by participants
6. Determining short- and long-range goals for relieving the problem situation
7. Determining a chronological sequence regarding what goals need to be pursued first and which can be postponed
8. Identifying alternative strategies for achieving the goals
9. Identifying criteria for selecting from among alternative strategies
10. Projecting the possible consequences of employing each strategy
11. Developing an action plan that details what strategies will be used, who will do what, when, where, how, and so on

The creative-thinking process encourages trainees to expand the limits of approaches available to them beyond those immediately evident, to include new possibilities that they might not have used or thought of before. This process also can include several steps:

1. Thinking very positively about the ideal outcomes they would like to achieve
2. Generating possible solutions without applying immediate criticism as to their viability
3. Building upon ideas thrown out by colleagues, combining worthwhile elements in two people's ideas, using conceptual breakthroughs in others' thinking to stimulate fresh approaches in their own minds
4. Comparing the situation they are in to those in other contexts that are analogous to it
5. Continuing to generate unusual, farfetched ideas even after an obviously useful one has been proposed: that is, not cutting off the listing of possibilities prematurely, while still operating within the scope of old ways of thinking

Enhancing the use of skills like these can add depth and variety to trainees' ability to analyze effectively whatever problems they face.

WHAT ARE PROBLEM ANALYSIS TRAINING METHODS?

The primary mode of developing ability in problem analysis is the case study, or variants of this form. This method teaches through concrete example. It provides trainees with a stimulus that takes into account the ambiguous, multifaceted, complex nature of many management situations. They must respond to the case in a way that requires the skills of problem analysis, so they experience how to address in an effective way *any* problem that might arise for them.

Every case study describes a situation containing a problem that cannot be solved in only one simple, obvious way. The problem is of a kind that could arise in many work settings. Hence, in considering how to respond to it, trainees are gaining insight into that kind of problem and into the process of problem solving in general. There are many alternative ways to present cases to a training group. To explore these options, let's take one case as an example. Imagine that you are working with a group of newly appointed supervisors and you want to explore the process of communication. You offer them the following case for study:

THE FRIENDLY CUSTODIAN

Al Jones is a custodial employee of the maintenance agency that services your company. He is black. Jones comes on duty at 5 P.M. to clean up the office, working until midnight. Often people in your firm stay late to complete projects; several are women.

Jones is a friendly fellow and has fallen into the habit of stopping for a few minutes with them, especially the women, as he passes by their offices, discussing with them current office gossip and his personal domestic problems as well. An unmarried female employee reported to you, and others, that he has asked her to get together on the weekend. Another said that recently she "accidentally" tripped on his broom, and he caught her as she walked by.

Some of the women say they feel uncomfortable with him there at night, but have nothing other than the two incidents mentioned on which to base that feeling. When talked to privately, most see Jones as harmless and as respectful of their wishes about fraternizing. They say he is no more forward or intrusive than several of your firm's office employees.

You are called in by your boss and, as his executive assistant, are told, "Jack, a couple of the women here have said that they are uneasy about working late with Jones around. He can be easily replaced, and they can't. I think we should ask the maintenance firm to get rid of him. Would you take care of that?"

You check up on Jones and learn that he has been a steady worker for seven years without prior incident. He also is an active member of the Building Workers' Union.

Let us explore the options available to a trainer in working with such a case.

HOW CAN CASES BE PRESENTED?

A case can be presented to a training group in a variety of ways:

1. *The medium.* It can be offered in printed form, as it is above. It also can be read aloud when it is given to them. A film or videotape can be made of actors portraying the critical incidents. At the Wharton School, students are given a written statement of a case problem and then they have an opportunity to interview an executive from the organization where the case situation actually developed and where the problem was (or is being) tackled. The impact of the case presentation (and the difficulties in making it available) increases as each of the above-mentioned approaches is employed.

2. *The format.* Our sample case is presented in relatively abbreviated form. Students are likely to want more information than is provided about the background and circumstances of this situation. When using cases, detailed information can be supplied in several ways. Sometimes it is provided within the case itself. For example, at the Harvard Business School, a number of extensively elaborated cases have been developed. Many provide highly technical data and are oriented primarily to graduate students of business administration. Their cases vary from a few to nearly 100 pages. The American Association of Collegiate Schools of Business and Harvard University's Graduate School of Business have collaborated to create the Intercollegiate Case Clearing House (Soldier's Field P.O., Boston,

Massachusetts 02163). Information about available versions of these published cases may be obtained by writing to the Clearing House. Cases are classified into six broad categories:

a. Controls, Accounting and Statistical
b. Finance and Financial Institutions
c. General Management: Policy and Social, Economic and Political Aspects
d. Human Aspects of Administration
e. Marketing
f. Production

Other cases available cover functional problems in data processing, foreign trade, and similar technical topics.

Paul Pigors (1976) developed the Incident Process of working with case studies. He provides his students with only a brief summary of a case study, such as the one given above. After this summary has been read, students are asked to make a short-term decision in the role of the person who has to cope with the incident. Then Pigors gives the group 20 to 30 minutes to ask questions of the trainer (who either has prepared the case or has mastered information given in a comprehensive case report written by someone else). The questions at first are directed toward finding out about the "what," "when," "where," and "how" of the situation. Clues also are tracked down if they seem to offer reliable insights into the "why" of behavior. When the factual information has been assembled, the students are asked to summarize it—to highlight key items for decision-making—in the organizational role from which the case is being analyzed. Then they use the information thus accumulated to review the basic problem presented in the case, asking "What is at stake here organizationally and for the persons immediately concerned? How shall we state the critical question for action, now? Is it a multiple issue?"

A final method for presenting information is a preplanned "sequential" case, in which only one phase of the action is given at a time. Then at a critical point in the story, there is a pause, so that the learners can predict outcomes or suggested courses of action. The story is then continued, and an analysis is made of the reasons for the divergence between the predictions and what actually transpired (Simmons, 1975, p. 187).

3. *The kind of case.* The kinds of cases used can vary considerably. A distinction is made between a "case history" and a "case for study." The former offers a detailed account of a completed event. Sometimes, it reports a successful approach to dealing with a problem, and thus provides a model to emulate; sometimes it reports a manager's failure, and thus provides a strategy to critique. The "case for study," like our example, breaks off before the situation has been resolved.

Some cases are accounts of events that actually occurred. Others are fabricated, or changed slightly from a real event, to suit the learning objectives of the training. Of course, the former are more "realistic" and allow for comparison to be made between the students' responses and what actually was done. The latter, however, can be tailored to the particular training situation but are vulnerable to oversimplification.

There is an ample literature of printed cases available in textbooks from which those appropriate to training goals can be selected; or trainers can write their own. Herbert Engel (1973) suggests these steps in the process of constructing a case:

a. Choose a situation out of the work environment, one with which you are familiar. It should be job related and possess intrinsic value as a potential learning exercise.
b. Evaluate or judge the situation. Do this by:
   (1) Analysis of available facts and inferences.
   (2) Deciding what the problem probably is and to what principle it relates.

For instance, a situation involving excessive waste of raw material perhaps would relate to the principles expressed in work improvement systems.

   (3)   Finding out, if feasible, how the situation was resolved. Since many problems are never completely solved or, if they are, perhaps erroneously, this factor is not vital to the construction of the case. Nonetheless, it is helpful to know what really happened.

   c.   Establish a fictionalized version of the original situation. Names, titles, places, and time are changed. Normally, the fictionalized version will encompass additional data. The new version must hang together as a believable entity.

   d.   Write up the case, including:
   (1)   The introductory section, which includes the essential background data.
   (2)   The "problem," which is either real or alleged.
   (3)   The predicament or roadblock to an obvious resolution of the problem. The incident which creates the situation is included within this section.
   (4)   The questions or "charge" to the users.

Finally, the students enrolled in a training program can provide cases for use in their own class. These can be solicited several weeks prior to the training or at the beginning of the session itself. Form 6-1 suggests an approach by which trainee case situations can be gathered. This last approach is likely to provide the cases most likely to be stimulating and useful to the participants. Cases proposed by trainees inherently would have many of the qualities of a meaningful case:

   a.   A situation like those the participants might face.
   b.   A protagonist or central figure with responsibilities comparable to theirs.
   c.   Antagonist(s) or opposing figures like people they might have to deal with.
   d.   A sense of what is happening *within* each person (thoughts and feelings) as well as in the relationships *between* the participants.
   e.   A situation in flux, one that has changed and that will continue to change as time goes on.
   f.   A situation subject to differing interpretations by the people involved.

WHAT ASSIGNMENTS MAKE CASE STUDIES USEFUL?

For learners to gain in their ability to use the skills of problem analysis, they must be asked to work on the cases presented to them in ways they wouldn't ordinarily use, in ways that direct them toward a deeper, more analytic examination of the case situation. There are several alternative methods by which learners can be asked to work this way with a case.

The first is most common. The trainees read the case, meet in small groups, and are asked to come up with answers to a few basic questions within a set time limit. To answer the questions, they must apply problem-analysis or creative-thinking skills to the case situation. In Form 6-2 we provide a list of generally applicable questions from which a trainer can choose those best suited to the case being studied, as well as the instructional goal being pursued. To provide a specific example of how this might be done, consider the list of questions below, which could be asked of a group working with our sample case, "The Friendly Custodian."

1. What do you believe is Jack's most fundamental responsibility in dealing with this situation?
2. What ideal outcome for this situation would fulfill this responsibility optimally?
3. What negative outcomes does Jack want to avoid?
4. What do Jack's boss, the women who fear Al Jones, the women who like him, and Al Jones want to happen? What do they want to avoid?
5. What events in this story most certainly occurred; that is, what are the facts?
6. What inferences have been drawn about each of those events by the people involved? What differences exist among the ways those people perceive the situation?
7. At what point(s), and how, could the situation have been eased before Jack's boss demanded that Al Jones be fired?
8. What must Jack attend to right away? What long-range issues must he work on to prevent this kind of problem from recurring?
9. What are Jack's alternatives in dealing with this situation? List as *many* as you can, without judging their relative worth as yet.
10. What criteria should Jack use for choosing from among these alternatives? What constraints limit his behaviors?
11. What do you think Al Jones, his boss, the women in the office, and the union delegate might do in response to Jack's various alternatives?
12. What would you do if you were Jack?

A second alternative is used in the "syndicate" approach to management training at the Administrative Staff College–Henley (in England). There students are presented with "briefs" describing in detail a specific case or a general area of management. These are reviewed in groups of about 10 members each (a "syndicate"). Each breaks down the problem into specific assignments which are allotted to individuals or to small teams of syndicate members. They do their individual tasks and then prepare reports for the syndicate. Their findings are incorporated into a written report which is presented to a plenary session of the course, where it is again discussed, together with reports from other syndicate groups (Adams, 1976).

When a number of small groups convene to report on their analysis of cases, their comments can become repetitive. Group 1 shares its findings, group 2 adds a bit more, and the remaining groups often have little to say that is different. Their involvement can be increased if the order of reporting is reversed after the next exercise of this type; that is, the group that reported last now reports first. However, this system still leaves some groups out each time.

To overcome this predicament, Engel (1973) suggests using *simultaneous* case studies. Two (or more) different cases covering the same topic or principle are assigned to the trainees. Half receive case 1; the other half, case 2. If the room has a divider, or if two adjoining rooms are available, the trainer can divide the entire class into an even number of small groups. Half of the small groups work on case 1 in one area, the other half on case 2 in another area. Both cases must be about the same length so that the time required for reading, discussion, and analysis by each small group is about equal.

Before starting the reporting process, the trainer explains that two different cases have been worked on. Reporting then begins. Groups 1 and 2, which worked on the first case, report; then groups 3 and 4, which had the second case, report. Since the principles involved in both cases are the same, the trainer is able to reinforce these principles from one case to the other. The interest level is high within the small groups, since they are not listening, in terms of the events in the cases, to a rehash of what has already been covered. Intergroup questions are encouraged so that details of the cases can be clarified.

At the Wharton School, after the executive has visited the class and been interviewed, the students spend the next six days meeting informally in small groups to discuss their proposed solutions. Each student then writes his/her own analysis and solution to the problem, also summarizing that report in a one-page letter to the executive. At a second meeting of the whole group, a student leads the discussion of the reports, forwarding to the executive the 10 which he/she considers best. The executive studies the 10 reports and adds written comments. Finally, on the eleventh day after the first meeting, the executive again meets with the entire class, comments on the written reports, citing individuals, and tells them about his/her own solution to the case problem.

Another, much more elaborate, variant on the case study is the Action Project. It was developed by R. W. Revans and was used, in one major instance, with the General Electric Company Ltd. of Great Britain. In this program, 21 managers with potential for advancement were selected for an eight-month commitment. Their training was centered around a project each would do. The project could be carried out within another branch of GE, within their own branch of the organization as part of their own job, or in an exchange with another organization. Each project had to fulfill three criteria:

1. The project should be concerned with a major business problem involving a broad understanding of the company. It should not be directed at the solution of problems which are exclusively technical.
2. The project should cover more than one function of the business, requiring the involvement, cooperation, and commitment of a number of managers.
3. The participant should spend approximately six to nine months working on the project. After initial agreement on the task, he/she would diagnose the problem, make recommendations, and then help to initiate the necessary action. It is desirable but not necessary for the project to be capable of being completed within the time allowed.

Managing directors at GE and at several outside organizations were asked to submit suitable projects which were available in their areas for visiting participants. They also were asked to submit names of qualified candidates. When matching participants to projects, an attempt was made to create a maximum mismatch between the candidate's previous experience and the demands of the project. If, for example, a person had been a production manager all his life, he was offered projects concerned with the marketing and policy side of the business.

The participants met as a whole group for formal full-time study for only two and a half weeks at the beginning and for one week at the midpoint. They began their projects with a lengthy (three-month) diagnosis of the problem they were to tackle. One day each week they met in a group with four or five others similarly engaged and with two project advisors (one from Action Learning Projects and othe other from GE) to discuss fully all that was happening to them during the other four days of each week that they worked. Clients with whom the participants worked and senior management at GE were included in their groups periodically, as well. After diagnosis, an equal period of time was devoted to implementing the preferred solution. Reports of the participants' experiences were written up, and when the project period was over, some returned to their old posts and others were promoted to positions of greater responsibility (Casey and Pearce, 1977).

From these examples, we can see that learnings from cases can be manifested in several ways:

1. In written or oral reports to specific problem analysis questions
2. In reports given to a larger training group
3. In letters or a report to the presenting organization itself
4. In actually taking part in diagnosing, planning, and carrying out solutions to the problem posed by a host organization

HOW ARE CASE STUDY GROUPS CONDUCTED?

Cases are most often analyzed in work groups of 5 to 10 people. The most important characteristic of group composition is heterogeneity. In a Henley syndicate, for example, members of each subgroup are carefully preselected to provide as varied a mixture as possible of expertise and enterprise. In other words, each syndicate might have representatives from areas of *expertise* such as marketing, production, research and development, finance, personnel management, and legal, secretarial, or management services. They also include people from various *enterprises*, such as government, industry, banks, armed forces, trade unions, and voluntary bodies.

Executives spend 90 days in a residential program at the Centre Européen d'Éducation Permanente (CEDEP) dealing with case problems presented to them and others they introduced from their home organizations. However, the 90 days of residential instruction are spread out over two years. They are divided into eight 10-day to two-week periods separated by three-month recesses, during which participants return to their respective companies. Each time they return to their jobs, they attempt to apply and test ideas and practices acquired at CEDEP. Upon reuniting after each recess, they bring with them information as to the productive results achieved or difficulties encountered in implementing what they had learned, as well as providing new case material for their group to work on.

In the Incident Process, Pigors (1976) recommends that the case presentation and information-gathering phases, which take about 35 minutes, be followed by a 20- to 30-minute decision-making period. It includes four parts:

1. Each member writes his/her own answer to the question: How would I handle the incident (if I used my best judgment), and what reasons support my decision? These papers are signed and turned in to the discussion leader.
2. According to differences in written decisions, opinion groups of like-minded members select a spokesperson or a role player. Each spokesperson polls subgroup members and works with them to answer the question: What is the strongest case that we can put together to support our joint decision?
3. Next, decisions are put to the test of a brief debate between spokespersons, or in role playing. Subgroup decisions and reasoning are presented, compared, and appraised.
4. Then the discussion leader provides information about another kind of test—the test of history. What actually was done by the person in whose role discussion group members have been analyzing the case? How did that decision work out in the immediate sequel? No attempt is made to teach a class solution.

Pigors allocates a second hour to consideration of the fundamental issues that underlie the short-term problem identified in the case. He suggests that his students discuss such questions as:

1. What shortcomings (or flaws in the case situation) seem to have been accountable for difficulties that showed up in the incident? (These are factors to work on.)
2. What factors (personalities, organizational relationships, previous managerial actions, etc.) can be identified as actual or potential forces that would tend to favor productive interaction in such a situation? (These are resources to work with.)
3. What kinds of long-term action might alleviate current difficulties and/or tend to prevent the recurrence of such an incident? (This kind of planning concerns goals to work toward.)

In most instances where cases are examined, the group discussion is moderated by a chairperson selected from among the training participants themselves. At Henley, the chairperson for each case project is selected by the college to lead the group in dealing with an area in which he/she is not familiar. A research scientist, for example, may be required to chair the syndicate for a study of marketing. He thus has to size up the issues in an unfamiliar area, draw out the expertise of colleagues, and see that they contribute relevantly to the task at hand. The chairperson in this context must plan the agenda and the use of time, which is always shorter than is comfortable; assign responsibilities for reading and other background work, so that maximum use is made of the cooperative effort of the syndicate; brief members going on field visits or who will be interviewing expert witnesses; see that appropriate conclusions are reached in whatever report or end product is required; and lead that syndicate in meetings with other syndicates. In these ways, the chairperson is developing skills essential to higher-level management and is heightening awareness of the problem-solving process itself rather than relying on the authority that technical expertise provides. In the

Henley program, and others, a secretary/recorder is appointed, whose prime responsibility is to coordinate or even write the group's final report.

The content of case discussions will be determined by the tasks assigned to the group. The process of those discussions will be affected by the group leader, the trainer's interventions, and the norms within the group.

Pigors suggests that four freedoms be made available during case discussion:

1. The freedom to try out ideas for size
2. The freedom to cite firsthand experience
3. The freedom to speak one's mind (when necessary even in disagreement, without regard to the status of the speaker with whom one disagrees)
4. The freedom to propose and lead experiments in conference method (experiments to clarify the nature and origin of disagreements and to establish common ground)

People examining a case are likely to begin with what is easiest: judging, approving, condemning the people described. Many will start with the assumption that nothing more incisive is expected of them than shooting down the bumbling people in the case. Gradually, the easy blaming and praising must give way to asking, searching, hypothesizing, learning. The discussion leader should guide this shift (Lee, 1954).

Trainers serve as consultants to groups working on cases. They attempt to steer the group through the full problem-solving process, asking penetrating questions when the group seems to be overlooking or hurrying through an important issue. The group chairperson's authority should not be undermined by such interventions. The group should not be protected from doing their own thinking, dealing with internal conflict, or coming to their own conclusions. Sometimes, they must be allowed to struggle through a problem, or out of an obvious dead end, for the learning they will gain from that effort.

A final topic for a case group is examining their own interaction, or the case of that study group itself. Their own discussion may be seen as an example of a work situation to analyze. It provides an arena for applying among themselves some of the behavior they have recommended for persons in their case. It is helpful to schedule at the end (or the midpoint of a long project), a discussion of how the group is working together—whether they are looking at the problems in the group in the same ways they are examining the case being analyzed; that is, are they actually doing what they are talking about?

Problem analysis, using primarily one of the many forms of case analysis described in this chapter, will develop in trainees the ability to move from a narrow specialized perspective on work processes to one that encompasses many viewpoints and a long-range outlook.

FORM 6–1   *SAMPLE FORM FOR ELICITING CASES FOR STUDY*

TO: Participants in Management Development Seminar

FROM: John Smith, Instructor

When we meet next week for our management development seminar, we will be discussing general principles of effective management and then exploring how they apply to our individual work situations. I would like us to deal with ideas and methods that are genuinely useful. I am writing now to ask your help in assuring that our discussions are realistic and relevant to your needs. They are likely to be if we deal with situations that actually arise in your work. Would you bring to mind a problem that you faced recently, or are currently facing, that you were not sure how best to handle? It would be one which could be dealt with in several ways, one which seemed to call for managerial skill, one for which you would have liked some guidance from an "expert," one which you would like to see us discuss in our upcoming workshop. When you have identified such a situation, would you refer to it when filling in the spaces below? If these categories get in the way of your describing your situation, do not hesitate to write it out in whatever way is most comfortable for you. Then send it directly to me. I will keep what you write strictly confidential. If I believe I can incorporate your situation into the seminar, I will alter the details you provide so that your anonymity is fully protected—unless you offer to identify yourself.

I.   The setting in which I work and my duties:

II. The people with whom I work and their duties:

III. How the problem developed, and the point at which I had to deal with it:

IV. The choices I had, what I did, what I hoped to accomplish, how it turned out:

FORM 6–2 *CASE-STUDY ASSIGNMENTS*

After reading a case study, students can be asked to analyze the problem situation it presents in any of the ways listed below. When applying these questions to a particular case study the names of the characters, their organization, and so on, would be specified. Here, to provide universally applicable questions, we will assume that the case has a central character, whom we will call the "protagonist," and someone who is presenting an obstacle to his/her job performance, whom we will call the "antagonist."

1. What are the basic goal(s) of the organization?

2. What role does the protagonist play in achieving those goals?

3. What outcomes does the protagonist want to achieve in this situation?

4. What outcomes does the protagonist want to avoid in this situation?

5. What do the antagonist(s) (or others involved in the case) want to achieve and to avoid in this situation?

6. What are the facts of the situation—the circumstances and events about which everyone would agree?

7. About what events or circumstances do people in this situation disagree?

8. List the steps that occurred as this problem grew to its current proportions. For each step, suggest what could have been done to prevent its having as negative an impact as it did or how the next stage in the sequence could have been avoided.

9. What aspects of the situation need immediate attention? What needs to be done about them?

10. What long-range programs or policies need to be instituted to deal with the problem or to prevent its recurrence?

11. What alternatives does the protagonist have in dealing with the situation?

12. What criteria might the protagonist use in deciding what to do?

13. What constraints, in terms of time, money, equipment, and staff, limit the protagonist's options?

14. What might the antagonist do in response to each alternative, and what effect might each have on the situation?

15. What sequence of steps would you take if you were the protagonist?

CHAPTER SEVEN
KNOWING OPTIONS

WHEN SHOULD TRAINING FOCUS ON EXPANDING OPTIONS?

The training methods discussed thus far have been concerned primarily with enhancing *awareness* of what is occurring in work situations. They stressed the "soft" outcomes of training. However, once a problem is understood, it then must be dealt with actively. We shift now to achieving "hard" or "action-oriented" outcomes. We will progress from a broad to a narrow view of this domain. This first segment deals with enlarging trainees' view of (and capacity to handle) the options available to them in their work.

This kind of training is suited primarily to people who already are experienced in filling their roles. However, if their work requires the use of judgment, if it involves dealing with situations which are handled quite differently by various practitioners in that field, if how the job is carried out can in any way be called an "art," then periodic training is likely to be called for that emphasizes "knowing options." Examples of clients for such training include managers, teachers, counselors, government officials, nurses, salespersons, supervisors, lawyers, and so on. In fact, for several of these professions, periodic continuing education is required by law.

There are two kinds of situations in which option-oriented training is most appropriate. One exists where people learned to carry out their roles under circumstances that have changed. In the changed environment their familiar approach no longer is adequate. This could apply to foremen accustomed to dealing only with workers like themselves, from their own ethnic, socioeconomic, or sex-role group. Now, they increasingly may have to supervise members of other groups, as their plants hire people formerly excluded from those jobs. It could apply to salespersons in rapidly growing suburban areas who must deal with increased competition and new clientele. It could apply to paraprofessionals in increasingly technical fields, such as law or medicine, who are assuming decision-making responsibilities. It could apply to public officials who must handle interactions with an increasingly vocal, demanding constituency.

Option-oriented training also is well suited when people recognize a need to sharpen their ability to *apply*, as well as to know about, new methods. Innovations in a field often are described in newsletters, books, and other print media that report current trends. Practitioners grow curious about them, but they hesitate to employ such ideas on the job until they have had some direct experience in seeing how they work, in trying them firsthand. There already exists an awareness of their potential worth, but developing an internalized or "tacit" knowledge of how and when to use the new approach must occur at a training event.

This aspect of knowing options is especially applicable for methods that must be used in interaction with other people. The initially awkward trials (and errors) that must be made if a technique is being used for the first time often cannot be carried out, ethically or pragmatically, with a paying customer. Hence, the workshop provides a safe arena for practicing the new system in a noncritical environment, for sensing how well it fits or how it feels to individuals before they incorporate it into their work role.

To fulfill these goals for training, students need to develop several abilities. First, they must know *what* it is. They must have a clear and thorough understanding of the option they are to learn. In other words, they must have a "cognitive map," a knowledge of its purpose, and what steps are required to carry it out. Second, they must have a sense of *when* that option should be used, how it relates to the other alternatives they have at their disposal, or the *contingencies* under which it is to be applied. Third, they must know *how* to carry it out. They must have practice in its use, especially in the midst of the give-and-take of everyday work situations.

The what, when, and how of knowing options are developed principally through two methods: (1) the informative lecture, and (2) simulation of the work situation.

HOW ARE INFORMATIVE LECTURES MADE EFFECTIVE?

Books on training generally discourage the use of lectures. They warn that lectures often are dull, patronizing, and unlikely to produce behavior change. (Many are!) Nevertheless, in practice, *more* training time is given to formal or informal lecturing than to any other activity. Since this is the case, we want to suggest how to make the most of this medium.

When the purpose of training is exploring options, the lecture is used to convey information objectively, about one (or more) available options. (We will discuss how to advocate an option in the next chapter.) The very first step in this process, often the most important one, is articulating exactly what the lecture is intended to accomplish. This goal, like any other, should be expressed in terms of the trainees' response.

A "statement of purpose" is essential because lecturers often think only of what they themselves want to accomplish and have unrealistic expectations regarding how their listeners will respond. For example, they may want to "cover" a lot of material, and they simply assume that it all will be absorbed. The purpose and the lecture, however, must be compatible. A barrage of information probably will elicit only a sense of how complex a topic is; a lecture confined to a few main ideas can elicit comprehension and recall of those ideas in the future.

Therefore, what outcome(s) the lecture is to produce should be established first. (Examples are: the trainees will know how to do something, will know how something works, will understand why something is done, and so on.) That purpose should be specific and attainable. Let us take as an example a situation in which a trainer of computer salespersons is dealing with alternative ways to approach potential customers. Her "statement of purpose" for a lecture might be: "After hearing this talk, the trainees will understand and be ready to role-play three ways of approaching customers; they also will know how to determine which way is most appropriate for each typical situation they face and in which sequence to use them."

Having formulated an explicit goal such as this, her next step is to adapt her message to her listeners. This begins with some thought about what they *already know* about the topic. It also includes their *attitudes* about the topic and about attending the lecture. A group of experienced, road-weary computer field representatives should be addressed differently than a group of eager new hires for the same company. Sometimes the trainees' background is not obvious or available and an explicit inquiry must be made. This can be done at the start by asking the group a few questions they can answer with a show of hands regarding how much they already know (or what they most want to know) about the topic. If based on these data, the lecture's purpose is most likely to be appropriate and attainable.

The next step is organizing and outlining the content of the lecture. People can follow a well-structured presentation best, especially if they are "set" to do so at the start. There are several ways to organize a lecture:

1. *Chronological order:* a step-by-step account of a procedure sequenced in time (for example, the series of steps or instructions for initiating a new computer account)
2. *Spatial order:* describing the parts of an object that occupies space (for example, the facilities in the company's headquarters)
3. *Topical order:* describing each of the naturally divided kinds or types of things you are addressing (for example, the common types of clients or accounts and how each are best encountered)
4. *Cause and effect:* describing how one action leads to another (for example, the goals of the first sales call and what behaviors help to achieve them)
5. *Problem solving:* describing what can go wrong and how to fix that (for example, common pitfalls in selling and how to overcome them)

The purpose for the lecture, its content, and the audience addressed must be considered when determining an optimum organization plan. For example, the chronological order would be best for beginning salespeople; the problem-solution approach would be better for veterans.

The pattern of organization selected should then be written down in outline form. Main ideas should be sketched out, and then subpoints can be filled in under each one. The main ideas, which the listeners are to remember, should be kept to a minimum. Supporting material can be as plentiful as needed to make each point clear and memorable.

There are many verbal and nonverbal ways that a main point can be made more meaningful. The following are some verbal approaches:

1. If the trainees need to picture a procedure more vividly, *details* should be described in concrete language and *comparisons* and *contrasts* with more familiar procedures should be made.
2. If they are to imagine what it is like to use the procedure in a situation, anecdotes of recent *specific incidents* can be reported and *hypothetical examples* can be examined.
3. If they are to understand and/or judge a procedure's overall value, *statistics* and *experts' testimony* can be used.

Trainees are most likely to comprehend and retain information apprehended through both the eye and the ear. Hence visual supports that amplify ideas are useful as:

1. Summaries written on a blackboard, a flipchart, or an overhead projector
2. Pictures, cartoons, or diagrams shown on an opaque projector or on slides
3. Demonstrations of procedures provided live or on film or videotape·
4. Actual hands-on experiences involving objects, models, or brief practice interactions during the lecture

All these procedures are ways of restating, clarifying, or making more vivid the lecture's main ideas. They provide means for trainees to see the topic in their own mind's eye the way the trainer does, and they are the "handles" for retrieving memories of that awareness later when the lecture material must be recalled and used.

When this material is organized and supported it must be put into form for presentation. Even the best ideas must be embellished in ways that gain and hold listeners' attention. To start off well, an "introduction" should be planned that will arouse interest and give direction for the talk. People are encouraged to listen further to what someone has to say if a device such as a joke, a specific incident, a startling or unexpected statement, a rhetorical question, or a quotation from a respected authority is used to seize their attention. Even more effective is involving them personally. This can be done by referring to how the trainer feels and/or how the audience might be feeling at the moment, by referring to problem situations they may have faced recently or are likely to be facing soon, or by asking them to ponder a question and then eliciting their answers or providing one that is fresh to them. In each of these ways their thoughts are being pulled away from other individually pressing matters and are being focused favorably on what is being said.

The first part of the talk also should provide an explicit preview of "coming attractions," of what will be said later. This will provide both motivation and guidelines for appropriate note taking.

Throughout the lecture, attention must be maintained by what is said and the style of presentation. More than any other method, a lecture is a performance, the trainer is the focus or "star," and the set, props, and script affect the outcome. Before beginning, therefore, be sure that the room and everyone's position in it are conducive to hearing and seeing the speaker. Check the equipment and the audibility and visibility of presentations, draw the audience to the front of the room, and arrange to minimize disruptive noise or interruptions. Have the lecture notes in convenient form. An outline is best. This can be handheld or put on the board in full view of everyone. (Writing out the lecture or relying on memory for your message is not recommended. The stiffness of the former, and the danger of forgetting in the latter case, are eliminated by speaking with an outline.) The outline aids in highlighting the main or essential points, so that people are helped to grasp the essence of your message. Emphasis also can be given to a point by articulating it more slowly or more loudly, by a preliminary two- or three-second pause, or by inserting a phrase like "My first main point is . . ." or "The most important thing to remember is . . ."

Audience attention is encouraged throughout a lecture if the content is presented in ways that involve them. It should be made very evident how the lecture material relates to trainees' own lives and what questions that interest them the material is answering. Lecturers who are sincerely convinced of the value of their message, who invest all of themselves in presenting it (by injecting their delivery with feeling and energy), and who care about how listeners react to it (by maintaining eye contact with them, by allowing for interruptions when questions arise, by demonstrating their careful preparation, etc.) engage even passively seated trainees in a psychologically absorbing communication experience.

The lecture should not exceed listeners' typical attention span (20 to 40 minutes). At the conclusion, pull together what was said. It is helpful to anticipate the close by stating, "In conclusion . . .," and then to sum up the points made and/or provide a moving statement or story that epitomizes the essence of the lecture's message. Thus, a sense of completeness is provided, a capsule is given for recalling the message, and final motivation is provided by emphasizing its value to them.

WHAT CAN SIMULATIONS DO?

A simulation is a practice situation setup in a training program which duplicates as closely as possible selected components of real-life work settings (and their interrelationships) so that participants can experience making and carrying out choices involving those components. Simulations are called "games" and "structured exercises" in some contexts. They differ from much case-study work in that the situation is a fictitious one, although analogous to actual work contexts, and the participants become actively involved in performing work functions during the process. They differ from role playing (which we will discuss in the next chapter) in that simulations usually exaggerate reality more, run for a much longer period of time, involve more complex interactions among people, and yield learning outcomes that are less under the control of the trainer and based more upon participants' own individual choices and inferences.

These characteristics, which distinguish simulations, suggest *when* they should be used. Thousands of simulations have become available, from a variety of sources, over the past three decades. Selecting from among them and/or creating one for a specific training event is a decision which should be based on the *need* it is to fill. We will suggest below some of the functions a simulation can serve and where appropriate, the kind of simulation that can best serve that purpose.

1. Although the research on simulations is scattered and skimpy, virtually all investigations, no matter what the simulation studied, agree that they are enjoyable, motivating, and involving. Thus, they provide a welcome break from more passive training methods, and often are inserted for just this purpose, especially in lengthy sessions. (They do consume long time periods, which can be boon or a bane, depending on the trainer's concerns at that time.) The usually light, playful mood created by many simulations, and the fact that they often are called "games," also can be detrimental to their effectiveness. Many people associate learning only with more formal classroom activities, see simulations as a frivolous waste of time, and do not take them seriously. This tendency must be

countered by stressing *why* a simulation is being used at the time it is being introduced to the training group and by debriefing the simulation in such a way that trainees understand how it relates to their lives. (Chapter 12 will help with the latter).

2. Although they are time consuming compared with other training methods, simulations also can compress a wide variety of work experiences (especially for positions which involve many responsibilities and many options) into a relatively short period of time compared to on-the-job training. The "in-basket" exercise, for example, involves a person being handed, sorting out, and responding to as many as 25 different written messages in a few hours' time. Thus, he/she must face and react to as many *different* kinds of challenges as might be faced in months in an actual work role.

3. Furthermore, when the simulation ends, the participants can look back at what they did and evaluate their actions in the light of a variety of criteria. They can examine the *content* of what they have produced. Many simulations involve the scoring of points, often represented by funds or votes earned, which provide a quantitative measure of performance. How well they do on this criterion can be related to the options or choices they used. The players also can review the *process* by which they made their choices or how they interacted with their fellow participants. For example, one common form of simulation involves asking each of several groups to build a structure using simple office supplies, such as paper clips, 3 × 5 cards, and Scotch tape. When these structures are completed they can be compared regarding preestablished criteria, such as their height, originality, and strength. The quality of each group's product can be related to the procedures used to integrate their efforts, such as how leadership was manifested, how creative ideas were generated, or how satisfied each person felt about his/her contribution to the total effort. Thus, the simulation task should be one that most efficiently calls for the use of the skills to be examined afterward. A common problem that arises, whenever there is competition and points are scored in a simulation, is that participants focus too much on winning and are sidetracked from the actual purpose of the game, for example, to explore options regarding group interaction processes. This danger can be averted if the rationale is explained at the start and they are asked to notice *how* their group is working together as well as *what* they are producing.

4. A simulation can focus participants' attention on specifically selected dimensions of a work role, thus eliminating the distractions that arise in more comprehensive training methods or in real-life settings. For example, Body Talk is a game published by *Psychology Today* that directs attention to the nonverbal aspects of communication. The Prisoner's Dilemma game is another common simulation that forces participants to choose between two moves, one that implies trust or cooperation with other players and another that implies distrust or competition with them. The danger in such activities is that in narrowing down the group's focus the complex nature of everyday reality is being distorted. Participants sometimes complain that simulations present situations that are too

closed, rigid, or uncreative and thus do not allow them all the freedoms they actually have under normal work conditions. This occasionally is true, but the discipline of dealing with only one dimension of work life at a time can open people's eyes to more of the options available within that particular sphere, and thereby widen their options in the long run.

5. On the other hand, the simulation can be used to *expand* participants' perspectives beyond the limited range of their previous positions or their own narrow, vested interests. Many simulations have this purpose. For example, some simulate a whole *division* of a company, such as Planned Maintenance, developed by Didactic Systems, Inc., in which the players are maintenance managers in a manufacturing firm who must concern themselves with all phases of small-equipment maintenance. Other games incorporate an entire *company*, such as the Manufacturing Game by McFarlen, McKenny and Seider, in which a manufacturing firm is simulated and players manage the company by establishing production levels, marketing strategy, and financial policy. In the UCLA Executive Decision Game, participants represent *competing firms*. By manipulating the budgets of their respective firms in such areas as marketing, design, production, and capital investments, they attempt to improve their competitive advantage. In the Industrial Park Game, developed by Monroe and Raser, players represent the various interest groups within a large *metropolitan area*, such as business people, middle-class residents, and environmental activists, who must negotiate to determine where and how an industrial park will be established. Crises is a simulation of *international* conflict, in which players serve on teams representing one of six fictional nations.

In each case, these game experiences provide opportunities to test how people think who must make far-reaching, complex decisions. They are useful when preparing trainees to enter or understand a realm of wider dimensions than they are accustomed to considering. Of course, as the situation that is being simulated broadens, more and more of its elements must be omitted for it to be comprehended and dealt with in a relatively brief period of time. This quality of parsimony can render the simulation overly simplistic and distort reality excessively. This danger must be considered and discussed when debriefing participants if games are used to broaden perspectives.

6. Learning new options can evoke anxiety among trainees, but simulations provide an opportunity to sample new roles in a playful, relatively risk-free environment. Participants can test themselves or experiment with different behaviors in a context like one they might enter, but one which is free of most negative payoffs for any errors made. Thus, their fears or concerns about entering the new situation or trying a new approach are likely to be eased after having the simulated experience.

Some simulations, on the other hand, help participants to see that some decision making is not as easy or simple as they thought it might be. For example, the Life Career Game, developed by Boocock, requires participants to plan the daily activities of a fictitious person (with the goal of maximizing that person's life satisfaction) over an eight-year period. There are decisions to be made in terms of education, employment, marriage, and family; and there are "unexpected event" cards in the game, such as being laid off, being promoted, being drafted, or having an unexpected child. Future options must be based on past decisions, and scoring is based on probability data derived from national statistics. This activity, like most simulations, is free of the actual consequences of inappropriate decisions and yet sensitizes players to how difficult making apt choices can be.

7. Simulations can sensitize participants to inner feelings and values in themselves and others of which they might otherwise remain ignorant. For example, in the game Starpower, by Garry Shirts, a society is built in which some people have a great deal of power, while others have little. Players experience the plight of the powerless and the corruption of the powerful because players with the most amount of power are given control of the game and are allowed to set the rules. Blacks and Whites, another *Psychology Today* game, is designed to provide participants with an awareness of what is involved in being black and poor and to suggest the nature of ghetto conditions. One popular form of simulation provides a list of brief biographical sketches of several people, each with different beliefs, abilities, and social or ethnic backgrounds. The players are told that they must choose only a limited number of them to be on a lifeboat, to use a rare kidney machine, or to enter a bomb shelter; hence, the others will perish. Sometimes the roles are presented as candidates for a job. The players' choices from among the group will reveal their own and others' values and prejudices. This exercise can develop self-awareness and sensitivity to individual differences among the players.

All of these activities, however, can evoke strong feelings in the interaction among participants, and sometimes the game can end with a nonplayful amount of ill will between the contending members of the group. Trainers should avoid using simulations such as these with group members who will have to work together in the future or they should allot ample time for debriefing the activity and allowing the heated feelings to be worked out in dialogue that clarifies how they arose and what their implications are for better understanding intergroup conflict in other settings.

If the aforementioned strengths and pitfalls of simulations are kept in mind when decisions are being made regarding their use, they can be appropriately integrated into training programs and can contribute greatly to participants' growth toward exploring a wider range of options in carrying out their work than they had heretofore.

HOW IS A SIMULATION CREATED?

Packaged simulations may not be appropriate for many training situations. Their cost, their length, their content, and so on, may render them unusable. If trainers still wish to include a simulated experience, they may have to create it themselves. This process often requires more effort than is called for in preparing most other training materials, but its rewards can make that extra time quite worthwhile.

Let us take a sample training situation and consider how one might go about creating a simulation to fit within it. In this instance, our example will be a two-day seminar for personnel managers that deals with interviewing prospective employees. The steps we take to develop this simulation provide a format that can be used for any other training context, as well.

The first step is identifying the instructional objectives for the simulation. Let us assume that, in the first part of our example seminar, the trainers introduced several theoretical and practical approaches to using the face-to-face interview process for forming optimally accurate impressions of job candidates. The trainers believe that their group needs a change of pace, a chance to try out their new skills in a risk-free environment, and some feedback as to their ability to carry out the recommended procedures effectively. They decide that a simulation would be appropriate for meeting these objectives, that there is none on the market that exactly suits their purpose, and that they will create one.

The next step is developing a scenario for the game. This includes a description of the work situation the players will be in, the roles they will play, and the pattern of interaction among them. These trainers decide that the setting will be a personnel manager's office, the participants will rotate among the roles of interviewer, job candidate, and observer, and that they will simulate a series of 10-minute interviews (time pressure being one of the factors they want the trainees to learn how to handle better). The trainers obtain access to the personnel files of a large organization similar in some respects to those in which many of the trainees currently work. They write up a description of that organization (changing the name and some minor characteristics) which they will provide to all the trainees. They also use their resource material to write descriptions of 15 employees as they were at the point at which they were first interviewed, and they get actual subsequent ratings on several job performance categories for each one (again, changing names and other minor features to render them anonymous). They include workers who proved to be poor, average, and outstanding employees.

The next stage is developing how the game will be played, the rules the players must follow, and an accounting system for the game (which includes procedures for decision making by people in the key roles, methods of providing feedback on the quality of their decisions, and ways for displaying the results of scores based on the decisions made). In our example, the trainers divide the seminar members into groups of five. Each person is given three folders, each of which contains a description of a job candidate (one sheet is a résumé given to the interviewer, the other contains information that only the person playing the role will know) and a sealed envelope containing that person's ultimate performance in several performance categories (for example, longevity with the firm, advancement, attendance record, performance ratings, etc.) They all also are given the same description of the company, the position for which the candidates are applying, a checklist for the observer containing the interview procedures recommended by the trainers, and a rating form for the interviewer on which he/she makes predictions about the future performance of the candidate based on what was learned during the interviews.

The players are instructed to read the general material about the company and the job to be filled and then to carry out five rounds of play, each taking about 45 minutes. In each round one person is to be the interviewer, three people are to be job candidates, and one is to be an observer. They are to rotate these roles for each round. The interviews are to take no more than 10 minutes each. They begin with the candidate handing the interviewer one of the résumés in his/her folder, and then answering whatever interview questions are posed as they believe the person who they are playing would reply based on how he/she is described in their folder. At the end of each interview, the interviewers must fill out a brief prediction questionnaire on which they must estimate that person's ultimate performance in that job. (These predictions are based on the criteria for which information has been obtained from the actual organization's files.)

At the end of each series of three interviews, the interviewer's ratings are compared with the data that had been obtained from the organization's files and an accuracy score is calculated for each candidate, based on the variance between the interviewer's estimates and that person's actual performance ratings. Also, the observers share their ratings about how well the interviewer followed the procedures recommended in the seminar. During the 15-minute period allotted for review at the end of each round, everyone in the group discusses his/her impression of how those interviews were conducted.

The final step in the process of creating a simulation is giving it a trial run to determine its effectiveness and to make final modifications. Thus, the trainers in this case should gather five people they know and ask them to carry out the simulation they have devised. They may learn that more information is needed in their role descriptions, that 10 minutes is too short a time to carry out an interview, that the process becomes repetitive and boring at about the fourth round, that there is little correlation between using their procedures and obtaining accurate candidate assessment scores, and most important, whether or not it is likely to achieve their intended learning objectives. They can use what they learn from their trial to modify the simulation material, to warn the players at the seminar about any problems they are likely to encounter, or to describe with greater accuracy the uses and limitations of the game.

The overall approach described here for creating a simulation may yield very different specific game plans depending on the training situation in which the simulation is to be used. Creating one's own material provides maximum assurance that the exercise will fit appropriately the time, people, and purpose for which it is intended.

HOW ARE SIMULATIONS
LED?

The trainers' role at the start, during, and after a simulation session is a crucial one. This instructional method thrusts the players temporarily into another reality. They will need a capable guide if they are to enter, remain, and draw insights from the world of the simulated situation. The guide must be someone who has explored that territory him/herself, who knows what is likely to happen there, and who believes in the value of venturing into that domain. Thus, trainers ought to have played the game already themselves, be familiar with the work setting being simulated, and be prepared to support and inspire the players who are hesitant about entering an unfamiliar situation.

Before the game is begun, the trainers should brief the group carefully. The introduction should emphasize *why* the simulation is being done, so that they see it as a "serious," useful activity and attend to the salient issues in the process (not merely get caught up in obtaining a winning score). Then the background or scenario should be explained—using vivid imagery so that the players can picture concretely the work situation they are in. Sometimes signs, maps, or charts hung in front of the room are used to help set the scene, to remind the players of the game's rules, or to record the ongoing scores of the teams involved. Next, the roles of the players must be assigned, the rules or procedures of the game explained, and the means for interacting and scoring points provided.

The participants should be given an opportunity to look over whatever materials are involved and to raise the questions needed to clarify anything that remains unclear. Generally, however, the information provided at the start should be the minimum needed to begin. This is because the players' ability to absorb data will be quickly saturated, and often the process of picking up the information and procedures needed to carry out the simulation can be a useful element of the experience itself. Trainees can learn a lot—from the trial-and-error process and from formulating and asking necessary questions—about the skills needed for moving into new situations and adapting to them quickly.

During the game, the trainers must remain close at hand and observe interactions carefully. They might even jot down observations they want to point out to the group during the postgame discussion. The trainers can help to straighten out any group that is proceeding inappropriately, answer questions about confusing procedures, and provide reassurance to people who at first feel uncomfortable about participating. They also can make on-the-spot modifications in a simulation. At times, these modifications involve simplifying a procedure which is bogging down the players; at other times, the trainers can insert a more challenging element in a situation that a group is handling with minimal effort; or they can provide an equalizing factor (or end a game) if it involves competition and one team has an overwhelming lead.

The trainers' role at the end of the simulation may be the most crucial of all. Players often have been absorbed only in the content of the game, in trying to accumulate points. Their attention must be shifted at this point to *how* they proceeded. The debriefing can take several forms. The trainer can launch a discussion by raising issues based on the learning objectives for the simulation. There can be observers on hand who can report on what they have seen. At times, these can be experts in the content of the game, that is, people who can discuss the decisions of the group(s) in terms of how they affected the group's "economic" outcomes. The observers also might be experts in organizational procedures or in group dynamics who can comment upon intra- or intergroup interactions. Nonexperts can serve as observers too. Their reactions usually will be more useful if they are given criteria or checklists at the start to use in guiding what they attend to, record, and report to the group.

The participants themselves can provide data to discuss at the end. They can be asked to prepare self-reflexive reports on how well they achieved their objectives, how they organized themselves, and/or how they operated as a group. Their report also might be in the form of an account of what occurred or a simulated report to another group, such as a meeting of shareholders, a board of directors, or administrators of the company. Thus, their report can contain insights about their own behavior, recommendations regarding how that company might proceed in the future, or even suggestions to the trainers about how the game itself might be varied or improved. (Further skills needed in debriefing simulations are explored in Chapter 12.)

Generally, it is most important that participants take away personally meaningful insights about how to make their own behavior more effective in similar situations when back at their jobs. This can be done through a discussion within their teams about what they each did that aided and what impeded the group's progress. It is important for them to surface, clarify, and work through any unresolved negative feelings that may have been generated due to the stress, time pressure, and uncertainty of the game's process. Discussion of the ways in which the simulation was and was not like a real situation is helpful in identifying aspects of their behavior that have practical future application. Lessons they would rather *not* learn often are dismissed with a quick disparagement of how analogous the game is to reality. Some confrontation of this tendency may be helpful, but the point need not be pushed in a public arena. Participants in simulations often report that the real payoff in terms of learning is felt days and weeks following the play of the game, as the exercise is recalled in the light of new experiences.

Loveluck (1976) suggests a self-report instrument that provides useful data to participants on their behavior during the game. He asks each person to identify how much they and every other member "influenced the group" (any other factor can be assessed this way, such as "contributed to group harmony," "offered useful ideas," etc.). Then the scores of everyone are shared and compared. In other words, one may learn that his self-rating regarding influence on the group is an 8 (on a scale of 10), but that everyone else rated him 6 or below on this factor. By subtracting one's own rating from others, a "consonance" score is obtained—

the higher the variance, the less consonant a person's self-image is with how others see him. The sum of the individual consonance scores provides a group consonance score. The players thus learn instantly how consistent their self-perceptions are with how everyone else in the group sees them. These comparisons among self and other ratings generate considerable group discussion. When Loveluck asked for these ratings at several points during a game, he found that each groups' overall consonance scores correlated highly with their economic performance scores as a simulated business. It is from procedures such as these that a simulation expands beyond being merely a game and becomes an experience in which players learn more about the options available to them.

Training programs that provide stimulating, practical lectures and simulations enlarge the participants' repertoire of options, that is, what they are able to employ in dealing with situations they encounter back home. They are more ready, therefore, to act in ways that are appropriate to the conditions or contingencies that exist. They are more informed, skillful, and flexible than they had been before the training experience.

CHAPTER EIGHT
ADOPTING A SOLUTION

WHEN SHOULD ADOPTING A SOLUTION BE EMPHASIZED?

We will deal here with those times when trainers' primary objective is to persuade trainees to adopt or use a particular practice. As in Chapter 7, we are concerned primarily with work roles which may be handled in several alternative ways. However, we now address instances in which trainers want to *advocate a preferred method* rather than encouraging trainees to be aware of and to try various options. This is a more directive, more focused, a "harder" approach. Its aims are more specific. They are essentially to shift attitudes, or to provide information, which will in turn lead to desired behavioral changes. The trainers have an image of why and how the participants should operate differently, and their program is intended to communicate their vision so that trainees adopt it, as well.

In most instances, this form of training applies to work roles involving human interaction—those, however, carrying *less responsibility* than the people with whom case studies and simulations are used (at least this approach applies to *simpler* interactions than the other training methods do). One can only advocate a "best" way to do something if the method will be applied to situations that involve only a few variables, have procedures that can be specified, and are relatively predictable. Some examples are dealing with complaints in a retail store, issuing traffic tickets, handling credit collections, and being assertive with negligent employees.

The trainer in this situation draws upon research findings, or time-tested methods, to devise a recommended approach to handling a common problem. Sometimes the trainers will propose a change in how the trainees' entire work role is perceived. They may be advocating, for example, a participative versus an authoritative approach to decision making, an assertive versus an agressive approach to handling customers, a person-centered versus a task-centered approach to supervision. At other times they may be advocating an approach to dealing with specific instances that workers encounter: for example, how to close a sale, how to lead a problem-solving group discussion, how to respond to an employee grievance, or how to handle an appraisal interview.

We assume (or determine) that the trainees do not already use the preferred method. Hence, the trainers' first job must be persuading or motivating them to view it positively, or even as a better method than the alternative they currently use. An attitude change must occur. This task calls for a theoretical or *persuasive presentation*. The next step is for the trainees to be willing and able to employ the new approach: a behavorial change. This generally is accomplished by *role playing* how it might be used. We will deal with these two approaches to training in this chapter.

HOW ARE PERSUASIVE PRESENTATIONS MADE EFFECTIVE?

A persuasive presentation is needed when trainers want to *change* what participants already are doing. The presentation, therefore, is not just filling a vacuum; it is likely to meet some resistance. The trainees have come to see one behavior as most effective for meeting their needs in a situation; the trainer thinks another would be better. How can the trainer's new vision be substituted for or integrated with their more familiar one?

The procedures involved in planning and presenting a persuasive message effectively are similar to those recommended in the preceding section for giving informative talks, but some additional facets need to be added. The first involves identifying the purpose or the response sought from the trainees. Here it is important to find out beforehand their current opinions on the training topic. This is essential because the degree of discrepancy between their views and the trainer's will determine, in part, how successful the persuasive attempt is likely to be.

Let us imagine, for example, that a trainer has been asked to persuade a group of experienced foremen to use a reflective (or active) listening approach when responding to workers' problems, rather than giving quick advice. (This method should help workers to think more independently and prevent misunderstandings.) It is wise in such a case to learn how the group members view their work setting, their own roles, and their subordinates now, how they usually respond to problems, how effective they believe they have been, whether they have ever heard of or tried more nondirective approaches, and how those have worked for them. These data can be gathered via informal conversations or a survey beforehand, or in a series of short self-introductions or an initial discussion in the classroom. What is learned in these ways can be used to develop the persuasive presentation.

Let us assume that the scale shown in Figure 8–1 represents where people stand on an opinion continuum—in this case, in regard to responding to problems. At one end is a completely "directive" point of view (the foreman as drill sergeant) and the other is completely "nondirective" (the foreman as counselor). Let's say that the training group's average opinion is very close to the directive end ("Where the group is"). You would prefer that they be closer to the nondirective end ("Where the trainer is").

Few peoples' beliefs are utterly rigid. Most have a range of views that they find "acceptable." It requires little effort to shift them that far in either direction from their starting point (the "range of acceptance"). There is a wider range that they might be willing at least to consider and try if they are exposed to new, persuasive arguments for it (the "range of persuasibility"). Finally, there are approaches that are so alien to their very basic beliefs about themselves, others, and daily life that they could never swallow them unless absolutely forced to (the "range of rejection").

To advocate a primarily nondirective approach to these foremen, even if the trainer believes in it wholeheartedly, is likely to elicit rejection, a "backlash" of resistance to the trainer and his/her ideas. It would violate their self-concepts and

FIGURE 8–1.

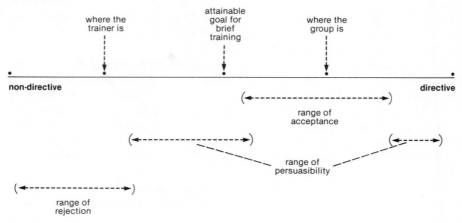

role scripts so radically that they could not accept it and would probably label the trainer an unrealistic fool for suggesting such a change.

However, if the goal were delimited a bit, to advocate only occasional use of nondirective leadership or a modified approach to it, they might go along with it. This goal would be within their range of persuasibility. It could fit with how they see themselves and their jobs, if they are persuaded to do so.

The process of persuasion, therefore, may be viewed as placing an attitude or a behavior within listeners' range of acceptance. This means that it has to be seen as fitting compatibly with their already existing beliefs. People seek consistency in their view of life and want to think that they are doing the best they can. So they tend to reject new ideas that seem contrary to old ones or ideas that portray them as having been "wrong" all along. The trainer's task when seeking change, therefore, is to link the desired approach in a positive way with values and beliefs the trainees already hold. If they see that connection, they will persuade *themselves* that the new approach is worthwhile.

There are several ways to achieve self-persuasion. One way is to remind the trainees of a series of beliefs they hold, affirm the value of those beliefs, and then indicate how the new method fits into a logical progression from those beliefs. For example, we could remind our sample group of foremen that they prefer thinking, independent workers, that people tend to continue doing what is reinforced, and that by giving advice they are encouraging dependency on them (the better the advice, the more reinforcing it is). This line of thinking probably will aid their oppenness to using nondirective responses. They are saying "yes" to the first two points, so they are likely to agree with the conclusion, since it is consistent with what already is obvious to them.

In addition, if someone else whom they respect advocates the new position, the trainees are likely to accept it more readily. (Having this viewpoint will be consistent with their regard for that person.) Hence, testimonials or quotations from experts in the field, or from people whom they see as similar to themselves, can enhance acceptance. A "reluctant" testimonial (from someone who says "I didn't like it at first, didn't think it would work—but now I must admit I was wrong") is the most effective form because that person seems least likely to be biased.

It is essential that the purveyor of the persuasive message be seen as believable. This applies to the trainer, especially, as well as to anyone else cited, quoted, or associated with the new idea. Credibility comes from a positive evaluation of the speaker's *expertise* and *character*. People who seem to know what they are talking about have expertise. This can be based on knowledge, experience, or demonstrated competence, (for example, "I've used this method myself many times, and my subordinates' performance has improved 50 percent"). Character is based on impressions regarding trainers' honesty or trustworthiness, their objectivity (or lack of a hidden agenda, vested interest, or bias), and their dynamism (the caring, energy, involvement that they demonstrate). The force of credibility might be summed up as: "The trainer seems to care about me, to be honest, to be well informed, to have compared this with other methods and chosen the best one. I'll give it a try."

Another approach to persuasion is heightening the trainees' sense of a need for change and offering a way to meet that need. People want to avoid unpleasant experiences, such as looking bad to others, losing job security, being annoyed, doing poor work, and so on. If you can link their current behavior with such states and your proposed alternative with obtaining more approval, job security, advancement, peace of mind, high achievement, and so on, they are more likely to find it acceptable. It is important that they see the desired outcome as contingent on doing what you advocate. For example, if the foremen come into the workshop believing that their staff ask questions because they are lazy or dumb, they will not try a nondirective approach. It will seem pointless. The foremen must be encouraged to see their own behavior as capable of influencing their subordinates in the desired direction.

If the trainees do enter with a somewhat disparate view from the trainer's, their opposition must be dealt with. Their perspective should be acknowledged and explanations for its shortcomings should be provided. Otherwise, when they leave and talk with peers, or try out the new method and run into problems, their old, more familiar views will predominate again. By refuting them, you are "inoculating" the trainees with information or antidotes to use should they get discouraged or should the new way be ridiculed. (Of course, this must be done respectfully. Using "put-downs" to demean traditional methods can feel insulting and increase resistance.)

In sum, when persuading a group to adopt a solution (when others are available and have been used) it is important to enhance its acceptability by increasing (1) its consistency with their other beliefs, (2) the trainer's credibility and that of his/her sources, (3) their sense of need for it, (4) their sense of its actual impact value, and (5) its superiority to other alternatives.

WHEN IS ROLE PLAYING USED?

Role playing serves primarily as an opportunity to rehearse or practice an interaction that is likely to arise in the near future. Thus, it usually is briefer, simpler, and more realistic than a simulation. Trainers also use it to achieve more concrete objectives; and they can plan, interrupt, or repeat a role play to steer it in the desired direction.

Role playing often is used to follow up a didactic message or a group discussion at the point where there must be a progression from knowing to doing or from thinking and talking about a process to using it. As an enactment of a scene that could arise in a workplace, it can fill several functions. If some trainees are to watch others role-play, it can offer a model of exemplary behavior to imitate, demonstrate errors to avoid, or reveal complications in a situation that the observers had not considered. If all the trainees participate in role playing simultaneously, it can offer them practice in using a method that is new to them, a chance to get feedback on how well they themselves handle a particular situation, and an experience whose dynamics can then be analyzed and discussed to develop deeper understanding.

There are several formats which fit under the general rubric of role playing. Each is somewhat more appropriate than the others for achieving specific kinds of learning objectives. We will consider the various types and relate each to the purpose for which it is best suited. To illustrate those uses, let us imagine that we are leading a workshop on assertiveness training for women managers.

Role-playing sessions may be either structured or spontaneous. A *structured* session is planned in advance; the characters' roles may be written out; and it usually is included to provide a demonstration or practice of a general procedure to be taught. For example, the women managers can be given a lecture on how to distinguish passive, assertive, and aggressive approaches to dealing with unreasonable requests. Then a demonstration could be provided of how each approach would be used to refuse a sexual advance. After that, the women could be divided into small groups to role-play the same scene they had just witnessed or one much like it. This would be a structured, preplanned role play.

A *spontaneous* session includes elements proposed by the training participants themselves. In our example, a time could be set aside for the trainees to role-play dealing with the particular requests they are likely to encounter in their own jobs. Or a role play can be set up on the spot. If, during a large group session in which assertive methods are being explained, a participant were to pose a perplexing situation that she faces, the leader could digress for an enactment of that situation. Spontaneous role playing is useful in developing greater self-awareness, dealing with unanticipated cases, and accounting for individual differences among the work situations of participants.

Role playing may be done by one group in *front* of the room or by all the participants in small groups *around* the room. The public enactment is useful as a demonstration or as a scene for everyone to analyze. It gives the trainer a chance to intervene in the process if more background information is needed, if the players reach an impasse, or to suggest alternative ways of proceeding. Putting trainees on display, however, risks their being self-conscious or embarrassed. Hence, it should only be done with volunteers and after a climate of trust and honesty has been developed within the workshop.

Role playing in small groups involves everyone simultaneously in the activity, allows for exploration of participants' special interests, and provides the privacy needed for discussing issues in vulnerable areas. Since the trainer is not on hand, these sessions can perpetuate undesired methods or be dominated by one member of the group. Hence, it is important to use them only after groundwork has been laid thoroughly—by covering recommended techniques, by providing explicit instructions about what the group members should do, and possibly by appointing an observer to each group that regulates the process.

Finally, in some role playing, all information about the situation and the people involved is *open* and available to everyone; in other situations some data are *covert*, available only in the role description given to each of the players. Open enactments are useful for practicing techniques to be used in a risk-free setting. Covert situations often are more realistic—we often have to deal with people whose motives or goals are not immediately apparent. (This often is called a "hidden agenda.") They force attention away from oneself and onto the other persons. What actually is on the players' minds emerges during the interaction. Role players enter covert situations feeling more wary, wanting to avoid misinterpreting other role players and looking foolish. Hence, to minimize inhibition, the covert approach also should await the development of mutual respect among the trainees.

HOW IS ROLE PLAYING LED?

Role playing requires that trainees try out a way of responding that they have not used before. At the same time, they are doing something that seems closely related to acting or performing. Both factors are likely to produce some self-consciousness, awkwardness, and even rejection of the activity itself. Role playing, therefore, must be introduced carefully. Enthusiasm of trainers who like and value role playing also is contagious and usually facilitates use of the technique.

Its value as a training technique, as well as its specific purpose at the point it is being used, should be clearly explained. The players' anxiety can be relieved by stressing that it is *not* a performance, that learning can be drawn from *errors* as well as accuracy in doing the recommended procedures, and that attention should be focused on what they *themselves* are saying or feeling, not on how they look to others. The trainers also might demonstrate how to begin and carry out a scene.

There should be a clear bridge between the role playing and what has occurred before in the workshop and/or the participants' work lives. In other words, they should see it as an extension of their prior learning (for example, a preceding lecture or case study) and as related to their real everyday needs. The latter connection is stronger if they themselves propose the problem or the situation to be role-played. These ideas can be gathered by surveying the group before the workshop begins for suggestions about situations they want to learn how to handle better, or by giving them a checklist of sample situations from which to choose at the session itself.

The next step is forming the group that is to do the role playing. Usually, this involves two parties: one person playing him/herself and another playing the customer, subordinate, job applicant, or whomever the trainee must deal with. Often, a third person participates as an observer (or, if it is a public role play, the whole class observes). It is best for people not to enact scenes with people they work with. Experimentation with new behaviors is best done with strangers. To mix a large group, the trainer first should calculate what is one-third of the group's total number; then count people off in seating order from one to the one-third total, starting over after that until everyone has a number but only three people have the same one; and finally assign scattered spots in the room for the three people with each number to rendezvous and carry out their role play. If the group does not divide evenly into the desired group size, the odd person or two can be asked to volunteer to act as an observer of the whole process and to comment at the end of the session about differences noted among the groups as he/she wandered about the room.

The work setting and the events leading up to the situation to be enacted should be described next. Doing so with vivid imagery helps everyone to picture where they are supposed to be and to get into playing their roles.

The players then need to be assigned and oriented to their roles. This can be done orally, if it is an open role play, or by their reading previously prepared capsule role summaries, if it is to be covert. There generally is no need to be concerned that people be aptly "typecast" in their roles. Men can even play women, and vice versa. The experience still can have its intended impact; and the players may gain a broadened perspective by being in the opposite sex's shoes for a while.

Observers should be given guidelines regarding what to look for. If a simple point is being illustrated in a brief time, this can be given orally. If the role play is concerned with several factors, if it promises to take more than five minutes, or if its intent is covert, the observers should be given a printed checklist with space for jotting down quick comments. Form 8-1 provides a sample format.

After the initial instructions have been given, questions for clarification should be entertained. If it is an open role play, responses can be addressed to the whole group. If it is covert, they must be handled one-to-one at the questioner's seat. At this point, too, a one-sentence reminder of what the role players are to do can help to launch them in the desired direction.

It must be emphasized here that the trainers' manner of introducing the role play will affect greatly how it is enacted. A firm, serious approach will encourage the dubious participants to do it as realistically as possible. Sometimes, the trainers are seeking a playful, disinhibiting, exaggerated approach. In such instances, the trainers should model a free, unrestrained, lighthearted style—and the players are likely to do the same.

The trainer should step back during the first few minutes of the enactment to demonstrate that the role players acutally are now on their own to carry it out. After their initial effort, however, several problems may arise that require the trainer's active intervention: (1) People new to role playing may step out of their roles and speak as themselves as soon as things get difficult (for example, "I'm not sure what to say now," or "you aren't supposed to say that"). (2) They may be observed to be playing their roles in an exaggerated, unrealistic, stereotyped way (that is, "hamming it up"). (3) They may be distorting the intended thrust of the role play by misinterpreting or adding elements to the characters' lives (usually drawn from their own) that are not applicable. (4) They may hit an impasse in their interaction in which they go over and over egocentric arguments and make no progress toward compromising or resolving the differences at issue. (5) They may move quickly to a disastrous outcome (such as someone being fired) that ends the scene abruptly. (6) They may stop or finish the scene and then, if it did not turn out as they would have liked, deny its value because it was not "true to life."

The trainer should step in at these points and ask the players to examine what they have been doing by asking, for example, "How are things going?," "What do you think the problem is?," "What change in your approach might help things go better?" Usually, the players can recognize and resolve their own dilemma. Occasionally, the trainer can use more directive interventions, such as reminding them of the role play's basic purpose and asking them to give it another try; providing some additional information or correcting a misunderstanding; requesting that they switch roles and try the scene again—this time with each player seeing it from the opposite perspective; or asking someone else to volunteer to take the place of the person having difficulty and to try another approach.

There are several other interventions that can enhance the outcomes of a role play, if employed judiciously. One is asking someone to be a player's "alter ego." This person sits beside the player and experiences internally that person's position in the scene. Whenever the alter ego thinks of a strategy, has a feeling, or wishes to insert a comment that would help the partner carry out the role's intention more effectively, he/she can intervene in a predetermined way. These ways include passing a note to the partner offering a suggestion, halting the action momentarily with a hand signal and making a comment in the partner's role, or taking over the partner's role in the scene for a period of time. This alter-ego method is useful when awareness and expression of the role players' *internal* cognitive and emotional processes are vital to the trainers' objectives for this activity.

Another intervention involves the trainer stopping the action and asking one player to talk aloud about how he/she is experiencing what is going on. This is like an actor presenting a soliloquy in an Elizabethan drama. The role player may simply offer a monologue in which the strategies and feelings of the scene are explored, or the trainer might interview the person (in his/her role) about what is going on in the scene. This approach often can help someone get beyond a habitual, narrow, or inhibited approach that is proving ineffective in that situation.

When the trainers note that the demonstration group, one or two groups in the room, have carried out their role play effectively (that is, the scene has drawn to an end or the essential dynamic within it has been played out and the intended point has been made), they should give a two-minute warning and then conclude the role-playing portion of the session. A role-playing group should be thanked for its effort.

At this juncture there often is some information that needs to be shared with the whole class. Small groups might report on what they decided, why that decision was reached, and/or how it might be carried out. If there was covert information that each role player had, those data could be shared with the others in the scene and with the observers. Sometimes it will seem better to air this information before there is discussion about the enactment; at other times it could be better to share reactions to what occurred first and then learn the additional information.

Finally, a discussion is needed about what was learned from the experience. This can be held with the class as a whole or within role-playing groups. In either context, several guidelines should be followed. The people from whom reactions should be solicited are: first, the protagonist in the scene; second, the antagonist(s); and finally, the people who had specific observation responsibilities. Their responses should be in terms of the learning objectives for the role play (again, certainly not about the players' performance).

Whatever comments are made should describe what those individuals *themselves* experience, rather than critiquing others (for example, "I felt uncomfortable when he raised his voice," rather than "He was too loud"). They should be made in reference to the *roles* others played rather than about the person playing the role. (People will not necessarily carry out a role in the way they ordinarily behave and inappropriate impressions can be formed if trainees assume and talk as if they were seeing enactments of player's actual everyday mode of relating to others.) Comments can be about the specific decisions the role players arrived at or about their communication in the process of decision making. These two kinds of comments should be kept distinct; and their target (that is, the exact moment or person in the role play to which each comment is referring) should be made clear, to avoid global inferences that are not really meant. The antagonist and observers can offer useful feedback to the protagonist regarding how they perceived and reacted to his/her behavior. These responses could well be the same as would arise in the minds of coworkers or consumers with whom they will be dealing back on the job.

If the trainer is coaching role players in how to behave more productively, he/she can ask the participants to replay the scene and alter their behavior in certain ways. For example, if the role play is a conflict that has been done destructively, the trainer can ask the protagonist to change certain word usage and nonverbal communication to increase the chances of productive conflict. In the debriefing, trainers should be sure to ask the antagonist how the change in behavior altered his/her feelings and responses. In this way, role players and the audience have a demonstration of their ability to alter interactions.

The trainer should conclude the session by thanking the role players for their effort, and even complimenting them for their willingness to try a new or out-of-the-ordinary way of interacting. The insights gleaned during the role play and the discussion might be summarized. Finally, the group might be urged to go ahead and actually try what they had been practicing when they return to work. However, players may need to be reminded that the new approach being used in the classroom role play is not likely to be done smoothly or to achieve the desired response the first (or every) time it is used in "real life." That approach may require much practice before it appears natural to the user, and it will not necessarily be a foolproof wonder-worker. Brief assertiveness training workshops, for example, should not be expected to produce an entire group of glibly assertive or universally respected people. In fact, one successful trial in a classroom role play does not mean that a new skill has been learned and is ready for use at work. Multiple enactments may be needed for a fresh approach to be genuinely internalized, and not everyone encountered thereafter will respond in the way the trainee desires. Practice and persistent use of the new method should increase participants' chances of dealing effectively with people in the future.

HOW CAN STRUCTURED
ROLE PLAYS BE CREATED?

A role play can be prepared prior to a training session when you know what situations the trainees will be facing, when you know the problems you want them to overcome, and/or when you know the behaviors you want them to perform. The first step in doing so is to identify the typical or critical incidents they must be prepared to handle. These should be ones in which conflict is likely to arise. Several kinds of conflict are possible. The trainee might be a role in which there is an inherent adversary, for example, in labor-management negotiation, in a political campaign, in bidding to win a construction contract. There might be a conflict between how that person and someone else views a situation, for example, persuading a customer to buy something or a board of directors to approve a proposal. The person might feel internal conflict between two or more goals, allegiances or emotions, for example, loyalty to a work partner and to the company, wanting a promotion and fear of more responsibility, wanting job security and to air a complaint.

The background leading up to the conflict situation should be described and provided to the trainees. This should be written in clear informal language. The second person perspective usually is used (" *You* are the foreman in a unit that produces . . ."). It should be concise, if possible taking no more than five minutes to read. It usually should describe the situation to be confronted in objective terms, with no preferred response implied. The situation should be one that can be enacted in one session and one that the protagonist has a decision to make that can be carried out.

All the role players should be given the same basic description of the scene. If it is one in which everyone usually does have equivalent information, this common background sheet is all that is needed. Usually, however, each person enters a situation with his/her own unique personal history, point of view, vested interest, expectations, and intentions for it which the others do not know. It can be helpful to write out a brief character sketch for each role player, which provides this private information and which is given only to that person. When the role players know who they are, what is going on in the situation, and what they are after, the scene is ready to be enacted.

HOW CAN VIDEOTAPING ENHANCE ROLE PLAYING?

Role playing provides a chance to carry out an advocated or customary behavior and to learn immediately and frankly how others react to it. With videotape they can also see and hear for *themselves* how they come across. This opportunity is especially appropriate for those who fill a very public role, whose outward appearance and demeanor are essential to their effectiveness (which can include everyone whose work is primarily interpersonal, for example, retail clerks, teachers, receptionists, bankers, etc.). It also is of value for people who deny the feedback others give them; that is, what they are told is so discrepant with how they view themselves that they cannot believe that it is true. Also, someone may be in a position of such power (or abuse that power) that the workshop participants, and even the trainer, would be hesitant to give that person honest feedback. In these instances, self-awareness is best enhanced when people see themselves perform typical job functions on a videotape.

This experience can be disconcerting. People usually do not hear their own voices or picture themselves as they actually are. Sometimes they like what they see; sometimes they don't. Therefore, when a role-played scene is televised and played back for the participants, some precautions are advised.

First, permission to televise someone should be requested, not assumed. Trainees should have the right to refuse this opportunity if they wish. Second, they should be allowed to view the videotape privately, or with only the trainer and their fellow role players present. This will minimize the "show biz" implications of being on television and permit a more authentic exchange about what is seen. Individuals should comment only on their own behavior, unless they themselves ask others for their opinions. These self-evaluative comments can be elicited by asking them what they *like* about how they appear, how they would like to *improve*, and what *help*, if any, they would like from the others present in assessing the tape or improving their performance. Since those being assessed are dealing with their own personal presentation of self, what changes to make are up to them. Others can say how *they* themselves react, not what the focal person *should* do. The trainer should model such nondirective feedback and ask specifically for these recommended kinds of comments, so that people are not hurt by what can be a very penetrating experience.

It is recommended, too, that trainees be allowed a second (or even a third or more) opportunity to tape and view themselves. This will help to eliminate any behavioral distortions from the first round that had been due to being "on camera." It also will provide a chance to use what was learned from that first experience. The second tape is very likely to manifest marked improvement in whatever shortcomings were noted. This provides instant reinforcement for the changes made and a more positive self-image to carry back to the job.

Trainees will be more enthusiastic about and competent in carrying out a predetermined set of behaviors if it is presented to them via an appropriately designed persuasive message and they are given an opportunity to practice it in a structured role-play situation. They need to value the new method and see it as well suited to themselves before adopting it as their customary mode of behaving. These two steps in the learning process work well in combination to achieve these instructional outcomes.

FORM 8-1   *OBSERVER'S CHECKLIST*

Purpose: To record what each person did that affected progress toward making a decision. In the column under the name of the person speaking, put down the number of the person to whom the comment was directed and a word or two that will jog your memory whenever someone says something that fits one of these categories. You will be asked to share your observations with the role players after the scene is over and they have aired their own reactions to it.

Behaviors   *Names of Role Players*

Asked a leading question	1	2	3	4	5
Interrupted					
Was judgmental					
Was supportive					
Owned an opinion					
Displayed flexibility					

(These are only a sample set of instructions and behaviors. Others, which suit the specific issues being addressed, may be substituted.)

CHAPTER NINE
LEARNING A SKILL

WHEN IS SKILL DEVELOPMENT APPROPRIATE?

The more concretely workers' jobs can be specified, the more likely it is that their training will emphasize skill development. This approach is most applicable, therefore, to employees who have a narrow range of responsibilities and few alternatives from which to choose in carrying them out. The people who fit this category include most manufacturing and industrial or blue-collar workers and the hourly or support personnel in office or retail work. Examples are machine operators, maintenance workers, bank tellers, store clerks, receptionists, and keypunch operators.

Quite often people in this group carry out their work in large part by operating a piece of equipment. Their training emphasizes learning how to use it properly. Their work may be said to be "machine-paced"; that is, they must adapt to the requirements of the equipment they are using or to the system in which it is used. This is in contrast to jobs in which machines are viewed as tools for implementing the decisions of the human beings who have them at their disposal. A printing press operator would be trained in skill development more, therefore, than would a publisher, a graphic designer, or a writer.

Training in skills can occur at several points in such individuals' work lives. The predominant juncture is upon being hired for a new job. This can occur when that person is first entering a field, when transferring within the same line of work from one position to another that requires a somewhat different kind of performance, or when being upgraded from a lower to a higher position of responsibility.

Training in skill development also might be advised for someone whose work is proving to be inadequate or substandard, as well as for someone who does not possess some fundamental skills needed for participation in another form of training. (The latter may be called a "pretrainee," for example, someone who is functionally illiterate or who lacks basic mathematical or social skills.) Finally, as organizations update or automate their procedures and equipment, long-time employees may have to be retrained in the new mode of operating. Skill training, therefore, can be a component in a larger training package, and it can occur at various points in a worker's career. Furthermore, everyone who has a technical dimension to his/her work will, when first encountering that equipment or task, be a candidate for skill training.

HOW IS SKILL LEARNING PLANNED?

The first step in designing a skill development program is determining exactly what skills need to be learned. To do so, the trainer must have access to someone who already has mastered the requisite competencies. This can be done by asking a manager in the sponsoring organization to identify someone (or better several people) whom he/she regards as an "expert" or as a successful user of the skills to be developed.

The trainer can elicit the specific skills to be taught by interviewing and/or observing the person who will serve as a model. Several approaches can be used in an interview to obtain the necessary information. The trainer can ask the informants to describe their work in a chronological sequence. They are asked to detail what they do from the point at which they begin their work, proceeding step by step until they reach the point at which the job is completed.

The trainer also can ask: "How do you know when someone does your job well?" or "What would you look for to determine when someone has been sufficiently trained to do this job well?" If we learn how the expert will judge the worth of the trainee on the job, we know what must be emphasized in the training process. The standards for evaluating someone's work usually have at least three components: (1) the time needed to complete a task (how fast?), (2) the quality of the performance or work output (how well?), and (3) the quantity or number of units completed (how many?).

A third approach is to inquire about the problems that are likely to arise in the course of carrying out the work and then about what should be done regarding each of them in the event that they occur. This is done by an "if so, then what" mode of interrogation. After the basic job description is obtained, the trainer asks about what could go wrong, what difficulties newcomers often have, and what variations on the basic process are likely to occur. For each contingency mentioned, the experts are asked what they and their peers have done in the past to handle them.

There are several precautions to keep in mind during this process. The first is that highly skilled employees often are conscious of and can articulate only a portion of the knowledge they employ in carrying out their work. There usually is a great deal that they "take for granted" or assume that "anyone would know." This might be called the "tacit" or subconscious level of their competency. The trainer must draw out from them as many of these out-of-awareness procedures as possible.

This can be done by asking "How *specifically* do you do that?" for every activity they mention. Whenever they use a pronoun or term whose referent is general or unclear (such as it, they, that thing, the tool), ask "What (or who) specifically are you referring to?" If they just name a procedure (such as "check that it is done properly," "be thorough," or "insert it carefully"), ask them to spell out exactly what activities go into doing it that way or exactly how one tells that the procedure is being done as it should. In these ways, the quick mental processes that the experts carry out without really thinking can be put into a form that the neophyte can use.

It is important, too, to differentiate the minimum acceptable performance level for entering a job from the performance standards of an expert. A job skill often has some basics which are required of everyone who is employed to do it. Then there are additional components which can be picked up as time goes on. To be as efficient as possible, trainers must not set objectives that go beyond what fundamentally is needed for beginning employees, although old-timers may have inflated expectations for them.

A second source of information for determining what must be taught is observations made of experienced workers performing their jobs. The trainers' naivete in this setting can be an asset. They can watch the workers' step-by-step performance from the point of view of a newcomer. The obvious, commonsense activities can be recorded in a notebook, in photos, or on videotape or film. What is not self-evident can be pursued through questioning. From this firsthand contact with the process to be taught, trainers can gain familiarity with what they must convey, and they can pick up nuances that the experts might neglect to mention in an interview.

Once the skills to be learned are broken down into a sequence of small, manageable steps, and standards for assessing entry-level competence in each of them are established, the basic preparation for training has been done. The final step in this phase is writing out the job description that has been developed and then returning to the manager and expert informants for a second check as to its accuracy. Despite whatever care has been taken, omissions, errors, or distortions may occur in the processes of interviewing and observing. These can be caught and eliminated if the trainers' perceptions and conclusions are checked out with the people who ultimately will assess the adequacy of the trainees' performance.

WHERE SHOULD SKILL LEARNING TAKE PLACE?

There are several characteristics of skill learning which suggest that training in this domain should take place on the actual job site. For example, the training period needed may be short; the organization may be too small to maintain a training staff; equipment and/or conditions involved in the work situation may be available only where the job is to be done.

On the other hand, in some situations it is dangerous, intrusive, or pointless to have untrained people at the job site. One example is when you must prepare a large number of trainees, whose needs for attention and guidance would overburden functioning workers who must take time out from their own responsibilities to coach them. Under these circumstances, a classroom training experience is needed.

Another factor helps to determine the most appropriate context for training. Training objectives can usefully be broken down into *tasks* and *skills*. Tasks are procedures that are highly specific and applicable to only one work situation. Skills are more general procedures that can be applied in several contexts. For example, typing is a skill; typing out an invoice in the style preferred by a particular supervisor is a task. Driving a bus is a skill; traversing a specific bus route is a task. Bookkeeping is a skill; carrying out the payroll routines of a unique company is a task. Cooking is a skill; following the recipes that fit the menu of a particular restaurant is a task.

Most often, skills are more appropriately taught in a classroom (or "vestibule" situation); and tasks are learned more efficiently on the job. Skills applicable on many jobs (such as taking shorthand, repairing television sets, or blueprint reading) can be taught most efficiently to large groups by professional trainers in a school setting. The students can then use their skills to obtain jobs with a variety of firms. Tasks, which are relevant only in one context, usually must be taught by the supervisor who will oversee their performance. That person most likely is available only on the job site.

Whatever can be learned in a classroom relieves the busy employer from taking time out to teach. In the classroom the requisite skills can be addressed in a concentrated manner. This is because for most jobs there is a mixture of two kinds of situations. Some situations call for trainees to be doing *routine* activities that are quickly mastered; others call for facing critical incidents that require decisions. The latter category of events can be covered in a few days of a well-planned training program which is free of the routine tasks. It might take weeks on the job for all the kinds of critical incidents to arise and for the necessary instruction to be provided each time.

However, in many lines of work the particular circumstances that might exist in each place of employment can never be simulated totally in a classroom. Warren (1979) suggests that decisions regarding training context be divided into a three-phase approach. Briefly summarized, he maintains that a classroom experience is recommended under the following conditions: (1) the more a job requires skills that are similar to those used in other firms (or units of the same company), (2) the more skills there are that must be learned to do the job well, and (3) the more the way a job is to be performed remains consistent over a long period of time (thereby allowing for a stable training program to be developed).

Classroom instruction has its shortcomings. *Skill* learning rarely is sufficient for all that must be done on most jobs. Hence, school or training program graduates usually are not able to step right into a job and handle all of its unique *task* requirements. First-line supervisors must assume supplementary training roles as a result. Some resent this role and fault the training program for being inadequate. How much the person doing classroom training should cover and how much should be done by the supervisor on the job is debatable. Each person often is disappointed with the other's contribution. For this reason there must be frequent collaboration between all parties involved in such training to parcel out responsibilities as appropriately as possible. The responsibilities of skill and task training also should be spelled out in the training contract (see Chapter 3).

HOW IS SKILL LEARNING ACHIEVED?

At this point, the skills to be learned and the context in which they are to be taught have been identified. The next step is actually transferring the required competency from the trainer to the trainee.

The first stage in this process is demonstrating or modeling what is to be done. An example of an effective worker must be provided for the trainees to know what they are striving to achieve. The first decision at this juncture is determining who will serve as a model for the process to be taught.

The ideal model must be someone who, of course, is competent in using the skills to be learned. The more similar that person is to the trainees, the better. The similarity can be in demographic terms, that is, someone like them in age, race, sex, local speech dialect, and so on. The model also should be someone not too far removed from the trainees in terms of experience. All these factors increase the likelihood of the trainees feeling confident ("If he/she could do it, so can I") and understood ("The model recently was in my shoes and knows what it is like to be first learning these skills"). It can be helpful, too, if the model is a warm, attractive, successful person—someone the trainees would want to emulate and join when the training is over.

Often the trainer is the person who provides the demonstration. When this is not possible, a guest expert can be invited to make a presentation, or a videotape or film can be shown depicting the performance to be initiated. The latter approach allows for the possibility of using several people as models. The more examples the trainees can see, the more likely they are to find a model to identify with, the clearer they can sense how the basic methods are carried out through a variety of different individual styles, and the more assured they come to feel about envisioning themselves acquiring the skills.

The demonstration can serve two basic functions. First, it can encourage or remind the observers to use abilities they already have. For example, it can remind people who serve the public to employ the basic standards of politeness and tact with which they are familiar. They can see how the models are dressed, how they introduce themselves, acknowledge the citizen's cooperation, conclude an interaction, and so on.

Second, it can help the trainees to learn procedures with which they had not been familiar. For this to occur, it is important that the crucial elements in the model's behavior be pointed out to the trainees. If the demonstration is on tape or film, it can be helpful to replay or show in slow motion the essential moments. The trainer might first point out the behaviors to be emphasized. Soon after, the trainees should be asked to note and describe those actions themselves. In some cases, the film or tape itself can be the major training device, especially if the trainee has a remote control switch to use in determining what episodes are to be replayed or slowed down.

Several precautions should be kept in mind when using demonstrations. It is important that models not use their roles to show-off to trainees all that they know and can do. Nor should a lengthy demonstration of a complex procedure be the only example available. One instance of the whole process to be learned can be appropriate if it is followed by short samples of each step in the sequence. Sometimes, the demonstrators' thoughts or inner decision-making process are a vital part of the skills to be learned. These can be explained after each segment of behavior has been demonstrated.

The trainees follow the observation stage by trying to carry out the procedures to be learned themselves. The trainer observes their performance and provides feedback regarding what they are doing well and what needs improvement. There are several principles to keep in mind during this period. These principles generally refer to the *points* at which the trainer reacts and the kind of *responses* given to the trainees as they approximate the desired skills.

The trainees' first attempts to do what is required are likely to include some accurate or desirable behaviors and some that are incorrect or inappropriate. At this point it is essential to highlight and reinforce what is being done *well*. This means making *explicit* what is correct in their behavior and providing a positive reaction to it. The trainer's positive reaction can be a compliment, checking off some items on a list of the required skills, or any other way of affirming that action. People differ in regard to the reinforcements to which they respond. In some instances, giving them attention and a sign of approval is sufficient. In others, making a more concrete reward contingent upon their doing well, such as money or accelerated progress through the training period, will have a stronger impact on their behavior.

It is important that reinforcements be given contingently, consistently, and with minimal delay. In other words, praise or rewards should come only after behaviors that are done well (contingently); they should be meted out fairly whenever and to whomever deserves them (consistently); and they should come as soon after the action to be reinforced as possible (with minimal delay).

Sometimes, the trainees only approximate, come close to, or omit just a small portion of the behavior they are to learn. In such instances, what they have done well should be reinforced, and they should be offered "prompts" regarding what else needs to be done. Prompts are hints or clues as to their next step in a sequence of acts. These can be given orally by the trainer or they can be instructions written on a card, poster, or clipboard that they use. If such prompts cannot be used on the job, they can be used as aids only during the early part of the training period. Then they slowly are faded out by a process of gradual elimination. Thus, trainees are nurtured along from whatever their starting point was, through a series of successively more accurate approximations using reinforcements and prompts, to the point where they can do whatever is necessary to carry out their jobs.

HOW ARE SKILLS IMPROVED?

Sometimes, training is mandated at a point when someone or a group is found to be doing substandard work. The trainer in this case is faced with a challenge in problem solving. Rather than simply having those people repeat the basic training program or designing another for them, the overall work situation should be analyzed.

The first step in this process is obtaining the information necessary for solving the problem. This includes a description of the *variance* between what the workers are doing and the standards for satisfactory performance. This can be couched in terms of the time taken, the quality with which the work should be done, the number of units completed, or the workers' apparent attitude regarding the activity. We must learn just what they are doing wrong.

Next, the trainer must learn about the situation in which the problem occurs. That is, where, when, with whom, and how the substandard performance is manifested. This information can be garnered from the supervisor, the workers' peers, or the workers themselves. It can be learned through written reports, interviews, or actual on-the-job observations.

The trainer's next step is learning whether or not the inadequacy is due to a skill deficiency. Mager and Pipe (1970) suggest asking: "Could the workers perform as desired if they really had to, that is, if their lives depended on it?"

Answering this question "no" suggests that the workers need training. Answering it "yes" suggests that some extrinsic element in the work situation is discouraging optimum performance. Mager and Pipe suggest several other issues that need to be considered after this initial determination is made.

We will begin with the situations in which a skill deficiency is present. Even in these cases, a complete training program is not always necessary. Sometimes, workers resume employment after a layoff, are transferred to a unit, or are assigned a task in which they once were proficient. However, since their skills went unused for a period of time, they have forgotten some of them. In this case, they may merely need some time to practice those skills, get used to using them again, or to "brush them up."

In other instances, people have been doing a task regularly, and have slipped into poor habits which never have been pointed out to them. In some jobs, for instance, speed has been rewarded rather than meticulous care (or vice versa). Suddenly, the supervisor is told to catch every flaw in the product or to speed up production. When standards shift or when inspections and feedback are intensified, people can be deemed inadequate who simply had not attended to that performance criterion carefully before. They do not need training; they simply need to focus on another aspect of their work.

It also is important to check whether the workers have been given adequate equipment or information to do the job. If the typewriter, lathe, or truck breaks down periodically and quantitative reports of output show deficiencies, it may be the equipment (not the worker) that needs overhauling.

Finally, before initiating training, one should ascertain whether the person to receive it is well suited to complete the program. Some work requires a kind of talent, intelligence, physical ability, sensitivity, or interest that a candidate possesses insufficiently to benefit fully from training. In other instances, the candidate is overqualified for the job and would be bored in it. These judgments should not be made rashly. They are difficult to make accurately and can emanate from the social prejudices of the evaluator rather than from actual limitations of the worker. They are best reached after a conference with the person in which alternative opportunities are explored and careful comparisons have been made with the histories of people who have completed the training successfully. People can be remarkably flexible. Generally, we suggest giving a person a chance to succeed rather than *a priori* judging someone negatively.

Now let us consider situations in which people *can* perform the skills they are assigned to, but produce substandard work, nevertheless. These usually seem due to a lack of motivation, laziness, or procrastination. Rather than jumping to conclusions about the workers' competency or character, it is helpful first to consider the context in which the work is to be done. In some situations, circumstances are such that it is not rewarding to do a job well, quickly, or on time. For example, if speed or quantity of output is rewarded by the company rather than quality of work, standards of precision are likely to decline. If any instance of an error is severely punished, rate of production is likely to be sacrificed for meticulousness. Taking a risk, sticking one's neck out, being considerate often will get workers in a strict bureaucracy into trouble with their superiors, so they don't do it. Yet the people they serve are likely to blame them for their caution and rigidity. If some chores bring immediate approval and substantial rewards, and others get little or no reaction from superiors, the latter are likely to be delayed. If work that is not done on a regular shift produces overtime hours and commensurate pay, the system is encouraging procrastination. Sometimes, workers do not know exactly how their supervisors are judging them, what is being looked for in their work, or what they are doing that is perceived as inadequate. They lack the data needed to do what is expected. In sum, the overall consequences faced by the worker must be examined before assessing why substandard work is being done. What seems like laziness to a distant observer can make perfect sense to someone on the scene who can see the whole picture. Once these considerations have been taken into account, an appropriate approach to training can be determined. Sometimes, the trainer must assess the trainees' entry-level skills and provide remedial instruction in deficient areas. Or, as may quite often be true, the change needed is not in the worker but in the context in which the work is to be done.

Skill development begins when specific work functions are first described. It continues through the period when trainees learn to perform them. It can be addressed anew when standards of performance are not being met. The trainer's contribution to this process differs depending on which aspect of skill development is being done. This chapter presented a systematic review of what those contributions might be.

CHAPTER TEN
INTEGRATION IN
THE SYSTEM

WHEN SHOULD INTEGRATION IN THE SYSTEM BE EMPHASIZED?

The work of most people in organizations interfaces with what others do. Every person is part of a larger system. Someone's efforts precede theirs; someone else's follow it. People observe and compare themselves to coworkers. Their human needs and their job responsibilities are met through interactions. Without effective cooperation, even the most talented people are rendered ineffectual. There ain't no more "Lone Rangers" (although even *he* needed Tonto); interdependency is inherent in most jobs.

If a training program is effective and participants are prepared to change their ways of operating, they will return to work eager to implement their learning. When they do so, those changes usually have implications for coworkers. They, too, will have to function a bit differently as a result. Imposed change is not always welcomed. It may even arouse subtle resistance, effort to keep things as they were, or denigration of the new approach. This reception can be frustrating to the enthusiastic trainees. Consequently, they may become hostile to their work environment or to the training they received.

Training cannot, therefore, be limited to just the acquisition of new skills. Some consideration often must be given to facilitating integration of those changes into the work system. People need to know not only how to improve their own work, but also how to interact effectively with peers, subordinates, and superiors on the job, that is, how to be proficient as "team" members.

Problems involving dysfunctional team coordination do not arise only after someone has attended a training program. They can exist whenever people in an organization must adapt to some sort of change. When a company grows, when someone new is hired, when an internal procedure or structure is altered, when society is unstable and social values are evolving, when someone is undergoing a personal or family crisis, after new equipment is installed, when work-related agreements shift (such as when a new labor contract is negotiated), or whenever the status quo changes, some adaptation is required.

Often, people make assumptions and judgments about that change that affect their response to it. Some may embrace it; others may hate it. Those individuals rarely talk through how they are reacting to it. Misunderstandings and resentments come about. These can cause conflicts that remain unexplored. Energy that could go into working out conflicts goes instead into interpersonal resistance, ill will, and even subtle sabotage actions.

At such points, intervention is needed that is addressed to how people work together. This form of training concerns the underlying process, rather than the explicit purpose, of the organization. In other words, whether they are making nuts and bolts or conducting foreign policy, every organization can face comparable people problems. These problems can be alleviated in one of two ways. First, people in the organization can be trained to become more sensitive to and flexible in handling their interactions with others. This is "human relations training." The intent here is developing awareness and skills; it is not situation specific. This kind of training is especially appropriate for managers whose primary daily responsibility is facilitating the efficient functioning of the work system—that is, the efforts of the people within it. Ability in human relations is essential for these individuals.

The second approach is for trainers to function as consultants. They enter the system for a limited time to help a group overcome specific obstructions to change, to clear up temporary communication breakdowns, and to assist in setting up arrangements within the system for preventing repetition of such problems. This is "team development training."

These two approaches are carried out in ways that are overlapping, but they each have distinct features, which we discuss in this section.

HOW DOES HUMAN RELATIONS TRAINING WORK?

Human relations training can take many forms. It can include all the training methods we have discussed in this book thus far. There is one approach, however, that is uniquely appropriate for preparing trainees to work with whatever human relations situations arise in the give-and-take of organizational life. That is the T-group.

This method of training was developed in New England during the late 1940s. Since then it has been applied worldwide. Its form contrasts dramatically with most traditional instructional methods, so it requires careful explanation to be understood and used appropriately. In fact, it is precisely in the differences between the T-group and complementary forms of training that its particular value lies.

The special qualities of the T-group experience are reflected in how it is set up and how it is run. A T-group is composed of about 8 to 18 people, all of whom, ideally, have not been in regular contact with each other outside the group. They meet for extended periods of time, a minimum of two or three hours at a time, in sessions scheduled throughout a full day or for as long as two full weeks at a stretch. There is no preset agenda or structure for the group. At every moment the members are free to say and do whatever they choose.

Each element in this format has an inherent purpose. The size of the group is meant to be large enough to include a variety of viewpoints and small enough to allow everyone to participate. The members' unfamiliarity with each other allows everyone to face a situation in which there are minimal assumptions, expectations, and habitual patterns of interaction imposed by a history of relating and an organization's norms. The members can even deal with each other without knowing what work they each do, their educational backgrounds, or their positions in their firms' hierarchy. They sit in a circle so that each person is facing and is equidistant from the others and so they can address anyone they choose. They often sit on the floor to allow equivalent physical freedom to move as close to or as far away from the group or an individual as they want. Being seated on the floor also breaks up habitual communication patterns that may accompany seeming to be seated in a formal meeting arrangement. They meet for long periods of time to allow for (1) the creation of a network of relationships among them, even a temporary "society" within the group, (2) to feel satisfied or dissatisfied with what happens in that context, (3) to change it in whatever ways seem best, (4) to see how those changes work out, and (5) to deal with the issues each person or the group chooses to address. The lack of agenda or structure permits unfettered social experimentation and heightens members' awareness that whatever occurs is their own creation and hence their own responsibility.

The learnings that occur in the T-group emerge from the interaction among the members. Since they are responsible for creating whatever occurs in the group, they must choose what they want to happen and how to bring that about. This very process of decision making forces trainees to clarify their values about how they prefer to deal with people. Ideally, the process enhances self-responsibility.

As they proceed to talk and act based on these decisions (even if they choose to say nothing), they are being perceived by the others, who form impressions of them. The group is encouraged to report these impressions. From this exchange, people learn how others see them. They also become aware of how differently each person can view an event that they all witnessed. This feedback can be unusually honest because the group members do not have work or social roles that are interdependent, as they are with their back-home associates. Furthermore, the group leader should be skilled at encouraging constructive, helpful feedback, and at discouraging its opposite.

When people have no job to do (other than to improve their own human relations) and when they are operating at a high level of honesty, they tend to become more and more *aware* of what is occurring among them. They see, in the interactions they observe and in their own encounters, the communication process at work. They see what ways of talking lead to understanding and trust and what ways lead to confusion and alienation. They see how the ways in which group decisions are made can lead to cohesion or to dissension. Their understanding of human relations processes grows steadily, and those lessons, based on concrete experience in a concentrated period of time, are deeply felt (and hence retained over time).

They have the opportunity, too, to act on what they are learning. They can compare their own customary behavior with what they observe in others; they can evaluate it in terms of the outcomes it produces for them in the group. They can tell much more clearly and immediately than usual what "works" for them and what is ineffectual. In a supportive group environment, where there is nothing to lose but a little of their arrogance, they can "unfreeze" their old patterns and experiment with interacting a bit differently than usual.

Not necessarily, but most often, these changes are in the direction of being more natural, more spontaneous, more "real." Trainees become aware that at times they use a lot of energy protecting themselves from threats that no longer are present in their lives. In being "safe" they were inhibiting themselves (and others) from using their full human potential. Common examples include women who have inhibited their firmness, frankness, and leadership ability; and men who suppress their feelings of warmth, stress, fear, and vulnerability. These self-imposed restrictions may have been appropriate in their childhood home or community. They may even fit most work situations. But when it comes to a time of change, conflict, or crisis, when people need to be maximally aware and behaviorally flexible, these suppressed parts can come in very handy. So another form of T-group learning is to rediscover, to grant oneself permission to use, practice, and develop skill in implementing disowned aspects of one's human relations.

It is evident that for the T-group to be useful, members must talk openly and honestly about how they are relating to each other in the group. Some of this will be obvious, rational, and well understood. But for the dialogue to represent fully what is going on, it must also include feelings, prejudices, intuitions, "gut-level" sensations, and issues people still are struggling to comprehend. The latter comments may be the most valuable. This is because people so often withhold them, and they go unexpressed.

As group members share and listen to people speaking their minds fully, they will become better able to discern more of what is going on within and between people back at work. They will see much in the dynamics of people's interactions that they had overlooked before. They will develop their own "radar" to pick up nonverbal hints of upset feelings. They will see more vividly how those feelings affect themselves and others at work all the time. They will know how to draw out from others more of what is inside them. They will know that this process takes time and requires skills of inquiry and active listening. They will know how to articulate their own views in ways that are least likely to elicit defensiveness in others. In short, they will be better able to engage in the kind of dialogue that is needed to introduce constructive organizational change most effectively.

HOW ARE HUMAN RELATIONS TRAINING GROUPS LED?

The kind of interaction that occurs in a T-group differs in several ways from what usually goes on between people. For this shift to be effective, one or two trainers are present to facilitate the process. They must know the territory the group is going to explore and how to guide them through it safely. The trainers' role has many facets, each of which we will discuss here.

The Trainer Is an Explainer

The leader's first responsibility is to be sure that all the participants know what they are getting into when they enter the group. As mentioned, this process is based on free choice and personal responsibility. It assumes that change is best achieved through communication and involvement. Consequently, to benefit most the participants must enter the group freely (that is, volunteer for it), and they must value participatory management to some degree. The T-group is for self-directed learning, not for imposing new behaviors or for converting someone who values a strictly authoritarian approach to dealing with people.

The participants also must be somewhat capable of freely exchanging feedback with others and of personal flexibility in responding to what they learn. People who are so vulnerable that any confrontation would upset them, or who are so rigid that they cannot imagine trying new things, are inappropriate candidates for this form of training. A T-group is likely to be neither therapeutic nor placid enough to meet their needs.

To prevent participants from being disappointed by the T-group, from possibly being hurt while in it, and from being so resistant as to be an unbending obstruction in the group, the trainer must explain its goals and methods beforehand. Such a briefing will help all members to be better prepared to benefit from their experience. It will help them to set personal objectives and to use the group's resources (its members) most effectively right from the start.

The Trainer is a Clarifier

The members' first task is to agree on what they want to happen in the group. Since they are free to do as they choose, it is helpful for people to state whatever goals they have and how they plan to pursue them. They also can ask others to help them in this endeavor and share how they are willing to help others accomplish what they want. This form of exchange will slowly build "norms" or agreements on how individuals and the group will interact to meet their needs. Quite often, people cannot immediately be explicit about what they want. When an individual or the group seems bogged down and uncertain about how to proceed with this, the trainer can help them clarify their preferences. This generally is done by questioning: for example, "What would you like to say (or *not* like to say) about your relationship with the people here at the end of this group?"; "In dealing with people at work, when do you feel less capable than you'd like to be?"; "What might happen here that you think would help you in handling such situations more effectively?"

The Trainer Is a Supporter

The T-group is intended for people to work on the human relations situations in which they experience difficulty. To acknowledge and explore them requires an admission of being less than "perfect." People often hesitate to reveal ways in which they aren't doing well for fear of a "negative halo effect," that is, concern that they will be viewed as incompetent overall. They will explore areas of deficiency only if they feel assured that they also are accepted as people and that their fundamental worth is not in question. The trainer must emanate this acceptance.

The participants must see the trainer as a friend, even to the parts in themselves that they themselves do not like. It is, in large part, the trainers' unconditional regard for them, his/her conviction that they are capable of learning and growing, his/her belief that there is no behavior that they are stuck with or that is out of their reach, that bolsters their confidence to use the group environment as a vehicle for learning.

The Trainer Is a Confronter

Trainers must work with an apparent paradox. On the one hand, they must accept the participants as they are. On the other hand, they must "confront" them, that is, challenge them to grow. Although trainers may seem to be in a double bind, this contradiction is only superficial. At both points the trainer is affirming the participants. In the first case their status quo, in the second case their potential.

Confrontations are statements or questions that encourage greater *self-*

examination. Trainers confront discrepancies (for example, between members' words and actions: "You asked him to respond honestly and now you're condemning him for what he said"), unnecessary restrictions imposed on self and others ("Why *shouldn't* he be quiet if he wants to?" or "What makes you think you're being too pushy?"), inferences about what is going on in others' minds (for example, "How do you *know* she really is angry at him"), avoiding responsibility ("Whose fault is it that you didn't interrupt them when you thought they were going on too long?"), and so on.

The Trainer Is a Model

Trainers are not aloof from the group's process. The members will look to them for examples of how competent communicators actually relate. If their behavior is not congruent with what is being attempted in the group, their effectiveness is diminished. What trainers *are* speaks louder than their words. Hence, trainers should tune into and express their own goals, their own deficiencies, their own needs in the group, their own satisfactions and dissatisfactions with the group, their own feedback to others, their own desire for feedback from others, and their own experimentation to expand their social repertoires. (This work, however, should be clearly distinguished from their performance of leadership functions. Comments made by the trainer from a participant role usually should be prefaced by a comment like, "I'm saying this for myself alone, not as a leader of the group.")

The Leader Is a Translator

When people are free to do as they choose and are speaking about unsettled relationships, their defenses can be down and they may be in a vulnerable position. The trainer is always watchful for interactions that can do more harm than good. Most can be translated into worthwhile contributions.

For example, people attribute responsibility to others for what happens in the group ("You are dominating us" or "You are holding us back"). At other times, people impose their own point of view on others ("You shouldn't get upset about that" or "You are too inhibited"). This "right/wrong" orientation creates "good guys" and "bad guys" in a group. The trainer attempts to translate judgments into reflections of the judge's value system. In such instances, it is more appropriate for the speakers to explain how *they* reached those conclusions than for their targets to defend themselves. Once owned and clarified, these comments can be rephrased into useful feedback that their receivers can consider without threat.

Sometimes trainees exaggerate the similarities among people in the group ("We *all* want to get along" or "We're *all* tired of this"). At other times, they exaggerate individual differences ("Everyone besides me seems so self-assured" or "I didn't want to object because I thought everyone wanted to do that"). In the former case, the trainers might encourage differentiation of views ("Do any individuals feel *differently?*") and in the latter, similarity of views ("Does anyone else *also* feel that way?")

The Trainer Is a Linker

This function is served when a concern is brought up and then left hanging. Someone may be annoyed or intimidated by someone else. If this is stated openly, those people or others in the group can at first be uncomfortable at the tension created and prefer to avoid exploring the issue. They can withdraw into silence, change the subject, or laugh it off, which can leave one or both parties with a lingering sense that something is "wrong" with them. The trainer, at such points, encourages and helps them to continue discussing the thoughts and feelings that lie behind their comments in the group. He supports them in "encountering" one another. Often, by disclosing more about themselves, they grow (and others in the group grow) to understand each other better, and the sequence of events that led to their alienation is "cleared up." Even if it is not, the trainer points out the courage it took to bring the matter up and that it is useful to learn how to relate and work in a group even with someone apparently very different from ourselves. Thus, that encounter is not framed as a "failure."

The Trainer Is a Weaner

At the start, the T-group members can be very dependent upon the trainer to intervene in their interactions. If they are to be able to handle such situations "on the spot" back at work, they must gradually be able to engage in a wide range of interactions and work out whatever problems arise *on their own.* Trainers, therefore, must gradually minimize and delay their interventions as the group progresses. At the end, the members should have incorporated many of the trainer's skills into their own behavior, and he/she is no longer needed.

After participating in a well-run T-group, trainees are much better able to accept and discuss changes (and the feelings change engenders) in themselves and others. They can use this ability to help integrate ideas and skills gained in training programs (or demanded by new job circumstances) into the workplace.

WHEN IS TEAM DEVELOPMENT NEEDED?

There are times when a trainer is called in to assist a group of people that work together (a "team") to operate more harmoniously. Some problems arise when there are breakdowns in how the system or work team integrate their efforts. Some "symptoms" of a need for team development include:

1. Unnecessary duplication of effort.
2. Some things just do not get done; they seem to "fall in the cracks" and performance or productivity suffers as a result.

3. People seem to be pulling in different directions.

4. People often have to check to see if things get done; decisions are not followed up as well as they could be.

5. Some people seem to be apathetic, just going through the motions; there is lots of grumbling behind the scenes.

6. Meetings seem to get bogged down; usually a few people do all the talking; others who could be helpful are quiet.

7. People think they have to be careful of what they say; they rarely stick their necks out.

8. Some people work very hard; others slide by.

If these concerns exist, it is likely that the job is not getting done as well as it would if there were better coordination among the people who work together. A team that is well integrated is one that is in agreement about three major elements in its work. These are:

1. What are we here to do (goals)?
2. Who should be doing what to accomplish that (roles)?
3. How should we be working together to get it done (procedures)?

The problems cited earlier all relate to one of these three issues. Problems arise when members of a team have not articulated or are not in agreement about their goals; when their roles are not clear or they have conflicting expectations of each other; when their procedures do not allow for members to understand, participate in, influence, and agree to the decisions made; or when there is inadequate recognition, support, and cohesiveness among the group members. The function of team development training sessions is to work through such problems and to help the group answer those basic questions about their goals, roles, and procedures.

HOW DOES TEAM DEVELOPMENT WORK?

The basic sequence of topics at team development sessions usually follows the list given above. There actually are many variations possible in team development training. We will offer a relatively standard approach here.

The first issue to address is the team's basic mission. Each person should answer the questions: "What are our (my) reasons for being here?" and "What are we (I) doing here?" This can be done prior to the meeting itself. This statement should articulate what each person is trying to accomplish as a team member in his/her day-to-day work and what the team as a whole exists to do.

When everyone has done this, the responses should be shared (perhaps recorded simultaneously on newsprint). Everyone's views should be out "on the table" before attempting to integrate them.

The next step is formulating a list or a statement that completes the following: "As *we* see it, our team's basic mission is . . ." This is done as a whole group, with the trainer serving as moderator and recorder. The first crack at doing this is likely to yield some vague generalizations and/or an unrealistically long list.

The group must next refine this statement of goals. The items that are expressed in "fuzzy" language may need to be concretized. This can be done by asking the group to identify what they would take as evidence (indicators) that each of their basic mission items is being achieved. They would emerge with "performance" goals, that is, items that include implications regarding how their degree of success or failure might be measured.

Let us take as an example a team meeting of a small-town health care agency staff. A mission statement might read: "As we see it, our team's basic mission is to promote optimal physical well-being for the residents of this town." A more specific performance goal would be "to offer six health maintenance classes this fall that are attended by at least 15 people each." The mission statement is inspiring, but the performance goal is something that can be done, seen, and measured.

If their list of performance goals becomes too long, the items may need to be prioritized. Some should be designated "high priority," others "moderate priority," and some "low priority." Those most likely to be in the first group include (1) any directly connected to the team's reason for existing in the first place (for example, "Provide visits with a nurse or doctor for everyone who is qualified"), (2) any that if not achieved could create a problem of crisis proportions (for example, "Keep our equipment supply needs filled"), and (3) any immediate, short-term items (for example, "Send an announcement of the fall class schedule to the newspaper").

Differences of opinion about priorities may emerge at this stage. However, airing and discussing them is preferable to having them manifested on the job. You may discover that people who may have seen each other as unreasonable or time wasting (a personality clash) actually may have very different views on what is important (a priorities clash). At the end of this stage, the team should have formulated and posted in a prominent place its integrated basic mission statement and a list of prioritized performance goals.

The next step is addressing the question "Who does what around here?", that is, role negotiations. There are several ways that poor role definitions can handicap the team's functioning. The first is role ambiguity. This would exist if team members are not sure of what they should be doing (for example, "I don't know if I should send out patient reminders this afternoon or prepare posters for our classes"); if they are not sure what others on the team think they should be doing (for example, "I don't know if I should point out things that should be improved or just mind my own business"); or if they aren't sure about what others on the team should be doing (for example, "When I get a case like this, I don't know who is supposed to handle it, Dr. Smith or Nurse Jones").

A second problem in role definition exists when the expectations of team members are inconsistent with each other. This, too, can take several forms.

There can be role conflict between oneself and others (for example, the physician wants the community health worker to limit her diagnoses and write-ups to *medical* problems; she wants to include the *social* problems of her patient population). Sometimes two or more other team members have expectations for, and make demands on, a team member that are inconsistent (for example, one physician wants the nurses to provide routine health examinations for teenagers seeking work permits; another physician objects strongly to nurses doing any examination and diagnosing work; the doctors do not confer, so the nurses receive conflicting requests). A third problem is role *overload*. The demands are not in conflict, but there is not enough time to perform them all (for example, the physicians also work part-time in hospitals and/or private practice; they cannot find time to examine all their patients *and* meet regularly with nurses and other agency staff).

All these problems in role ambiguity and conflict can sap the energy of team members, causing task inefficiency and quarrels that also might look like personality clashes. They must engage in role negotiation to clear them up. This requires having all the people involved in a given role problem to share information about what they need from each other to get the job done, and what help they can offer each other in performing the various role demands they make. This give-and-take in the interest of more cooperative, efficient team performance should yield informal "contracts" between the negotiating parties that specify the role responsibilities of each person.

This process often is started with the exchange of *written* messages between the team members. At the training session, or before, participants prepare brief written messages to each person with whom they interact. Each message includes two main elements; (1) what the receiver does that *helps* the sender in doing his/her job, and (2) what the receiver could do *more* of, or *less* of, to help the sender do his/her job better. Each part should include some explanation of *why* that action is helpful and each should define the action as precisely as possible. For example, instead of saying "I need you to be more honest and open with me," it would be more meaningful to say something like, "In order to help me know how I should deal with work permit applicants (why?), I need you to give me a detailed list of what I should ask them and how I should examine them (what?)."

Participants in team development may be hesitant to admit their confusion or to ask someone to operate differently. Including affirmations will help, as will reminding them of how a situation can deteriorate if it is not cleared up. The written exchanges also help to facilitate understanding, consideration, and resolution of potential difficulties.

After these messages have been exchanged, volunteers should be elicited to respond orally to the requests they receive. Each person's response can be in several stages and forms. The first step is clarifying the message with the sender. If the request is obvious or confidential it need not be reported to the group, although as many should be aired as possible.

The next step is responding to the request. This can be in the form of an *immediate agreement* (for example, "That's a good idea, I'll do it"). It also can be *agreed to conditionally* (for example, "I can do that if you or some other team member can do something to help me"). An *alternative* can be suggested (for example, "I can't do that, but I can do something else that will help solve your problem"). Finally, the request can be *negotiated* (for example, "I don't think that is an appropriate request; It's Mary's job; I don't have that information").

Once the two people have agreed as to what will be done, they should jot down a note that records what each will do. In its full form, this informal "contract" might include four parts: (1) the problem definition, (2) what person A will do, (3) what person B will do, and (4) a check-back date. Each person should retain a copy.

Sometimes the agreements made at the meeting involve simply planning to get together over coffee to hash out the details of a complex procedure. Thus, not every role negotiation episode evolves a contract. The parties can agree to meet afterward, can give each other permission to do something, or can make even very minor adjustments that will help things be more clear and efficient between them.

If the group is small or the meeting is long, one person usually reads through all of his/her written messages and works out all the subsequent agreements before proceeding on to the next person. If time is short, it is best to have everyone share with the group a summary of the messages received and of their responses to them. At that time appointments can be made among small groups for working out any issues that appear to require a longer negotiating session. Sometimes one of the parties involved can suggest that a third person, perhaps the trainer, be present to facilitate their problem-solving process.

Whether the problems requiring negotiation are worked out in the presence of the whole group or at a smaller meeting, the participants should use a sequenced problem-solving approach. The trainer might aid them in learning and implementing this procedure. It proceeds from analyzing the problem (its "symptoms" and possible causes), to generating alternative solutions, to selecting the best alternative, to deciding how to implement it, and finally to determining how and when to evaluate how it is working.

It is important, too, to be sure that participants are aware of which problem-solving *stage* they are at, *who* needs to be involved in the decision (people who can provide useful information and people who can develop commitment for carrying out the decision), *how* the others need to be involved (*directly* in making the decision, *consulted* for information or opinions before the decision is made, or *informed* about the decision so that it does not come as a surprise to them afterward), and *when* the decision will be made (including the timetable for getting it done and who will be responsible for "managing" the process, that is, for making sure that it gets done by the agreed-upon time).

There is one last step in assuring that the agreements made in the team development meeting will be carried out. The participants may need to review the forces in their situation that are helping them to fulfill their performance goals and those that are hindering them. These can be divided into three categories: (1) things to do myself, (2) things to do with others on this team, and (3) things to do with others and the environment outside this team. Some of the factors in the organizational environment of the team (for example, certain company policy) that may hinder optimal functioning were discussed in Chapter 2. When conducting team-building sessions, trainers should remember to do so from a systems framework so that trainees are aware of the elements they are capable of affecting in the session and ones they are not.

By spelling out the factors that might affect a plan of action (both pro and con), participants can more realistically foresee how likely it is to be carried out successfully and what they can do to improve the chances of its working.

Both T-groups and team development are most relevant when close collaboration among people is required to get a job done. Since people are the most complex, the most unpredictable element in an organization, these approaches to training are the most challenging in the trainer's repertoire, yet ultimately can be the most rewarding.

HOW ARE TRAINING ACHIEVEMENTS PRESERVED?

A final consideration in the reintegration phase is including activities *within* standard training programs that help participants maintain whatever changes they have made. Lippitt and Lippitt (1978) contend that "the designing of support systems for the successful continuity of change efforts is perhaps the most significant test of the competence and professional quality of the consultant" (p. 25). Trainees will need environmental support at work for fresh attitudes and behaviors. Therefore, we conclude this chapter by suggesting several methods for helping trainees successfully reenter their back-home settings.

Throughout the training session, as we have said, trainers should discuss the utility of their material by using examples relevant to the particular audience with which they are working. As the training draws to a close, they also should allot time for considering problems trainees may experience when they return home, and if possible, ways of using the training content itself to handle those problems.

The latter suggestion is particularly helpful when the subject matter of training is effective communication. For example, trainees may have learned about the importance of openness for clarifying their relationships. They may expect, as a result, that when reentering their home environments, others will applaud their openness and respond in kind. Their new approach, however, comes with "strings attached": They demand implicitly that their co-workers reciprocate. If they do not, the trainees may deride them for being closed, thereby using their newly gained openness to divide them further from coworkers rather than creating better integration of effort.

Near the conclusion of the training, an effective exercise is to lead trainees on a guided fantasy in which they return to their home environments. During this time, they imagine specific situations in which they will use what they have learned, responses they expect to get from significant others in their lives, and how they will handle any problems that arise. The fantasies are then discussed and the imagined problems and possible responses explored in detail. Such scenes also can be role-played, so trainees can practice responses and assess which are likely to be most helpful.

Another activity that might be included at the end of a training program (especially one that has been lengthy) is identifying support people in back-home environments with whom trainees can discuss whatever problems arise and from whom they can get continued reinforcement for their changes. In some cases, people who participated in the training can form ongoing support groups. In others, trainees can identify people in their normal environments (social, family, and/or work) who are likely to be supportive of their growth. It is important for trainees to be reminded that not everyone will welcome their changes, especially when those changes might affect long-standing, interpersonal relationships. In such cases, it usually is not helpful to try convincing others of the value of the training or that they themselves should attend to learn how to improve as communicators, accountants, or whatever. This approach often is perceived as condescending and is likely to be met with resistance, apathy, or hostility.

A means of encouraging transfer of learning is to plan some form of *celebration* at the end of training. Change is often more effective when successes are recognized and when learning is fun. Celebrations serve both goals. They can include a party, a skit, or creation of a symbolic ritual that epitomizes the purpose of the training.

Trainees also can plan a celebration of their new learning in their back-home environments. If this event includes people with whom they work or live, trainees will be building an ongoing support system at their home base. For example, trainees could agree with their supervisors on a time to share the learning of their training, informally or formally with coworkers, if that is suitable to the nature of their reentry group.

Another reentry activity is *goal setting*. This involves identifying a specific and limited problem the trainees would like to address in their normal work or home settings and stating *concrete, behavioral goals* that may help them solve their problems. For example, after an assertiveness training course, a woman might say that she plans to ask for three things she wants from her husband in the following week. She then might *identify the resources* she has for meeting her goal and the obstacles to achieving that goal. Resources might be her new skills, her desire to maintain her assertiveness, reinforcement from friends, and basic support from her husband. Possible obstacles could include fear of unpredictable responses from others and changes in her marital relationship, uncertainty about her new image, and family members who do not support the changes. The final step is *planning action steps* for enhancing the resources and overcoming the obstacles. For example, she may practice her skills in less risky settings at first (with a trusted friend), keep her support group informed of what she is doing, and let her husband know of her goal in order to encourage him to view it as positively as possible and to be prepared for the changes. She can deal with the obstacles by negotiating new roles with unsupportive family members or by reducing the dependence she has on them to support her new behavior.

To increase chances for achieving their goals, it may be important for trainers to remind participants to consider how well training and back-home environments are matched. For example, executives may attend a workshop in which the goals include learning the value of trust and the power of taking responsibility for personal choices. The workshop norms may have included openness, honesty, and exploration of self and others on an intimate level. Although these ideas can be used in business settings, trainees need to remember that the manner and pace with which new ideas are introduced play a big part in their acceptance. For example, expressing strong personal feelings in the next board meeting, whose members have the interaction style of *Star Trek's* Mr. Spock, probably will not be met with resounding approval. The more disparate the training and work environments, the more slowly and carefully trainees need to introduce major changes.

HOW CAN TRAINING BE FOLLOWED UP ON THE JOB?

If the trainer is working with an intact work group, plans can be made during the training for a formal review of progress after the training. Lippitt and Lippitt (1978) use the term "periodic maintenance plan" to refer to reviews that serve the purposes of reminding groups of their goals, helping them monitor their success, and establishing different, more realistic goals when necessary (p. 25).

If trainers are outsiders working within an organization, they may want to identify a person early in the training who can take over many of their functions after the training. Built into their contract can be an agreement that the trainers will work with that internal consultant for a certain number of hours to help with specific follow-up procedures.

Depending on the nature of the training and client group, a credible person outside the organization also can take over the follow-up function. For example, we worked with a number of cities doing community development work. It was not possible (because of time and financial constraints) to stay in touch with all the communities, but there was a person already in the larger system who could. He was the human resources director for the State League of Municipalities, whose role became advising communities about handling their subsequent problems. This kind of arrangement should be established prior to the training and is most effective if the local follow-up person's orientation and goals are close to those of the trainers.

For some goals to be realized, participants need to establish new institutional channels in their back-home arenas. For example, we conducted a long-term training program in several small communities for the purpose of building indigenous cohesive groups, made up of people from diverse socioeconomic backgrounds, who would influence local government decisions about social programs. It was not enough to have them function as a group and make effective decisions during the training. We needed to include time for them to develop a group structure (hierarchy, officers, committees), plan meetings for after the training, and develop a strategy for presenting themselves to the city council to petition for formal recognition as an advisory board. By becoming a legitimate institutional channel (an advisory board), the group was more assured of continued influence, public visibility, and, therefore, more interest from local citizens than if they only had operated as an informal group.

If the training is interpersonal in nature, people also can establish mechanisms for reaching their goals. For example, couples who have attended Marriage Encounter are asked to set aside a particular time of day for communicating about their relationship and disclosing feelings to their partners. The agreed-upon time, in essence, becomes a follow-up procedure for helping couples maintain the intimacy achieved in the workshop.

Finally, changes incurred during training are most likely to be reintegrated and used in the back-home setting if there is some kind of public commitment to make changes. For example, the training and its goals can be publicized prior to the event and after its completion. Company or local newspapers often are used for publicity. Public commitment may come in the form of a person letting a friend or coworker know of the changes he/she desires, for example, losing weight or stopping smoking, or setting new priorities for time use. It is more difficult for people to change their minds and deviate from plans if they have told others, whose regard they value, of their intentions (see Kiesler, 1971).

In some cases, the trainer is employed to follow up workshop participants' efforts personally. This can be done in several ways. A simple method is writing or calling trainees to discuss possible problems and to ask for feedback on the training. This method is easier when the trainer has worked with intact groups or organizations.

Second, trainers can build an agreement into the training contract to conduct follow-up interviews with trainees and, if feasible, their coworkers or cointimates (depending on the nature of the group). Purposes of the interviews can be to check on progress toward goals, to answer questions about problems, and to evaluate the outcome and long-term effects of the training.

A final suggestion has to do with giving information obtained during training to key people in an organizaton. For example, a large company was conducting a series of workshops for middle managers in several divisions of the organization. The communication skills the managers were being urged to adopt were not congruent with the management philosophy of the company and the communication styles of the top executives. Consequently, many of the trainees confided to the trainer that they were confused and even threatened by the discrepancy between how they were being treated and how they were expected to communicate after the training. It was important for the trainers to report this information to those sponsoring the training, with the recommendation that either top management also be trained or that the training stop, since it was creating more problems within the company than it was solving.

The kind of information relayed to important people in an organization does not include trainees' personal responses and ideas. The trainer is not a spy for top management. However, we believe that information that comes from a large group of people and affects the entire training effort can be passed on ethically. (Other activities that can serve as follow-up activities are described in Chapter 14.)

With this chapter we come to the end of the training cycle. The material provided thus far in this section offers a comprehensive, systematic set of training procedures and guidelines for implementing various phases of training. The trainer now is armed with a complete repertoire of skills and methods for conducting effective learning experiences.

CHAPTER ELEVEN
THE OVERALL
TRAINING PLAN

In Part II we described when and how to use various methods of training. A training program, however, is more than simply the sum of its parts. They all must be interwoven into a unified design. The workshop into which each step fits must provide a well-integrated cohesive experience in which all parts harmonize to achieve the overall objectives. Factors that affect integration include how methods are selected, sequenced, and presented. We will discuss all three in this chapter. To illustrate the points to be made, we apply them to the following example of a training situation.

A concern recently given widespread recognition is the effect of *stress* on human performance. Excessive stress can have a debilitating effect on an individual's health and decision-making ability. When stress is suppressed (and people feel tight and inhibited inside), they are prone to inappropriate outbursts of temper, to feeling alienated from others, and to tunnelvision or rigidity of outlook. In some professions, where stress is prevalent, unhealthy outlets are common, such as excessive drinking, smoking, or eating. Hence, recognition of stress-provoking situations and symptoms of stressful responses, as well as learning how to relieve stress in oneself and others, can be a valuable focus for training.

The legal system is one setting in which stress is endemic. When an adversary relationship exists and much is at stake, stress rises among defendants, lawyers, and judges. Imagine that you are asked to offer a one-day workshop on managing stress at a statewide convention of judges. They can choose this event from among several offered at the same time. You are at the point of planning how you will approach it. Since their time is precious and this is an "elective" for them, you want it to be both informative and enjoyable.

HOW ARE WORKSHOPS
BEGUN?

The training event actually begins long before the participants and trainer meet. It is affected by how the program is established, how it is advertised, and how trainee needs are assessed, as well as by many other events that occur prior to that first meeting. These steps are discussed in other chapters.

Here we pick up this process when the trainer and participants initially make contact at the start of the workshop. It is best for the trainer to arrive a bit before the official starting time. This period can be used for double-checking the facilities and room arrangement, for setting up audiovisual equipment, and for establishing an instructional "home base" on a table or lectern on which the instructional plan and materials for the day are comfortably arranged.

We find ourselves using that time to feel as settled in and as familiar with the environment as possible. Chatting with early arrivers helps us to loosen up and to learn whether there are any recent current events that are affecting the trainees. We find that this early small talk enhances our confidence and rapport with the group (since there often is a correlation between early arrival and participants' degree of enthusiasm about the program), and it provides a quick orientation to the group and its immediate concerns.

We acknowledge and greet each person arriving in as personal and direct a way as possible. We think of them as coming to share what will be a special (and perhaps stressful) day for these reasons: Training is an antecedent to change of some kind; it is an "out-of-the-ordinary" experience, a potentially exciting and creative encounter; people are coming together who are strangers and yet will be affecting each other before the day is out; a new minisociety will be formed in that room; they will deal with a new leader, a new role for themselves, new kinds of activities, and higher expectations for performance afterward.

These conditions themselves generate stress to which participants can react in several ways. They can see the workshop environment as a dangerous, threatening place and defend themselves from it by creating an inner wall, by putting up their guard, by approaching the workshop very hesitantly and cautiously, or they can see it as an appealing and challenging environment and reach out toward involving themselves in it by listening attentively, by pondering the ideas presented, and by using the energy that stress stirs up in them to plunge into workshop activities with enthusiasm. Some enter the room already oriented to one approach or the other. Many are on the line between the two, and upon entering immediately look for clues as to the kind of experience it will be, so that they will know how to react. The training actually begins the instant participants lay eyes on the trainer. The first few moments of trainer-trainee contact are crucial in determining whether a relatively open or closed stance will be taken toward what is to occur.

People seat themselves where they choose, write their names on a card placed in front of them, and we begin at the scheduled time, if that is at all possible. Each of these elements is purposeful. Self-selected seating indicates their freedom to be as close to or as far from us as they want; prominent display of names, which we use often, promotes dealing with people as individuals; and keeping to the time schedule means that we are conscious of and stick to the agreements we make. Thus, we are setting norms, or patterns of relating, which we believe are conducive to effective training.

Our first comments address directly the uncertainty that exists at the start. We explain why this training session is being held, what will occur here, and how they can expect to benefit from participating. We share how we became involved as trainers, how we plan to interact with them, and what *we* hope to gain from the experience. We know that at this point they are sizing us up as people, as well as getting the content of our message, so we try to be as real, frank, and straightforward as we can. If we are not pretentious or guarded, they are less likely to be, and the workshop will be an authentic one.

During these comments, too, we are establishing a businesslike "contract" with them. There will be an exchange of "resources" going on, and it will operate within certain limitations. We tell them what the workshop's objectives are, what we have to offer for them to be met, and what they will have to contribute toward achieving those objectives. We also explain the conditions under which this exchange can best occur, such as the explicit time periods needed for this work, the kinds of activities it takes to do it (such as reading, frank and honest discussions, involvement in simulations, etc.), and the risks involved (for example, feeling a bit awkward when using the new approaches for the first time). Then we propose that continued attendance at the workshop implies knowing what will be happening and agreeing to live within that contract. If dropping out is not an option, people are free to subscribe to some portions of the contract and not others. The essence here is being overt and clear about what agreements underlie being in the workshop, and then sticking to them as it progresses.

We usually follow this introduction with a request for a brief comment from each participant. This might include their names, work situations, and any one of several pieces of information, depending on the situation. Most often, we ask them to share: "What specifically would make this workshop worthwhile to you?" Their responses give *us* a chance to quiet down and size *them* up for a while; they provide us with a sense of the group's interests and level of enthusiasm; and they tell us what each person is looking for, so that we can address those persons when making comments especially relevant to them in the course of the session. During this period participants, too, get to hear the variety of concerns people bring with them and can be more understanding if portions of the session deal with topics that are of little interest to them, but vitally concern others. If we had no part in setting up the program, we also ask: "What led to your attending this workshop and how do you feel about that?" This gives people who were *told* to come a chance to express their resentment or fear about being "selected." We indicate that we understand and accept those feelings, thereby allowing us to move on to making the best of the situation we are in together. (See also Chapter 4 for how to deal with anxiety about facing change.)

The strains that accompany the start of a training session also can be eased in other ways. Some people deliberately insert jokes into their opening comments to lighten the atmosphere. Others do a "warm-up" or "get-acquainted" activity early in the session that loosens up the stiffness or formality of the situation. For example, participants can be asked to print on a sheet of paper their name, job, hometown, what "turns them on" (favorite activities, books, movies, public figures), and what "turns them off" (what they avoid, dislike, feel angry about). Then they affix these to their chests with a piece of tape and mill around the room, greeting each other, and quickly garnering profiles of what everyone else is like. This process can end with them forming dyads or small groups with others with whom they want to work on the first exercise of the session.

There are numerous variations on opening activities. There is much room for trainer choice within the essential steps of deciding what should be accomplished during this period and then planning how that will be done. Whatever the purpose, be as direct and up-front as possible with the group about your intentions.

HOW ARE TRAINING ACTIVITIES SEQUENCED?

The outline of a comprehensive training program that we introduced in Chapter 1 also provides the most fundamental approach to sequencing. In other words, most programs should begin by considering the need for training, proceed through each step around the circle (see p. 00), and end by integrating the new learnings into the overall organizational system. Although this pattern provides a basic framework for making program planning decisions, it does not resolve all sequencing issues. Several other criteria should be incorporated in an overall program plan. These are variety, an exposure continuum, and correlation of performance scores. We will consider each in turn.

Variety

Trainees' attention to and absorption of material are enhanced when there is variety in how it is presented. Variety can be achieved by moving along the continuum of methods suggested in Chapter 10 and by considering several other factors as well. The overall training plan should be examined, and modified if necessary, to incorporate variety in (1) abstraction level, (2) source of information, (3) structure, and (4) facets of learning. We will consider each in turn.

Abstraction Level. Most work processes can be discussed in highly abstract terms (that is, *general* principles that apply to many situations) and through less abstract terms (that is, *specific* examples that apply only to particular instances). In our workshop for judges, for example, we would discuss the way stress generally is created and manifested before we would consider how it might appear in any one of the particular situations judges face in their work roles.

Any phenomenon can be viewed at several levels of abstraction. A person's drinking problem, for example, can be discussed in terms of how it affects a particular situation, the elements that exist in all the situations in which he tends to overindulge, the overall nature of the alcohol abuse syndrome, or the factors in contemporary society that lead to use of various consciousness-altering substances by the population as a whole. Each level has value. Each calls for use of different cognitive processes. Most people prefer to examine a problem predominantly at one end of the abstraction ladder or the other. In a workshop, however, to maintain maximum interest and useful learning, all these levels should be included.

Generally, the sequence followed is from the general to the specific. Knowledge of underlying principles should guide concrete applications. This process is called deductive reasoning. However, on occasion a session can begin with presentation of one or more critical incidents which can be discussed and used as the basis for inferring general propositions that apply to all instances of that type. This is called inductive reasoning. Mixing both approaches and utilizing various levels of abstraction deepens and gives variety to workshop learning.

Source of Information. A training program may be viewed as a vehicle for exposing participants to channels of information about its topic that would not otherwise be available to them. In most sessions those channels include the trainer, the instructional materials, and the group of participants themselves. These sources should all be tapped and mixed in a stimulating sequence.

Trainers can present what they know; various media can be used to supplement those ideas; and participants should be asked to contribute the knowledge that they bring about the topic, as well. In our sample situation, the issue of stress is one that most thoughtful adults have already considered. A workshop functions to bring additional attention and a broader range of ideas to bear on the topic than is commonly provided in ordinary conversation or in the popular media. To repeat what participants already know is often experienced as patronizing and boring.

Furthermore, human tolerance for receiving input is limited. Ideas presented by the trainer will stimulate thoughts in the training group. These need to be expressed. Interest is maintained when there is a balance between input and output for the participants. The training plan, therefore, needs to include a rich variety of experiences that move briskly from trainer contributions, to supportive illustrations using various media, to reactions, comments, and questions from trainees (that is, information emanating from a variety of sources).

Structure.   We spoke in Chapter 1 about the complementary functions of "hard" and "soft" approaches to learning. The former tend to be structured, linear, and directive. The latter are spontaneous, holistic, and intuitive. A well-planned workshop includes a mixture of each.

Participants want to know that the trainer knows where the program is headed, has planned how the group will get there, and is in control of the group's progress. If these are the only qualities they sense in what is occurring, they may feel overly pushed, programmed, or regimented. They also want to feel that there is room for accommodating to the unplanned issues that they raise, that the trainer is flexible and responsive, that they have some voice in determining what will happen.

Comprehensive trainers offer a prearranged schedule for the overall session, make prepared presentations to the group, and cut off discussions that linger on topics tangential to the main focus. However, they also relax this disciplined approach from time to time in the course of a workshop to ask for comments on a topic, for feedback on how things are going so far, and to allow for deeper exploration of an issue that seems to stimulate the group more than they had anticipated when planning the schedule. Thus, they mix hard and soft approaches as the situation seems to call for them.

There are a couple of points at which a shift from hard to soft seems most appropriate. These occur immediately after a thought-provoking experience has occurred. The experience might be a lecture that included controversial ideas, an exercise to which participants responded in a variety of ways, or a case study that presented an ambiguous situation. At these points, when trainees are aroused and have viewpoints to express, a soft receptive mode is most appropriate. Another juncture is immediately after a break in the session. During the informal interaction that occurs over coffee or lunch, participants often raise issues among themselves or ponder what had been presented in the preceding session. They are likely to generate questions that need to be explored before they can attend fully to the new topic to be raised in the upcoming portion of the workshop. Hence, we begin most sessions by stating: "Before I launch into what I had planned for the upcoming session, did anything come to mind over the break that you would like us to consider?" In this way, they are invited to "clear their decks" before setting forth in a new direction.

In sum, shifts in structure, from directive to receptive to directive again, and so on, as the session progresses, are another way to help in maintaining participant interest level and involvement in the learning process.

> *Facets of Learning.*   As mentioned earlier, there are three basic facets to learning about a topic: the knowledge to be gained (cognitive), the attitude or value one has about the topic (affective), and the ability or skill to use the knowledge in action (behavioral). A comprehensive training program provides a mixture of all three.

In our example workshop, dealing with managing stress, there would be some theoretical explanation of the way stress works (cognitive), some consideration of how it affects the legal system—to emphasize the importance of giving time and energy to working on this issue (affective)—and some instruction and practice in the use of techniques for dealing with stress (behavioral). Omitting any of these three, or dwelling too long on just one, would reduce the effectiveness of the workshop.

Generally, these facets are introduced in the order: affective (*why* learn this?), cognitive (*what* is to be learned?) and behavioral (*how* is it used?). However, in the course of a workshop they can be deal with in other sequences. Sometimes, an affective "sermonette" is needed to rekindle the trainees' enthusiasm or to counter a cynical argument; sometimes an additional piece of information is called for; sometimes demonstration of methodology is appropriate; sometimes all three are called for when answering a participant's query. The cue for determining when each is needed is to listen for the issue at the heart of a question; that is, is the person asking *why* something is important (affective issue), *what* is true about the topic (cognitive issue), or *how* something is done (behavioral issue)? By planning and spontaneously incorporating all three facets of learning as appropriate, the workshop will be sufficiently varied and comprehensive.

Exposure Continuum

When trainees first get together, whether they are at entry level or are seasoned professionals, they are likely to feel somewhat self-conscious and want to "look good" in front of their peers. This concern can produce a sense of caution or reserve during the "image-creating" period at the beginning of the workshop. Some people deal with this phase by seeking a quick opportunity to display their abilities openly and so seem utterly uninhibited at the start. However, whether they are reticent or flamboyant, it is important to remember that trainees are likely to be playing it safe, revealing only what will be approved, during the early stages of a workshop.

At this point, activities should be planned that are likely to relieve rather than exacerbate their concerns about appearance. Thus, a training plan should be reviewed for the degree to which it moves from simple to complex material, from easy to more challenging activities, from discussion of participants' past successes to examination of situations in which they experience difficulty. As they feel reassured that they are accepted, as they note that the norm in the group is to acknowledge the legitimacy of human shortcomings (and the legitimacy of *success* as well), and as they have a chance to demonstrate mastery over some aspects of the workshop topic, they will become more willing to work openly in the more risky domains beyond their entry level of competence.

To begin the workshop on stress management, for example, by asking the judges to share cases in which they were *not* able to handle their own or others' stress buildup would be inappropriate. Since they are likely to be proud, reserved people, the discussion would be leaden and false. It would be wiser to ask for instances in which they dealt *most effectively* with the stress of litigants and lawyers, first, and then how they cope with it in their own lives. (People talk a bit more easily about third parties than they do about themselves.) After being acknowledged as fundamentally capable professionals, they would be more willing to address areas in which they need to grow. (As discussed in Chapter 4, personal change seems paradoxical in that people must feel accepted before they will voyage into new areas.)

Similarly, lectures and activities at the start of a workshop generally should be easier to comprehend or complete than those inserted later. It takes time for trainees to trust the trainer and the group enough to be comfortable asking questions, to disagree, to share personal applications, to explore problematic situations. Therefore, controversial or complex material should be presented after a solid background of agreed-upon principles and straightforward exercises has been laid. Activities involving spontaneous role playing, self-disclosure, or instructions that are difficult to understand also should be postponed. In sum, the workshop sequence should progress from calling for exposure of socially acceptable aspects of self to dealing with more risky, challenging material in which exposure of one's less polished aspects are likely.

Correlation of Performance Scores

A final criterion for sequencing the workshop agenda is the degree to which the parts are interrelated, that is, skills learned in one area often are very similar or closely related to those needed for performance in another. Hinrichs (1976, p. 845) suggests that when subcomponent performance scores are available, correlation coefficients should be determined between them. (He offers the example of aviator training. Correlations were determined between scores on various key subcomponents of training, such as instruments, gunnery, and navigation.) A grid is then developed like the one below for a skill made up of five component tasks:

	a	b	c	d	e
Task a	—	.35	.32	.40	.43
Task b		—	.70	.17	.52
Task c			—	.10	.45
Task d				—	.38
Task e					—

These correlations suggest that some tasks are more highly interrelated than others (for example, b and c). We might expect that skills learned in doing b would transfer readily to performance of c. Therefore, these two tasks should be placed close together in the training sequence.

By rearranging task order in the matrix (the magnitude of the coefficients should increase as one goes down the columns and decrease when one goes across the rows), a sequence can be created in which each task is maximally related to those that precede and follow it. In this case, transfer of learning is most likely when training is sequenced in the following order:

	c	b	e	a	d
Task c	—	.70	.45	.32	.10
Task b		—	.52	.35	.17
Task e			—	.43	.38
Task a				—	.40
Task d					—

Whenever quantitative pretest data are available, it can be placed on a grid in this way to help determine the optimal training progression.

HOW ARE TRAINING ACTIVITIES SELECTED?

The foremost criterion for deciding which activities to include in a training program is how suitable they are for achieving the program's learning objectives (which are based on trainees' needs). When a choice must be made among several *equally* appropriate activities, several other factors might be considered. These are (1) specificity of objectives, (2) trainer experience, (3) trainee experience, (4) trainees' prior contacts, (5) trainee similarity, (6) budget, and (7) time. We will discuss each in turn.

Specificity of Objectives

For some programs, desired learner outcomes can be stated precisely; for others, the trainer's mission is less clear. For example, a trainer briefing judges on recent U.S. Supreme Court decisions would have a more precise aim right from the start than would the trainer dealing with stress management. The latter is a general topic area, subsuming several subtopics from which one or more can be selected for special emphasis. When objectives are inherently precise, instruction is more straightforward and the activities primarily are in the "choosing and applying a solution" category. When objectives are set at the discretion of the trainer and trainees, it is advisable to include activities that allow for diagnosis of trainee needs, exploration of alternatives available within the topic area, opportunities for subgroups to branch off and pursue areas of particular interest, and large-group discussion periods in which questions can be raised on topics related to the central theme of the training. These experiences allow for an appropriate match between the group's needs and the points within the parameters of the general topic area most relevant to them.

Trainer Experience

Activities chosen must fit within the repertoire or expertise of the trainer. Trainers will be most effective in implementing an activity if three preparatory steps have been completed:

1. They have *participated* in that activity themselves as trainees. One needs to know what it *feels* like to engage in a case study, a role playing, a simulation, a team-building group, and so on, in order to sense how much instruction, support, and coaching trainees need to carry out these activities effectively. Only through prior personal involvement can one intuit just when to offer input and how detailed it should be either at the start, during the process, or when forming conclusions at the end. Furthermore, trainers' experience should take place in a variety of contexts and in sessions that are more intense than the one they are to lead. The greater the breadth and depth of trainers' experiential background, the better prepared they are to anticipate, be unruffled by, and deal appropriately with whatever ways the trainees react as they enter into what for them are new, sometimes confusing, experiences. (It would be expeditious and helpful to our royalties if trainers could feel fully prepared immediately after reading a book like this. However, training is a complex, multidimensional art form which requires deep, tacit knowledge that cannot be gleaned solely from this kind of linear verbal material. Experience is essential.)

2. They must be well informed about the *theoretical base* for the activity, that is, the principles of learning that underlie its design and implementation. After people first engage in, enjoy, and learn from an activity, they often leap to the conclusion that henceforth it should be incorporated in every workshop, for every group. They can become advocates for that procedure, imposing the same instructional solution on whatever training problem they encounter. Instead, trainers need to be informed about all that is reported in the theoretical and the research literature regarding *when* each method is appropriate, *how* it is implemented, and *what effect* it is likely to have on participants. This background includes differentiating training methods from superficially similar practices that actually have a different focus (for example, distinguishing T-groups from psychotherapy and distinguishing communication misunderstandings from actual instances of deception or mistreatment). In each case, the former is appropriate for training and the latter is not.

3. They should have *co-led* the activity with an experienced trainer. What a participant sees in the workshop often is only the result, not the process or underlying structure, of the trainer's thinking. Trainers usually do not reveal what actions have been considered and rejected. Nor are all the actions deliberately taken always observable. For example, how trainers form groups, give instructions, respond to questions, time activities, or position themselves in the room are often consciously thought out, but may be taken for granted or seem spontaneous to trainees. The novice who is a coleader can learn during planning or postmortem conferences what the trainer was thinking at these points. Coleaders also can get feedback from their more experienced partner about their own initial attempts to use particular methods

and their probable effect on the group they are leading. Collaboration and dialogue with other trainers throughout one's career expands awareness of the dynamics and options available in using various training methods.

A trainer's repertoire of methods is limited, therefore, to those for which he or she has been a participant, studied the theoretical and research literature, and coled with a more experienced trainer.

Trainee Experience

Whether or not trainees have engaged in activities before also affects which are chosen. Generally, the more familiar the activity, the more effective it will be. Trainees unused to role playing, for example, can be so self-conscious about doing it right and not looking foolish that they do not really benefit from the experience of trying out a new behavior.

When a new activity is being introduced, it should be structured simply and instructions as to its use must be made clear and precise. For example, when launching a small group discussion period on the qualities of a supervisor with an *experienced* group, they can be asked to "Take 15 minutes to come up with a list of what you believe are characteristics of competent supervisors." A group that *has not* participated in such discussions before might be asked: "Each of you should write out what you think are five characteristics of a competent supervisor. Then convene your group. Select a leader and a recorder. The leader should ask each person to read his/her list aloud. The recorder should jot down the characteristics which are on everyone's list. Then discuss those that appear on several person's lists, one at a time, and see if you can all agree on their appropriateness. Discuss and decide upon as many as you can in a 15-minute period." Such a step-by-step plan would be reassuring to a novice group and stultifying to veterans.

For some activities, prior experience can be a handicap. There are a number of activities that should be one-time-only events. Most structured simulations and problem-solving activities are intended to exaggerate a process for those who were unaware of its impact (for example, the effect of a competitive versus cooperative approach to problem solving, the demoralizing effect of bias based on social status or race, the distortion of information as it is passed from person to person). Once someone has participated in such an activity, they know what is to come and either tip-off their fellow group members, act artificially, or just feel bored. Similarly, veteran trainees sometimes pick up and use training jargon, adopt a jaded "I've been through it all" manner, and compare your training program to their past glories, all of which can be alienating to others in the groups. For this type of participant, new approaches are better than repeating what is familiar.

Should repetition of an activity for some participants be unavoidable, that can be turned into an asset by altering those experienced participants' role a bit. They can be asked to compare the upcoming activity with their previous experience to see if the process and outcome do indeed turn out to be the same. (This "legitimizes" the inevitable comparisons that will be made.) Or those persons can serve as "expert" observers or commentators for the activity. Thus, their familiarity with it is viewed as beneficial and made useful to the group.

Trainees' Prior Contact

In some training groups, trainees are meeting for the first time. In others, they have already worked together or have had prior contact in professional circles. Their degree of pre-or posttraining contacts should affect what activities are chosen and how they are run.

Usually, when trainees are strangers to each others, the activities can call for more disclosure of problems they themselves have on the job. When acquainted, case studies of people similar to them are better. The reason for this distinction is obvious: people can be reluctant to reveal fully their own short-comings (or their real feelings about others with whom they work) in front of people whose impressions of them, whose gossip, whose actions are likely to affect them and their livelihood in the future—at least until an unusual level of trust has developed in the group. An exception, of course, is the team-building group wherein relations at work are so bad already that they must be brought out into the open to be dealt with.

A special concern in regard to open discussions is the training group in which some people are present who supervise others in the group. The subordinates' behavior is bound to be influenced by the presence of those who have power over them. They are likely to defer to the higher status people and remain quiet if the supervisors are vocal and opinionated. Or they can be more active to show off to the boss what they can do. To allow for authentic talk to occur, small groups that are homogenous in regard to status can be formed. Keep in mind, however, that the division along lines of rank is thereby emphasized. Asking the supervisors to grant their employees "immunity from prosecution" can help, at times. But generally, a status mixture within workshop groups is best avoided by careful preplanning—unless the workshop's specific intent is to deal with communication across status lines.

Among trainee groups in which some people have had prior contact, another danger is their remaining stuck in old ruts. For example, people very familiar with each other often will sit together in class and during discussions reinforce points of view each has long held. To move dialogue beyond these old routines, seats for small-group work might be switched so that people who are least familiar with each other get to work and talk together. This shift allows everyone the opportunity to obtain fresh perspectives and feedback, to act somewhat differently than they usually do (if they choose to), and to speak more frankly than they might with someone in their intimate social world.

The more similar and in close contact trainees are, the more relevant content must be to their particular local needs and the more specific examples are needed from their own context. Vague across-the-board generalizations are less likely to be seen as relevant. The trainer also is likely to be confronted with the perennially insoluble problems of their situation (which they may *not* really want him to solve). They will know why every new idea would not work and are likely to support each other in a resistant collusion, blaming problems on everyone but themselves. See Chapter 13 for ways to handle this kind of situation.

Variety of Background

When all trainees are relatively homogenous and have a common set of needs (for example, entering a job that is new to them all), their program can be more structured and content centered than it would be if they were a heterogenous group with varied backgrounds. With a mixed group, more time must be given to discussion sessions in which variations are considered that allow application of the material to each person's home/work situation. Mixed groups also provide an opportunity for participants to talk with people who do similar work in other settings and with people who work in roles that are complementary to their own (for example, production and marketing people, civilian and military people, etc.). Since it is impossible to please all trainees all the time, when working with a heterogenous group, the theme of the session needs to be one they can all relate to, that theme must be adhered to, and activities must be incorporated that give trainees a chance to bring up their local issues and to explore them in small groups with each other.

Budget

Training must be cost-efficient, and selection of activities is likely to be affected by the training budget. Warren (1979) states that cost of activities can be computed by summing three factors:

1. *Preparation.* How much will it cost to develop the program using this method, and how long will it take? The decision to create an activity oneself or to buy an off-the-shelf item from a training source hinges on this factor. The actual cost is affected, too, by the degree to which the activity can be used in the future with different groups and instructors.
2. *Aids and materials.* What will be the cost of buying or renting equipment for audiovisual aids, case materials, workbooks, machines, simulators, and so on? Fees for consultants, guest speakers, and co-trainers would be included here.
3. *Presentation.* What will be the cost of the training facilities, instructor fees, and trainee salaries (or tuition, if outside sources are used)? When computing personnel costs, the number of training hours must be multiplied by the number of trainees, and then this number must be multiplied by the trainees' hourly wage or salary. Included, too, should be wages for the time required to get the trainee to the place of training and then back to the job again (for a training session lasting one hour, this could mean doubling the expense: a half hour to get there and a half hour to return). Instructor time costs also should include the time required to set up at the start and to wind up at the end of each individual training session.

When the cost for an activity has been arrived at, a well-informed decision can be made regarding whether or not to include it in a training program. Its benefits must warrant the expense. Too often, the cost and the value of training programs have been viewed as directly related. This formula may apply to machinery, but it does not fit human functioning. Many expensive fads touted in the training literature have proved to be of limited value. A company's wisest investment for improving the cost efficiency of training is hiring a knowledgeable trainer who is skilled in matching worker needs and training methodologies, rather than buying fancy equipment and having it inappropriately used.

Time

Finally, the time available for a training program affects the selection of activities. The learning objectives should determine how *much* time is allocated. Time needs go up if behavioral and attitudinal goals are set. To simply provide trainees with information requires the least time; to teach new behaviors requires more time; to change their attitude or belief systems requires the most time. For example, to inform the group of judges about recent research on stress (a cognitive goal) might take a couple of hours; to teach them several useful methods of stress management (a behavioral goal) might take an additional four hours; to allow them to raise concerns and discuss specific situations, as well as to provide practice experiences through which they gain the confidence and the timing to use the methods well (affective goals), might take an additional eight hours.

Each learning goal implies particular activities, each of which have time implications. Content or cognitive goals suggest using informative lectures, for which people have short attention spans. Behavioral goals imply coaching through performance of new procedures, for which longer sessions are palatable. Attitudinal goals imply discussions and practice sessions, which hold people's interest the longest.

The spacing of sessions affects activity choice, for example, whether the training program will run all day or for a series of shorter sessions scheduled weekly. To maintain interest, longer sessions allow, even require, an emphasis on experiential, hands-on activities; in shorter sessions didactic presentations can predominate. When widely spaced sessions are scheduled (for example, weekly or monthly), it is wise to suggest "homework" assignments. These can involve reading, on-the-job observations, trying out newly-learned procedures, and so on. These are difficult to incorporate into an intense retreat program where sessions are separated only by coffee or lunch breaks. This difference suggests that when more new material must be learned, more widely spaced sessions are advisable; when a more fundamental attitude change is sought, more compact sessions are recommended. For example, sensitivity training—which is intended to alter the basic approaches trainees traditionally have applied to dealing with others—is low on content complexity and high on attitude change; hence, it usually is done on one-day to two-week retreats. Computer programming workshops—which require much information to be transmitted, but about which personal beliefs are virtually irrelevant—usually are taught in weekly seminars. Time clearly is related to the purposes and modalities of training.

HOW ARE TRANSITIONS MADE?

Training proceeds in stages, and the trainer is responsible for handling the transitions from one stage to another. Several guidelines can be applied at these junctures.

The major issue is timing: Sessions should be experienced as neither too long nor too short. A training episode generally has a beginning, middle, and end. Most often, a task or topic is introduced; it is explored in a learning activity; and the essence of the lesson is summarized. A session that is too abrupt is one cut off during the period of exploration; a session that is too lengthy continues after the essential point has been made and accepted. There are several ways to avoid these two extremes.

The first is to articulate in the instructional plan (see Form 11–1) what the basic goal of each training episode is. That helps guide knowing when it has been reached. The second is to be as sensitive as possible to the participants' "energy" level. It can be heard in the hum of their voices as they meet in a group and in their postures, facial expressions, and hand and foot movements when they are facing front. Signs that energy is dissipating should be cues that a shift or a break is needed. It is better to err in the direction of cutting things off too soon and providing a brief break (rather than extending the session for too long). The people still actively exploring the topic can continue on their own; the others are content. Overly lengthy sessions please some but frustrate the quick learners and those with short attention spans.

As a safeguard against overlooking signs of weariness or completion, invite members of the group to signal to you when they complete a task or feel a need for a break. Such a request need not be honored immediately when one person makes it. At that point, ask others if they have heard or done as much as is useful. If most agree, a respite is warranted.

Intermissions can be structured in several ways:

1. The group can be released to do whatever it wants.
2. They can be asked to think about the topic to be considered at the upcoming session—perhaps even be given a flexible assignment regarding it, such as coming up with a response to a controversial question in that area.
3. A few moments can be taken for some stretching, enlivening exercises; for example, touching one's toes and then slowly straightening up and arching backward a few times loosens up the spine. Giving brief head, neck, and upper back massages in pairs can renew a lethargic group.
4. Another approach is suggesting a way that people with similar interests branching

off the main topic can get together in corners of the room to discuss at leisure their mutual concerns.

5.   During the break participants can be invited to meet individually with the trainer to discuss matters of personal concern that they would prefer to keep private.

HOW IS TRAINING CONCLUDED?

The final moments of a training program can linger long in participants' minds, so it is wise to plan that period in advance. The most obvious function for the close is summarizing what the trainees are to take away with them. These basic ideas are best elicited from them and any omitted can be filled in by the trainer. They can be reinforced by being put into writing and displayed prominently. Occasionally, even a summary of the content can be condensed still further into a phrase or a statement that epitomizes the very essence of the learning experience. For example, the workshop on stress management can be concluded with a summary of causes, symptoms, and treatments for stress. Then that summary can be further encapsulated in a phrase, such as "When the laws of the body are honored, society's legal system works better, as well."

The process of interaction within the training group also can be summarized at the end. Trainers can share how their observations of the group or feelings about being with them changed as the workshop progressed. Sometimes the training theme can itself be illustrated through the group's process; for example, "We could see how we became more human, more relaxed and receptive as the stress among us was reduced. This can happen in every facet of your work setting."

The participants should be given an opportunity to structure the conclusion or get in their own last words before the end of the session. At the start of the last segment of the workshop, the trainer might say: "We are entering the home stretch. At this point think again about what you hoped to learn at this workshop and about the situations in the future in which you might be using what we have been discussing. Notice if anything seems to be missing, or remains unsettled in your mind and take this opportunity to ask for it to be covered or cleared up." This gives each of them some responsibility for making the experience a fully worthwhile one. A short period also can be provided for this at the very end by saying: "We are nearing the close—there are only 10 minutes left. Is there anything you would like to ask or say to the group before we separate?" Sometimes someone will offer a reaction that expresses the quality or meaning of what has occurred better than any preplanned summary can do.

It is important that closing clerical tasks not dissipate the impact of the workshop's termination. Feedback sheets, final exams, and recording of attendance or academic credit data should be done just before or clearly after the sign-off between the trainer and the group.

It is a helpful practice to shake hands or otherwise incorporate an individual leave-taking ritual with each participant. The memorability of the training session is enhanced by the warmth and intimacy of the participants' interaction with the trainer.

HOW IS THE INSTRUCTIONAL PLAN ORGANIZED?

A training session is a step-by-step sequence of events designed to lead participants from their entry point to achievement of the intended objectives of training. Everyone involved—the trainer, trainees, and the program's sponsor, as well as someone who in the future will want to know what was done—will need some map or guide to the steps along that path. The most appropriate guide will provide all the information needed in a parsimonious, useful way (see Form 11–1).

The key pieces of information are the why, the what, the how, and the how long of each step. People's efforts are best focused when they know the "why" or the purpose of what they are doing. Hence, the instructional plan specifies overall goals for the entire experience and particular goals for each distinct activity within it. The "what" is the content. Procedures for outlining didactic material were provided in Chapter 7. The "how" is the instructional method used, and "how long" is the time allotted for each episode.

By detailing all this information, sponsors and participants know what they are getting into, and trainers have a clear reminder of the sequence they are to follow throughout the session. A useful guide for determining how specific to make the instructional plan is imagining another instructor trying to reproduce an essentially identical workshop using only this plan as a guide, or imagine a trainer offering a related workshop looking at your plan to assure that connections are made but overlap is minimized. If you have provided adequate information for these purposes, the plan is complete.

FORM 11–1   *THE INSTRUCTIONAL PLAN*

Purpose: This form suggests a format for laying out in terse form the essential ingredients in a training program.

   I. Title:

  II. Trainer(s):

 III. Sponsoring organization:

 IV. Description of participant group:

  V. Date and times:

 VI. Place:

VII. Overall training objectives:

VIII. Training plan

Time Period	Goal	Method	Materials Needed
1.			
2.			
3.			
4.			
5.			

 IX. Evaluation procedure

CHAPTER TWELVE
FACILITATION SKILLS

Although some instructional methods fit best within particular phases of training, one set of skills cuts across the use of all methods and phases of training. That is "facilitation skills." These involve *gathering accurate information* about how people in training are relating to each other, to the trainers, and to the materials being presented and *intervening to clarify* the interpersonal dynamics of the training sessions. Facilitation skills tell us how the content and methods are working and how to improve the training session as it goes along.

Facilitation skills are needed whether the training is primarily technically or process oriented. For example, a trainer may be conducting a technical skills program on budget planning. Facilitation skills guide the trainer in assessing how the participants are learning and how they feel about the program. From that assessment, alterations can be made in the content, the speed of the presentation, or the method of training. If the focus of the training is process oriented, to develop communication skills, the trainer will be able to use the information gathered for directive interventions, such as giving participants feedback on how well they are using the communication skills being taught within the training session itself.

Effective facilitation involves several elements:

1. A comprehensive orientation to self and others
2. Observation skills for gathering information

3.   Intervention skills for clarifying interaction
4.   Self-development of the trainer

Figure 12–1 provides an overview of key elements in the facilitation process and furnishes examples of the kinds of skills and orientations possible.

WHAT IS A COMPREHENSIVE ORIENTATION TO FACILITATION SKILLS?

To describe a comprehensive orientation to training (Chapter 1) we used the terms "soft" and "hard." Those terms also can be applied to facilitation skills. A soft orientation is most effective for gaining perspective and information about (for *diagnosing*) the interpersonal dynamics of training sessions. Trainers, therefore, should employ that orientation first, followed by a hard orientation for narrowing the meanings of the interaction and intervening for clarification (for *changing* those dynamics).

For example, a trainer may be observing (in a "soft" mode) how a work group completes a task during a team-building exercise. The trainer notices initially that people joke a lot and compliment each other. By remaining "soft," by waiting and watching the entire group over a longer period of time, the trainer may also notice that each "round" of jovialness is preceded by strong criticisms. Waiting for patterns to emerge and being open to a wide range of information (nonverbal as well as verbal cues) is the value of the soft mode of facilitation. It enlarges attention span and the amount of interaction perceived. The trainer hypothesized (accurately) that the group interaction had more to do with relieving the stress of struggles for control and influence than with affection, as the initial interaction might have suggested.

FIGURE 12–1   Model of Facilitation.

Skills

		Observation	Intervention
Orientation	Soft	Noticing a range of verbal and nonverbal cues of self and other; noticing group themes, patterns, images; noticing incongruencies in communication	Formulating tentative guesses about meaning of behavior; reflecting behaviors that are observed without interpretation; simply changing a response to a person or group without giving direct feedback
	Hard	Pinpointing specific behaviors; interpreting meaning and consequences of behavior; judging likely outcomes of repeated patterns	Confrontation of specific behavior; suggestions or advocacy for change; teaching a specific skill; stopping self from a biased intervention

It may be helpful to review the characteristics of soft and hard orientations so that trainers will understand how to use them for facilitating training programs. In Chapter 1 a soft orientation was described as an open, aware, receptive stance, increasing open-mindedness and flexibility. A soft orientation enhances trainers' ability to perceive people and events in a systemic way (as described in Chapter 2). A hard orientation is important for sorting out, categorizing, and judging information—narrowing and defining the meanings of behavior. Both orientations can be recognized by physiological, perceptual, and psychological indicators (Friedman, 1978). We find these indicators helpful in two ways: (1) by noticing their own mind/body state, trainers can know which orientation they are in, and (2) they can alter their orientation when the need arises. For example, a trainer may be making a number of interventions which seem to bounce off the group, or which even seem to irritate them. Most likely the trainer is in a hard orientation inappropriately. Instead, he/she should shift into a soft orientation and wait for a fuller, more accurate sense of what is happening in the interaction. Then his/her interventions will be more to the point.

The *physiological* characteristics of a soft state include a relaxed, centered body, indicated by low blood pressure, heart rate, and blood flow to the muscles. Breathing is slow, even, and deep. Eyes have a quality of softness rather than a quailty of tenseness and staring. In contrast, hard listening is characterized by higher blood pressure, increased heart rate, shallow breathing, and contracted muscles. The body is ready for action and there is a quickness of response.

Perceptually, soft listening is nonjudgmental and nonfocused. It includes a heightened sensitivity to a diverse set of stimuli, such as voice tones, gestures, facial expressions, postures, group spatial arrangements; and involves hearing another's entire message, rather than quickly jumping to conclusions about its meaning. On the other hand, hard listening is focused. There is selectivity in perceiving communication messages and a quickness to respond and to offer solutions.

Psychologically, when trainers are listening softly, they are interested in interpersonal needs of safety, security, and closeness. In order to listen and perceive others' needs accurately, trainers must be in a low need state themselves, making few demands on the one to whom they are listening. In other words, soft listening is accepting and tolerant of where trainees *are*, rather than pushing them to be or do something else. As such, a soft orientation is important for using the paradoxical theory of change (proposed in Chapter 4). In contrast, hard listening is related to interpersonal needs of power and control. That is, when trainers are coming from a hard orientation they are directing participants to move in a certain way and are interested in efficiency, structure, and precision. Responses that emerge from hard listening are often prescriptive and sometimes judgmental.

As described, soft and hard orientations influence trainers' awareness, which, in turn, direct kinds of interventions they make. Comprehensive facilitation includes an ability to use and sequence soft and hard orientations appropriately.

WHAT ARE ESSENTIAL
OBSERVATION SKILLS?

Observation skills involve the ability to recognize specific *behaviors* from which learners' states of mind and modes of interaction can be inferred. This recognition requires a soft orientation. There is human tendency to jump to conclusions about others, often from a single external cue, and then assume that one's interpretation of that behavior is reality. People then act upon their hunches about the meaning of observed behavior, often without even knowing what the behavior is on which they are basing their conclusions. Skilled trainers should be fully aware of what observations led to their interpretations, be prepared to describe them, and then remain tentative about their conclusions. For example, a participant may use a loud, aggressive voice each time he/she speaks. If that tone is interpreted as hostile, the trainer may respond with aggression, which may, in turn, create or increase the aggression of the participant. The participant's voice tone could as likely mean that the person is scared or that he/she simply has learned this particular style of communicating and is unaware of its impact on people. If trainers assume that they "know" what behavior means, or are unable to identify the behavior to which they are responding, they may create or accentuate a problem they are trying to solve.

A major advantage to observing behavior in a soft way is that trainers will have more data about interpersonal interactions. They will take in more aspects of trainees' behavior and withhold judgment about them. Soft listening is especially needed when first meeting a new group of trainees. Jumping to conclusions from past experiences (a hard approach) *sometimes* is appropriate for a familiar type of group. The trainer's accuracy, however, is limited to those particular audiences.

Focusing on observable behavior also provides trainers with the information they need to give useful feedback to participants. Several characteristics of effective feedback are (1) describing rather than evaluating behavior, (2) separating inferences about others' motivation from their observable behavior, and (3) owning feelings and perceptions about others. To meet those criteria, trainers must be able to focus on a wide range of behaviors, distinguish what they observe from the interpretations they make, and state their tentative hypotheses to the participants. This approach is more open and riskier than convincing participants the trainer's interpretation of their behavior is accurate. It is also more helpful in enhancing productive change.

Finally, focusing on behaviors and giving specific behavioral feedback to participants provides them with a "mirror," a reflection to them of how they appear. Thus participants are free to use the trainer's feedback to "observe" and assess their own behavior. They can discuss with the trainer what that behavior *means* to them. From a full discussion of their behavior and its impact on others, trainees are practicing "learning how to learn," that is, how they can continue to assess the impact of their behavior on people in their everyday lives after the training program is over.

An example may clarify the point. Some simulations that evoke competitive interaction (Win As Much As You Can and Starpower are examples) can give rise to resentment among participants, even in those who typically do not express or accept angry feelings. When discussing this type of game participants often say, in very loud voices, that they had no strong responses to the experience. A typical mistake is for the trainer to argue with them (however subtly) about whether or not they were angry. On the other hand, skilled trainers report what they observe (the loud voice, for example) that suggests a strong emotional reaction. Participants who hear how the trainer arrived at that conclusion can understand better how others might interpret and respond to their behavior. Again, by simply reporting specific observations the trainer facilitates awareness and acceptance of self, rather than trying to win arguments about the meaning of a particular behavior.

One common malady of the training profession, which blocks developing finely tuned observation skills, is the tendency of some trainers to go beyond what can be commonly observed, to seek being seen as "gurus," and to impose insights about trainees' behavior on them. Bach and Goldberg (1974) call this malady "mind raping," or controlling another's behavior by defining what it means. By acting "as if" they know more about participants' behavior than the participants, trainers may decrease participants' sense of choice, confidence and control. Trainers also create dependency, which obstructs the basic goal of teaching people to learn how to learn.

What, then, are skills that can be used when observing people in the training program? Neuro-Linguistic Programming (NLP) specifies in detail the ways in which trainers can make better use of their senses to perceive clues to how people think or make sense of their world (see Bandler and Grinder, 1979). For training purposes, the senses of hearing, seeing, and feeling/touching are most important.

The trainer should have a finely tuned *ear* for listening on several levels. The most obvious is listening to the content or meaning of what participants are saying through their words. A great many people stop at that level. However, it contains only part of the available information about how people are thinking and feeling. More subtle information is conveyed through the *voice tones* and the *kinds* of words used by participants.

Voice tones can be congruent with or *contradictory* to the verbal message. The latter suggests that the participant is attempting to disguise his/her state of mind. The participant may say, with a low, hesitating voice, that he/she understands a point being made. If the trainer ignores the tentative tone and proceeds with the rest of the material, the participant might well be lost for the rest of the session. Trainees' voices may indicate any number of feelings—being nervous and scared about speaking up, feeling resistant to believing the material, and so on—and those cues can be responded to in a number of ways. The point here is that vocal tone carries information and should be attended to for purposes of reading participants' affective states in the training session.

The kinds of words participants use also can provide important information.

For example, in a workshop on conflict management, one person said he did not understand why he was involved in constant, competitive conflicts at work. The trainer noticed that as he talked, his language was filled with words like "the *targets* for my next management strategy," "*nailing* people on certain points during staff meetings," "the necessary *battles* in the organization." The kinds of words suggested a competitive, aggressive orientation to others. The trainer's feedback to the person centered around having him listen to his words. He needed to examine the framework within which he perceived the others with whom he worked and notice how he helped perpetuate the competitive conflicts. Heretofore, he had thought it was only others who were "starting" or "causing" the destructive conflicts in which he was engaged.

The visual sense—seeing—provides exceptionally useful data for perceptive trainers. Soft seeing involves attending to the whole person—the myriad of nonverbal cues the person is sending out and whether they are congruent or incongruent with what is being said. Soft seeing involves a quality of *noticing* others' behavior, rather than *catching* them in incongruities. Noticing is a gentle way of being with people and enhances awareness and acceptance. Catching others in incongruities often produces defensiveness or guilt that undermines the goals of training. Eric Berne calls this playing the game of NIGYSOB (Now I've Got You, You S.O.B.), in which one person catches another making mistakes. The payoff for trainers is that they gain a superior position, but they may lose growth in rapport or insight.

Seeing not only means attending to the trainees' body language, but also involves tuning into what participants themselves see in their own minds' eye, what images come up in their streams of consciousness. Attending to participants' impressions and images can be helpful for assessing the atmosphere of the training session and for giving feedback about risky topics. In the example given above, about the trainee's description of conflict, the trainer could explore with the participant how he envisions conflict—as a war between people. As the trainer reflects the images implied in the participant's descriptions, he is asked to join in noticing this "painting" emerge. In this way, the trainer seems to be talking about something external to the participant (what the trainer sees while listening to him). Feedback often is perceived as less risky in this form than when given directly to people about their behavior.

A similar technique also can be included deliberately in training sessions by asking participants to draw pictures of concepts. For example, we have asked people in workshops to draw pictures of "conflict." The discussion then centers around attitudes toward conflict that are reflected in the drawings (for example, a fiery, unstructured drawing may mean the trainee conceives of conflict as destructive and chaotic) and the consequences of those attitudes on how conflict is handled in everyday situations.

The third channel for gleaning information about the dynamics of training is kinesthetic sensations or the physical feelings within the trainer or between the trainer and participants. Physical feelings can be interpreted as messages from one's own "intuitive center" that there are covert, usually riskier, responses within participants that are being ignored. To use feelings as indicators of interpersonal dynamics, trainers must clearly distinguish their own subjective reactions from the reactions of others. (The consequences of a lack of clarity about feelings are discussed later in this chapter.)

Sensing feelings also means exchanging messages with participants through touch. In personal growth workshops, touching exercises often are built into the training program, on the assumption that touch can minimize the feelings of depersonalization and alienation between people. In other kinds of training, touching may be done more subtly. For example, simulations can be planned that involve nonrisky touching. In one community development training program, there were people from diverse backgrounds who previously had perceived each other as enemies. One of the first simulations planned was Starpower, in which participants were required to shake hands while bargaining. We have found that it is difficult for people to continue objectifying others and engaging in destructive conflict when they are touching them and feeling their humanity. We have noticed also that when an exercise involving some form of touch between participants is used at the beginning of a potentially volatile program, participants much more quickly reach the point where they can interact directly in a nondefensive way.

It is important to note that most people need to be given permission to touch (or not to, as they choose) since it is a risky form of interaction, open to many cynical interpretations. Including touch in the "rules" of an exercise lowers people's risk since they do not have to take responsibility for their decisions to touch.

Trainers also can subtly touch participants to offer assurance. When someone has volunteered for role playing, for example, trainers may lightly touch the person's arm or back as they give instructions. If trainees are resistant or hostile, we also have used touch to make nonaggressive contact with these the persons are participating. The main criteria that should guide the use of touch are the trainers' comfort with touching and their ability to perceive the other's comfort.

WHAT ARE EFFECTIVE INTERVENTION STRATEGIES?

Interventions are based on observable information gathered about trainees' interaction and the meanings attributed to those interactions. When attributing meaning and explaining behavior, trainers and participants move into a hard orientation: they are taking a more focused, directive approach.

Meanings are guided by the kinds of theoretical systems trainers use. From a systems view, one of the ways trainers make sense out of behavior is to notice patterns in the interaction among participants and between themselves and participants. For example, the trainer may notice that certain men in a training program interrupt the women frequently, but seldom interrupt the male participants. Similarly, if there is a male and a female training team, those same men may interrupt the female trainer but not the male. The pattern can be pointed out, and the meaning of the behavior can be discussed. The trainer may indicate that interruption patterns often define power relationships between people and that they are particularly frequent between men and women. Men, culturally, are considered more powerful and dominant and, therefore, interrupt; women are considered submissive and therefore let themselves be interrupted. Discussion may center around the behaviors; the impact they have on people, groups, and productivity; the ability of either men or women to change the pattern, if desired; and *not* on whether the behavior is good or bad.

Providing a theoretical perspective and relevant research can be a useful form of intervention when the trainer is encouraging exploration of observed behavior patterns. The theory and research provide the group with explanations of behavior observed in the training sessions. As Abraham Maslow has said:

> To the seeker of knowledge about persons, abstract knowledge, scientific laws and generalizations, statistical tables and expectations are all useful if they can be humanized, personalized, individualized, focused into this particular interpersonal relationship. The good knower of people can be helped by classical "scientific" knowledge; the poor knower of people cannot be helped by all the abstract knowledge in the world. [Maslow, 1966, p. 11]

WHAT DOES SELF-DEVELOPMENT HAVE TO DO WITH EFFECTIVE FACILITATION?

The observation and intervention tools discussed in this chapter require sensitivity to phenomena and people by the trainers doing the perceiving and intervening. In other words, trainers themselves, in the final analysis, are the best (or worst) tools they have. With greater self-development, therefore, the trainer can choose and implement more styles of training (structured, unstructured, hard, soft), interact effectively with more kinds of people, and be more adaptable to change when the training program needs it.

What, then, is the self-developed trainer? Fundamentally, that person is aware and accepting of a wide range of feelings, thoughts, and behaviors. The parts of self trainers accept in themselves are the parts they can deal with openly and nonjudgmentally in others. Similarly, the parts of themselves trainers deny or condemn are the ones that will be ignored, judged, or otherwise turned away in others. For example, if trainers are uncomfortable with anger, they cannot remain centered and aware when that feeling arises in others. If trainers have not learned to deal with conflict, when conflict arises between participants or between a participant and the trainer, they are likely to avoid it by talking people out of their feelings, refusing to recognize that conflict exists, or by suppressing it, intimating that conflict is negative and unproductive.

Good preparation for trainers is noticing what emotions are not typically part of their everyday lives and working on developing recognition and acceptance of those feelings. A specific exercise is for trainers to ask themselves, "Who am I not?" and to generate a list of characteristics that usually are not applicable to them. Characteristics typically disowned by people learning how to be trainers include deviousness, authoritarianism, and dishonesty. By not acknowledging the existence of these traits, they make it harder for themselves to contact the positive dimensions of each. For example, deviousness is closely allied to expressing creativity or getting what you want. When trainers censor any hint of deviousness, they also give away a great deal of potential creativity. In the same vein, authoritarianism is one form of direct, straightforward communication. Being direct (and having nonnegotiable demands at times) is important when negotiating a training contract, adhering to a training schedule, directing participants to do certain tasks, and being unwilling to cater to people in training who are continually disruptive.

The point is that there are positive and negative ways of being creative and direct. Deviousness and authoritarianism involve using these talents inappropriately, overdoing them, being "stuck" in them. However, denying those *manifestations* of creativity and directness can often result in censoring the positive qualities also. Clearly, we assume that embedded within every disowned part of a person is a positive quality that is needed in some circumstances. The goal of integration is to reown as many human qualities as possible. Then we are free to use them when necessary to maintain, rather than deny, our own or others' "rights" to self-determination. We maximize self-development when we can *choose* when to use each part for maximum flexibility in training.

The consequences of self-development or internal integration (and lack of it) are fairly clear. First, it affects the body. More integrated trainers have more energy and are more relaxed than those who are trying to live up to many prescriptions or "shoulds" for behavior. Reich (1949) and Lowen (1976) believe that bodies take on the characteristics of disowned parts of the personality. Reich gave the name of "muscular armor" to those groups of muscles people keep in chronic tension so as not to feel unwanted dimensions of their experience. Tenseness, in turn, lessens the ability to sense feelings and listen openly to others (Friedman, 1978). When one is in a tense state, other people are likely to appear threatening; and that perception diminishes the ability of trainers to practice effective observation and intervention. Conversely, relaxation is important for soft observation and gathering accurate information. Greater integration also encourages congruent communication (consistent verbal and nonverbal messages); increased choices and flexibility of communication styles; and positive regard for others.

For integration, trainers must have an "up to now" perception of self. That perspective means that who they *have* been is not who they *must* be. They believe themselves to be in process, always available to change and growth. Trainers, therefore, are observers of themselves, noticing and watching their internal processes and continually exploring new potentials. This perspective is important since encountering new situations and people in each training venture can evoke new aspects of feeling, thought, and/or behavior; and to interact effectively with many different kinds of people in various professions requires a learning, flexible, multifaceted human being.

We contrast this view with the assumption that actualization is a finite goal that can be reached. Trainers who operate on that assumption must be "on top of" everything that comes up in order to be in control. In turn, to be in control means that *new* thoughts, feelings, and people will be threatening, will tend to throw trainers "off guard," and, therefore, will be suppressed. Thus, the integration cycle is reversed: The body is tightened to suppress responses; perceptions of self and others are rigidified; only safe, familiar feelings and behaviors in self and others are attended to; others are ignored or disdained; communication is increasingly incongruent since the disowned parts "leak" through the nonverbal channels in contradiction to the verbal communication; honest, open communication becomes more difficult since those qualities are based on acceptance of self and others, and on and on.

Self-development, then, is a basis for effective observation and intervention skills. Trainers cannot simply buy these skills like tape recordings to insert in themselves. Instead, they must understand and have developed the consciousness that is congruent with the skills. It is important to note that a multifaceted view of the self does not mean that trainers are chameleons—unrecognizable in each new situation. Rather, self-development means that trainers do not identify themselves with one image, style, or particular attitude. They identify themselves with observing their accepting, ethical "center" and then accumulate an ever-growing repertoire of methods to use depending on the situation they face.

WHAT ARE GUIDELINES FOR INTERVENING IN TRAINEE INTERACTIONS?

Based on our theory of change (Chapter 4), the descriptions of effective observation, intervention, and trainer self-development, we propose the following practical, behavioral guidelines for observation and intervention that are essential to effective facilitation.

FACILITATION GUIDELINES

I.   *Wait*: Learn to recognize your initial responses to others and then wait for more, from yourself and from others.

   A. Wait for people to say all they can say about the issue they are addressing.
   B. Wait until you can feel the "essence" of what they are saying/feeling.
   C. Wait so that participants can feel their response. Often the trainer rushes in to relieve tension or to dissipate anger or boredom. *Let* people experience what they experience; at the same time, notice your response to them.
   D. Remember that you may not have to *do* anything about peoples' responses except understand them.
II. Keep the behavioral and inference levels of observation distinct:
   A. Notice the behavior you can actually observe (see, hear, touch, smell) from self and others in the moment.
   B. Notice the interpretations you are making of those behaviors.
      1. Use phrases like "My observation is . . ." and "My guess is . . . ." to separate what you can observe from what you interpret.
      2. Ask trainees to be specific about what perceptions led them to their feelings and conclusions.
      3. Ask trainees to go ahead and guess aloud what others are thinking and intending. Use these guesses to clarify assumptions and then to check them out.
III. Stay in the present, both observing and processing.
   A. When you begin to think about what you'll say next or worry about a past response, you miss a great deal of information in the moment. You are also more likely to search for interactions you expect rather than processing with observable behaviors.
   B. To stay in the present, ask "what" and "how" instead of "why." "Why" questions necessitate a "because" answer which connotes justifications and responses can be discussed. Trainers can even create "games" by using this additional information. For example, if a participant appears irritated by a training activity, ask *what* is irritating or *how* he/she experiences the irritation, rather than asking why the person is irritated.
IV. Focus on what *is* happening, not on what should be.
      Instead of saying to a person "You shouldn't be feeling threatened," respond by reflecting the feeling you hear and asking the person for more information about the feeling. For example, the trainer may say, "By the sound of your voice and look on your face, it seems you are upset by this exercise. Can you tell me what you are responding to?"
V.   Give self and others permission to feel and think what they are feeling and thinking. Acceptance, paradoxically, allows change.
      For example, participants may indicate disbelief of the applicability of new ideas to their situation. Instead of being defensive about the disbelief, trainers can say: "Sometimes ideas are not applicable to all situations. Can you say how you think they fit and do not fit your particular work setting?" This kind of response puts the responsibility of sorting the new information on the trainee, rather than on the trainer, thereby avoiding unproductive arguments.
      Other possible responses that give permission to trainees include:
   A. If you or others are labeling a person (for example, uptight, aggressive, uncooperative), give permission to label openly so that the trainees' responses can be discussed. Trainers can even create "games" by using this process. They can have participants mill around, greet people, judge other participants the way they would in everyday life. Afterward, discussion can center around how people arrived at the labels they gave others and what impact the label is likely to have on the development of their relationship.
   B. When people express feelings that typically are thought of as negative or

unacceptable (anger, resentment, boredom), ask them to stay with, and even to accentuate, the feeling in order to understand it more fully. For example, participants may say, "I know I should not be angry with others in my group, but . . .." The trainer may ask the participant: "What does the anger feel like? What would happen if you let yourself be openly angry?"

C.   If you suspect that participants are censoring a type of experience, give personal examples of that experience in your own life. Your disclosure will give others implicit permission to accept similar responses in themselves.

VI.   Encourage people to take responsibility for their responses. Self-attribution is a basic requirement for awareness, acceptance, and potential change of responses.

A.   Turn questions into statements. Sometimes questions are requests for information; other times they are perceptions which are not being owned Such questions create defensiveness in others. Example: "Don't you think that . . .?" typically means "I think that . . ." An intervention, after someone has asked a question, may be to reply "That seems to be true from your perspective" or to ask "Is that true for you?"

B.   Use semantic interventions:
Encourage trainees to use "I" rather than "It." For example, "I feel good" rather than "It feels good when you do . . ." "I" indicates the person recognizes that the feeling is a part of self. Change "I can't" to "I won't" or "I have to" to "I choose to" so that the person is conscious of choosing rather than appearing to be forced.

C.   If someone insists that an activity or a person is irritating, you might check with others participating to see if all were as upset by the activity. In so doing, people may understand that irritation is not the *only* response to that situation and that their anger is their own.

D.   Projection exercises can help people to understand the categories they use to judge themselves. For example, trainers may ask participants to describe their favorite and most disliked objects in a specific room in their homes. Afterward, participants are asked which of the positive and negative characteristics also apply to themselves.

VII.   Be willing to be influenced.
The essence of interpersonal collaborative change is *mutual* influence. Being able to affect others, even the trainer, supports participants' sense of personal power. Without power people typically have two responses: apathy/boredom and/or aggression/violence.

VIII.   Follow and use the energy of the group rather than resisting it.

A.   If the group is rowdy and loud, structure a physical activity that addresses issues in the group and uses their energy. For example, if a group is dealing with trust issues, the trainer may suggest a trust walk to utilize the energy of the group.

B.   If the prevalent atmosphere is competitive, you could structure exercises that demonstrate the effects of win/lose approaches to conflict. For example, trainers could suggest that trainees develop a scoring system for the group that reflects its areas of covert competition, for example, trainees then would be directed to score themselves or certain other trainees on factors such as intelligence, beauty, and openness. This could be followed by discussion of the impact of the competition on group cohesion, personal self-esteem, and so on.

IX.   Clarify your own personal feelings and perceptions of the moment so that you do not project them onto others and so you see others' responses more "clearly."

A.   Recognize body tensions that can distort your perceptions. For example, before and during training, focus your awareness on each part of your body, checking out where you are tense. Try tensing and releasing those particular muscles and breathing deeply in order to relax.

B. Recognize the implied demands you make on others: your need to control, to be right, to be liked, to be included. Your needs, particularly if unrecognized, will color your perceptions and interventions. To check out these demands, you can ask yourself before the training what interpersonal needs you have not had satisfied lately and be aware they might arise in training. You can also notice during training what topics you seem to get stuck on or upset about and what kinds of activities are particularly satisfying to you. This does not mean that trainers should not have needs or get them met. It does mean that an *awareness* of them helps trainers decide whether or not getting their needs met during training is appropriate.

C. Too much internal dialogue in an effort to figure out how to intervene may interfere with your ability to observe what *is* going on. If you notice that you are lost in thought about what is happening in an interaction—essentially having a conversation with yourself—breathe deeply and refocus on the actual interaction.

D. Use your body responses as a gauge to the atmosphere in the room. For example, if you are tightening up, check out whether threat exists in the room. If you are reacting to someone vehemently, you are probably trying too hard to convince that person of something. Stop and do not make your comment before paraphrasing the thoughts and feelings of the other, indicating that you value his/her viewpoint, as well as your own.

X. Be aware of your own and others' tendencies to see/feel experiences dualistically. That is, people believe that there can be only one way that they *really* feel, that they are wishy-washy if they have feelings and thoughts that seem contradictory. For example, if a person is feeling sad *and* angry, encourage him/her to attend to both feelings at once, or one and then the other.

A. Relay to the person that it seems that he/she is also experiencing another feeling that you picked up by his/her voice tone or other clue. Indicate that feelings are not mutually exclusive and that more than one can arise in the same situation.

B. Be aware of your own tendency to choose between seemingly contradictory responses in yourself and share both sides of those ambivalent feelings with the group.

C. Reframe issues to enhance acceptance and choice. For example, if you have conducted a structured experience involving competition and cooperation, trainees could be building a case for competition as the *right* response (probably because they behaved competitively). The argument is based on the assumption that people must choose between competition and coopera-tion. A reframing intervention could come in the form of suggesting that right or wrong is not the issue, that both responses are appropriate at certain times. The trainer could then ask the person when he/she would consider each response appropriate, why, and with what consequences. The person then has a way of choosing behavior rather than a rigid role to apply universally.

XI. Do not make learning about self heavy-handed—people have lived a long time before they met you.

        Humor that comes from insight into self and others seems to give people distance from themselves so that they can compassionately examine what they see. Wise humor emanates from *watching* self and other, instead of *catching* self and other. Interventions from watching gives people permission also to watch. Catching creates defensiveness.

XII. Focus on and recognize the positive aspects of trainees' contributions. For acceptance and change, people must know first that they are worthwhile. Then they will be able to risk the exploration of self needed for potential change.

   A. If people are complaining about becoming confused or alienated during a session, you should accept that state, affirm that their perception of it is important, and suggest that it would be helpful to give further observations about how alienation occurred for them. You thus have "framed" the trainee's response as a strength rather than as an attack on you as an instructor. You also have encouraged the person to seek further information about a discomforting situation so that he/she might act on it.

   B. To avoid discounting others' feelings, use "and" more often than "but." For example, trainers may reflect to participants that they seem both excited *and* anxious at the start of a program. Both feelings are possible at the same time and need to be recognized to be dealt with.

XIII. Three typical responses that block good facilitation (increasing awareness) are judging, helping, and explaining.

   Judging: scorn, laughter, jeering, ignoring, moralizing, convincing the other you are right.

   Helping: trying to get rid of "bad" feelings; saying a person "shouldn't feel that way" which talks the person out of his/her feelings; reassurance ("It's not that bad"); comfort when it is not needed, setting up a competitive game or situation and then denying the strength of the trainees' responses.

   Explaining: telling someone what his/her motives are or analyzing why he/she is doing or saying something; communicating that you have the person figured out or diagnosed which typically sets up a win/lose argument or a power struggle over whose interpretation of "me" is right.

Facilitation skills thus encompass a great deal of what we have previously described about the training process. Their effective use is based upon trainers' valuing comprehensive training, a systemic view of people and organizations, a paradoxical theory of change, and matching training methods to their appropriate phase of training. If trainers develop their facilitation skills, they will be able to work through the problems that arise as the training is being conducted and to adapt their work to a great many situations and people.

CHAPTER THIRTEEN
SPECIAL PROBLEMS

Although trainers may have a good theoretical background, know many methods for carrying out training goals and objectives, and even have developed competency with facilitation skills, there are several distinct tasks and problems that may crop up that require additional know-how. We provide here specific suggestions useful in dealing with some problems we have encountered. These involve trainer *credibility,* as it is established before the training, and *conflicts* that arise during the training.

HOW IS TRAINER
CREDIBILITY ENHANCED?

In previous chapters we have discussed trainer credibility in terms of establishing the training contract and doing training. However, there are several activities that need to occur immediately prior to training that if handled well, can maximize the trainers' effectiveness. These activities are the pretraining publicity, introduction of the trainer at the training session, and the trainer's personal presentation of self.

Publicity

Publicity refers to the information participants get about the training and the trainer before the actual event. To set the stage for effective training, the trainer should take into consideration *when, how, by whom,* and *where* the training is advertised and *what* is included in the publicity. In some instances, trainers will be advertising their own programs through brochure mailings. Although it is important to do professional brochures and make clear, legal contracts with agencies handling registration and facilities, it is not our purpose to go into detail about that kind of advertising. We are focusing on the kind of publicity done by the contact person or organization that has hired the trainer.

When Is the Publicity to Be Done?   Training programs should be announced in advance to give participants a chance to think about the upcoming session and get prepared, but not so early that the excitement about training becomes lost.

Advance notice serves several functions. It allows people time to plan and rearrange their work schedules, if needed, for the training. It is difficult during training to overcome the resistance of people who are told that training is important for their professional development *and* are told an hour ahead of time when and where the training will occur. Trainers cannot always control this error, but they would do well to remind the group or organization of the need for advanced planning.

Advance notice also gives people time to ask questions about the trainer, the process, and the goals of the training. New educational experiences often are accompanied by fear—fear of not being competent, of failing, of being put down by those higher in authority. Advance notice provides an opportunity for dealing with these fears. If the training is for a heterogeneous, public group, advance notice and publicity, of course, helps to ensure that the training program will be well attended.

How Is the Advertising to Be Done?   Advertising can be done through person-to-person contacts and in written form. In organizations, personal contacts by people in power positions, or those who are opinion leaders, are the most effective channels of influence. These people may be in formal or informal positions. They may be top-level managers or line workers who have been at a company a number of years and thereby influence many other workers. Information about the training, therefore, also needs to be circulated in both formal and informal communication channels—through the company newsletter and/or through the company grapevine. Several managers have said repeatedly that the most enthusiasm is generated about training when organizational leaders talk about it with excitement in terms of how the training can help with participants' real problems and with increasing their skills. The trainer should, therefore, be aware of and solicit the help of opinion leaders in the training groups.

Publicity about training should also be written, since written communication often carries with it an implicit message of importance. Both oral and written communiqués about the training should emphasize strengths participants bring to the training, as well as the deficiencies that will be addressed. To focus solely on weaknesses that are to be "fixed" by the training can increase participants' fears, which, in turn, can trigger resentment about the training, resistance during the training, and/or apathy—all of which make effective training difficult.

The communiqués, both oral and written, should also include the purposes and, when possible, information about the actual content of the training. For example, when one of our colleagues does communication skills training, he distributes a three-page handout describing the social skills to be learned in the training. With this material in hand, people usually come to the training more confident about their knowledge of the topic and more ready to respond than when they spend the first hour or so of the session being introduced to the topic.

If an extensive handout is not possible—such as for short training programs for heterogeneous groups—we include in the written communiqué at least a paragraph discussing the overall importance and the main goals of the training.

It is especially important to use advance written information to defuse suspicions and uncertainty about threatening topics. For example, the publicity for conflict training focuses on the potentially *productive* means of managing conflict. Similarly, advance information for training in such areas as race relations and male/female communication should be designed to reduce the threat. Publicity can help by emphasizing the value of trainees' previous experiences, the *benefits* as well as the limitations of those experiences, and the possible advantages to trainees of obtaining additional insight and skill for dealing with problems they currently face in the targeted area. If threat is not decreased, nor trust increased before and during such training, participants are usually very cautious to prevent being perceived as racist or sexist. The training, therefore, cannot genuinely consider the attitudes and behaviors it was designed to address.

Both written and oral communication about the training should be done congruently. For example, one of us conducted a communication workshop for a large company. Participants were told orally that the training on participative management was very important for their jobs. The training, however, was planned during the busiest time for the trainees, when they were finishing production and shipping products. In order for them to attend the training on participative management "voluntarily," they had to work until midnight to finish their assigned tasks.

The tension created by the incongruencies of the topic of the workshop (participative management) and the management style with which the training was advertised, and between the importance of the training and its scheduling, were too much to be overcome in the single afternoon training session. After the first half hour, when there was obviously a strong undercurrent in the training, the entire time was spent dealing with the trainees' resentment about the multiple and incongruent messages they had received. At that point, the trainer was in a precarious position—helping the trainees discuss their feelings without derogating management. It is illuminating to transform those circumstances into a learning experience by asking the participants to explore the communication in which they are involved. This approach addresses the underlying issue within the context of the overall training goal. It also illustrates how much appropriate facilitation skills are needed when events occur out of the trainer's control.

By Whom Should the Training Be Publicized?   Someone who is respected and trusted by the potential trainees is the ideal advocate for training. One mistake trainers often make is to have the chief executive office (CEO) of a company, organization, or group be the spokesperson for the training. The CEO must be supportive of the training and be part of the planning, but he/she may not have the skills or the trust of trainees to establish pretraining credibility. People with both position power and the trust of the training group should publicize the training. If that is not possible, it may be advisable for trainees to draft announcements for the CEO. The way training is described often will "set" participants' attitudes toward it. Thus, it is vital that they receive communiqués congruent with the training objectives.

An example will make the point. One of us was conducting a three-day seminar for secretaries in a large company. The primary goal was for secretaries to learn the skills needed to become administrative assistants. While interviewing, the training team formed an impression of the CEO as a fairly sexist person, who wanted the secretaries (all of whom were female) to assume administrative responsibilities but never to question the opinions of their managers (all of whom were men). The double bind they would be in was obvious not only to us but to the secretaries as well. After carefully negotiating the goals of the training, it was important that the CEO *not* be the one describing the pretraining publicity.

Where Should the Publicity Be Done?   Publicity is most effective when it is distributed via the channels of communication accepted by the people who will be the participants. Sometimes those channels include a company or organizational newsletter, bulletin boards, brochures, newspapers, or announcements in business or social meetings. Again, the trainer needs to be aware that the medium can overshadow the message. For example, if a company newsletter is believed to be a tool of top management, training publicized only there probably will be perceived as an instrument of top management; and the trainer may encounter resistance. One form of resistance is to avoid giving the trainers information they need to assess the problems of the organization or group, which in turn decreases the effectiveness of the training.

It is obvious, by this and other examples, that the trainer often is stuck on the horns of a dilemma, especially when working for a large organization. The trainer is hired by top management and needs its support to make important changes and/or to address relevant problems. On the other hand, management is often part of the problem, so the trainer does not want to be seen solely as an extension of that group. The role of the trainer and how the training program will be presented to the trainees must, therefore, be carefully and openly negotiated in the training contract (see Chapter 3 for a discussion of contracting).

What Should the Publicity Contain?   Information that will orient and affirm the trainee and enhance the trainer's credibility should be included. The informative background material should describe the goals and content of the training so as to encourage forethought about them, increase motivation, and affirm the potentially positive outcomes of the training. Information that is likely to enhance the trainer's credibility includes the title he/she holds, previous experience, and groups to which he/she belongs (see King, 1975).

Sponsors of training usually are eager to include credentials of the trainers—education, previous work, and so on. An exception, however, sometimes occurs when women's credentials are "overlooked" both in written materials about the training and in the actual training session. For example, the male trainer may be addressed as Dr., and the woman, with the same credential, by her first name. The oversight may be totally unconscious, as a result of the traditional status of women, but it is important for women to be assertive in having their credentials be as prominent as those of male trainers. There are productive ways of confronting the oversights, several of which are discussed in the section on conflicts around sex differences.

The second kind of information to include in the publicity is previous experience of the trainer, especially in contexts similar to the current training. Mentioning specific organizations, groups, and people for which the trainer has worked, time spent with this training topic, and the trainer's publications are important for credibility.

Finally, it is important to include organizations and groups to which the trainer belongs that are familiar to the particular audience the trainer is addressing. Those groups could be professional affiliations, university teaching assignments, and/or former employment in situations similar to the current training context. The general purpose of mentioning these groups is for the trainer to demonstrate an understanding of the problems and aspirations of his/her audience.

Introductions

Oral introductions of the trainer at the beginning of the training can be extremely important. If an introduction is done badly by an unskilled speaker, the trainer may spend the first hour recovering the credibility lost in the introduction. Therefore, the trainer should inquire about who is to introduce him/her, about the person's speaking skills, and the relationship the speaker has to the training group. Sometimes it is appropriate to suggest that another person give the introduction. The latter should not be done if the change will cause more problems than it will solve. Often, however, the contact person for the training is not the one doing the introduction, and can, therefore, be talked with openly about its importance to successful launching of the training. The trainer should also talk, by telephone or face to face, with the person introducing him/her to establish rapport.

The actual introduction should include much of the information already discussed—credentials, previous experience, and so on. In addition, it is often effective to include some personal information about the speaker (a story, anecdote, information about personal background) that will begin closing the interpersonal gap between trainer and audience. For example, one woman, who conducts conferences for managers of volunteers, makes excellent introductions. She is credible to her audience—well known in the field of volunteer management and an author in her own right—and she lets the audience know that a three-dimensional *person* is about to address them. She adds some of her own perceptions of the person and creates nicknames that capture the person's essence (for example, "so without further ado, I give you the Texas Tornado").

When the person making the introduction also has the responsibility of introducing the training, it is wise for the trainer to furnish him/her with written material about the program. One of our mistakes, again, underscores the importance of this last piece of advice. The CEO of the company doing the secretarial training, discussed above, was to introduce the trainers and the training program. With a patronizing style, he talked for 20 minutes about how proud he was to have his secretaries in attendance. The air was one of a father taking care of "his girls," an attitude which, of course, contradicted the goals of the training. In his long talk, which was supposed to have lasted two minutes, he mentioned the trainers coincidentally.

Personal Presentation of Self

First impressions are important and can be lasting. Therefore, the way in which the trainers present themselves is particularly important at the beginning of the training.

Research on interpersonal attraction is of help on this topic (see King, 1975). The overriding basis for initial attraction is similarity: of looks, attitudes, and beliefs. Since trainees, initially, have only external appearances with which to form impressions, the dress of the trainer is important. The style of dress should be fairly similar to that of trainees. If the norm of a company, for example, is for male employees to wear three-piece suits, then a suit is appropriate for a male trainer. An absentminded professor look—baggy pants that are too short, coat that is too tight, and tie that matches none of the above—will probably not increase credibility. Dress is sometimes more difficult for a woman. If her dress is too tailored, she often is thought to be masculine. On the other hand, if her dress is typically feminine, she loses credibility. There are styles that combine the two extremes, and women may do well to spend time assessing the styles that fit them and the context of training. Experienced female trainers, fashion magazines, and fashion directors at large department stores can be consulted for suggestions and alternatives in women's clothing.

It should be noted that we do take exception to many of the books that tell women how they *must* dress for success, believing as we do that people can demonstrate their personal power better when they develop their own individual style of dress. The point, however, is that trainers (male or female) should be aware of the dress norms of their trainees and be attired similarly enough to enhance a sense of "common ground."

There are exceptions to the foregoing rule, and they have to do with groups that have certain expectations of the trainer. An example is a janitorial staff for which we conducted supervisory training. It would have been demeaning to them for college professors, about whom they had a certain image, to come dressed as janitors. Suits were inappropriate, but so were work clothes. The same admonition was once given to a group of VISTA volunteers by community organizers. The trainers told the VISTAs that their well-worn jeans and work shirts would not be well received by poor people in small communities who had specific norms about dressing up to meet new people and going to public meetings.

Language usage, as well as clothing, can affect rapport and credibility with an audience. Even mild epithets used with a church-affiliated group, for example, are not likely to be well received. Communication is aided by an informal presentation using everyday language. Barriers can arise when a trainer uses strong language to shock the audience and demonstrate power over them.

A final note: Women probably need to be more aware of their language usage than men. Their behavior as professionals is still more open to negative interpretations than is that of their male counterparts. Women, like all groups that traditionally have had low public power, must be especially careful to read their audiences accurately and assess their responses. This is not to say that women should play a "feminine" role. However, women need to remember that they are breaking stereotypes in their role as trainers. More is said about this later.

The third area of importance for personal presentation of self is punctuality. In Chapter 11 we talked about arriving at the training site ahead of time to assess the facility and to be ready to receive the participants. Punctuality implies that the trainer cares about the training. Conversely, being late suggests disrespect for the trainees and often creates a tense training environment that takes double effort to overcome.

HOW CAN CONFLICT BE HANDLED?

Thus far we have discussed establishing credibility prior to training. Another kind of special problem has to do with conflicts between trainer and participants and among participants during the training. In most training literature, the perspective usually taken is that there are "problem" participants who need to be "taken care of" with special techniques. We find it more helpful to analyze training problems from a systems framework so that trainers can see the part they play in conflicts and can know their range of choices for dealing productively with interpersonal conflicts.

In this section, therefore, we first describe a systems view of conflict and then use it to analyze kinds of problems that typically arise in training (see Table 13–1 for a summary).

For analyzing conflict, we believe that are at least two key dimensions: assessing the goals of people in conflict (including our own), and being able to use a wide range of strategies and tactics to move conflicts in productive directions.

TABLE 13–1　Handling Conflict in Training Groups

DIAGNOSING	RESPONDING
1. Assessing goals of conflicts 　• Content 　• Relational	1. Divide means of reaching goals from needs people are trying to satisfy 2. Be aware of range of human needs (affection, control, inclusion) 3. Listen for intensity of communication to decipher needs 4. Listen for repeated patterns of communication 5. Listen for incongruities in patterns of communication 6. Stay in touch with others and self in conflict by paraphrasing and breathing
2. Assessing strategies to use	Strategic choices include: 1. Avoidance 2. Escalation 3. Maintenance 4. Deescalation
3. Typical conflict issues in training groups 　(a) Authority conflicts: 　　• Dependence 　　• Counterdependence	 1. Escalate conflict by being a catalyst 　• Pick a fight 　• Rigidify instructions 　• Constrict time for activities 2. Deescalate conflict 　• Wait and do not respond 　• Use humor 　• Alter-ego participants (speak the unspoken message) 　• Discuss the interaction 　• Ask for further information 　• Coopt participants 3. Escalate/deescalate 　• Dissipation—let the monopolizer continue at length 　• Diversion—seek others' opinions 　• Dramatization—mirror peoples' styles with humor 　• Give people what they need—recognition, influence, etc. 4. Avoidance 　• Physical avoidance 　• Put counterdependents together 5. Maintenance 　• Agree on how conflict will be handled 　• Voice hidden concerns
(b) Conflicts about sex differences 　　• Discrimination around fees 　　• Sexual (flirting) responses	 1. Directly clarify fees 2. Ignore the response 3. Divert them through humor 4. Talk frankly about them

TABLE 13-1   Handling Conflict in Training Groups (*continued*)

DIAGNOSING	RESPONDING
	5. Be aware of sexual signals you may be sending out
• Differential treatment of male and female trainers (interruptions, etc.)	6. Male/female modeling of peer communication
	7. Have male direct the interaction to the female
• Put-downs of female through language, jokes, etc.	8. Use humor
	9. Reverse roles
	10. Use more dominant behaviors
	11. Clarify your goals
• Put-down of males through sexist accusations, in-jokes, anger	12. Understand women's perception of professional roles
	13. Clarify communication around sex roles
	14. Reempower participants by letting them take the lead and give feedback about sexist behavior
(c) Conflicts arising through communication games	
• To prove others are not O.K.	1. Provide positive recognition of self and others
	2. Refuse to counterblame and put others down
• To prove self is not O.K.	3. Communicate congruently
	4. Provide feedback on games

There are two kinds of goals in any conflict—content and relational. The content goal usually is defending a viewpoint on the topic being debated. Relational goals have to do with "how I see you, how you see me, and how I see you seeing me"—in other words, how we define our relationship. The relational definition will, in turn, affect the meanings attributed to the opinions being argued. For example, if I do not trust a person, I will interpret a request for a loan differently than if the request came from someone I do trust.

Content goals are often more openly stated than relational goals, but that does not mean that they are more clearly stated. For example, a trainee may insist on shorter training sessions. The request could mean a number of things: that the person has a hard time sitting for a long period of time, he/she has other work obligations, or he/she feels threatened by the material. In other words, the statement of the goal (shorter sessions) is only the *means* to a goal that is not yet clearly identified. To negotiate the conflict, the trainer must know the need the trainee is trying to satisfy. With that understanding, there may be other and better solutions to the problem than shorter sessions. Depending on the need, solutions could be as varied as using more active exercises in the training, starting at different times during the day, or giving greater support to the trainee during the session. Trainers need to learn to separate the stated goal from need the trainee is trying to satisfy, so that more solutions to problems and greater flexibility are achieved.

For several reasons, relational goals often are more difficult to discern than content goals or difference of opinion. First, many people are not consciously *aware* that they have unmet relational needs. Second, even if they do recognize them, they often do not have *permission* to ask openly for what they need. People grow up with many messages about expressing needs, one of which is: "It is childish (or weak) to be needy." Finally, many people do not have the *skills* to get relational needs met; they do not know how to articulate them in a way that does not seem to put the other person down, or whom to ask, or when it is appropriate to ask.

It is helpful for trainers to know classifications of needs so that they have some handles for assessing relational goals in conflict. Schutz (1958) discusses three needs he believes all people have in common. They are inclusion, control, and affection. Inclusion has to do with how close or distant, involved or uninvolved, central or peripheral people are with each other. Control has to do with having influence, power, and competency in relation to others. Affection has to do with liking, loving, and being supportive of others and self.

Because expressing needs feels risky for most people, they may do the opposite of what they want. For example, some people who want *affection*, but fear rejection, become aggressive when they need affection. Some who want to be *included* in an activity withdraw instead. The pattern establishes an unsatisfying, self-fulfilling prophecy, but the person feels safe since he/she has rejected before being rejected; withdrawn before being asked to withdraw. Satir (1972) categorizes four communication styles that are indicative of doing the opposite of what the person wants: the blamer, placater, distracter, and computer (see Form 3–4).

Trainers can become more sensitive to expressions of needs. For instance, they can listen for the *intensity* of voice and nonverbal expression. In discussing the process of Gestalt therapy, Polster and Polster (1973) emphasize listening and watching for the "figure" to emerge from the "ground" to understand the important messages a person is communicating. Intensity highlights the figure— peoples' key feelings, thoughts, and unspoken goals—amidst the background of their words and other messages. For example, a man may be talking in a flat tone about how many things are wrong at work. You notice that each time he talks about someone not appreciating his work, his face looks sad, which is the most intense cue in all the messages. You might surmise, therefore, that the interpersonal need is for appreciation and affection.

The trainer can also listen for consistent *patterns* in the flow of communication. For example, you, as trainer, are getting resistance from a participant. You notice that each time you say something with an absolute tone of voice and without qualifiers, the person argues with you. You might surmise, therefore, that the person has control needs that are not being met.

Finally, as we have said previously, listen for the *incongruities* among overt and covert patterns of communication. For example, one woman had a high-pitched voice and smiled as she talked about the problem she was having with her subordinates; they were lethargic and unconcerned. In the training program, we noticed that every time someone disagreed with her, she very sweetly talked them out of their perceptions by saying their disagreements must be simply a semantic problem and that she was sure once they got all the facts they would see it her way. Her demeanor would not suggest a high need for control, but her communication patterns and incongruencies did. In the long run, her subordinates lost any sense of having control and responded with apathy. If the trainers heard only her overt goals, wanting employees to be more active, they would have missed her covert relational need for control, which was, in fact, predominant.

In order to gather the detailed information suggested, the trainer should remember two things: stay in touch with the people in conflict and stay "centered" (by breathing freely and deeply). Conflicts are stressful, and increasingly so if the trainer is one of the parties in the conflict. There is a tendency, therefore, for the trainer to feel attacked, to pigeonhole the others involved as "troublemakers" or "oddballs," and to engage in a subtle struggle for dominance with them. In contrast, staying in touch means not taking a rigid position vis-à-vis the trainees, but continually attending to the verbal and nonverbal behavior of self and others to understand what is going on. Trainers' observations and fantasies can provide useful information about the conflict. For example, "I see you making fists as you talk, and I imagine you are angry about what is happening," or "I feel myself tightening up and distance between us growing."

The simple mechanism of breathing deeply helps trainers stay centered, rather than withdrawing or lashing out. You may notice that when people are stressed, they often withdraw by cutting off their own feelings, and their breathing gets shallow. The trainer should pause occasionally for a relaxing, settling deep breath, and when appropriate, recommend to trainees that they breathe deeply to stay in touch with their thoughts and feelings.

It also is important to know some strategic choices for influencing the direction of conflicts once participants' needs have been identified. These are avoidance, escalation, maintenance, and deescalation (Hocker and Wilmot, 1978). Each strategy can be used productively in specific kinds of conflict and is discussed in relation to kinds of conflicts below.

WHAT KINDS OF CONFLICTS ARE COMMON?

Conflicts arise around many issues in training and take many forms. Three general kinds of conflict present special problems to the trainer. These center around authority issues, sex differences, and communication games. The commonality among the three is that they all involve ulterior, incongruent messages. Therefore, the goals of the conflicts are largely unspoken and difficult to discern.

Authority Issues

Responses to authorities can be divided into three categories: dependence, counterdependence, and independence (Bennis and Shepard, 1970). *Dependent* responses to the trainer include submissiveness, apathy, withdrawal, and in general, doing exactly what the trainer says without questioning or assimilating the information. *Counterdependent* responses include rebelliousness, hostility, argumentativeness, and condescension, and in general, doing the opposite of what the trainer says without questioning the information. *Independent* responses involve listening openly to the information presented, sorting it in terms of past and present experience, questioning it in light of that experience, and assimilating the information that seems useful.

Independent responses are usually most productive and they usually are straightforward. Conflicts stem from dependent and counterdependent responses because they express an ulterior need for control. Both actually give power to the authority by having him/her make decisions: the dependent needs an authority to follow; the counterdependent, to resist.

Trainers who have high control needs and little flexibility often will trigger dependent and counterdependent reactions. They tend to take even more power away from participants, when the underlying issue is already a feeling of powerlessness, which exacerbates the conflict. Instead, the trainers' goal should be to reempower trainees.

The four conflict strategies listed earlier provide trainers with choices and flexibility of response. The use of the strategies have empowerment as their goal, allowing participants to reown their own responses and decisions. We provide below examples of authority conflicts and possible responses for managing them productively.

With dependent participants the trainer might escalate conflicts. One tactic is to be the *catalyst* in the conflict. For example, one of us was working with a large group of women, doing conflict management training. They were mostly dependent and could talk each other out of all conflicts (and thus bury them prematurely). Interestingly, the problem for which they wanted training was that their work relationships were smooth on the surface but fraught with covert conflict—rumors, backstabbing, and so on. This is often the case with dependent people. They pursue their power and control needs covertly; thus, relational issues are difficult to address. The trainer chose to *escalate* a conflict to illuminate the participants' relational style. She did so by being a *catalyst*, involving herself in a conflict. She disagreed openly with some participants and refused to be talked out of her perceptions. Participants then escalated their strategy of saying there was really no disagreement—probably just a matter of semantics—to which the trainer responded with still another disagreement. Fairly soon, the pattern was obvious; and their habitual conflict styles, goals, and consequences could be examined.

Another way trainers can be catalysts on the issue of control is to increase the rigidity of instructions. Have participants move around a lot; tell them they must improve; and when they do one thing, change the instructions. The purpose is to heighten their awareness of how much they will take before they will openly discuss control issues. This strategy helps create a "here-and-now" situation in which they can examine how they feel and what they say to themselves as they delay expressing their growing frustration. Of course, trainers can use themselves as catalysts to clarify interaction only if they understand the overall goal of the strategy and are not caught up in their own personal power needs.

Conflicts also can be escalated to enhance participants' awareness if the *rules and time of interaction are constricted* when people in training are fairly lethargic and reserved. For example, a simulation that calls for quick decisions under competitive circumstances will often increase the intensity of the interaction and reveal covert patterns. Simulations such as Starpower, Win As Much As You Can, Broken Squares, and Coin Exchange are good examples.[1]

A second strategy, principally for dealing with counterdependence, is deescalation. For example, we encountered a great deal of resistance with one group of law enforcement officers. The rebellion was manifested in in-jokes, refusal to respond, and difficulty in "hearing" even the simplest instructions, such as where to move in the room. The trainer deescalated by *waiting*—for them to finish joking, to decide to move into small groups, and so on. One tendency in that kind of situation is for trainers to become agitated and critical. That response, of course, is a collusion with the ulterior conflict; that is, if the trainer is critical, the trainees have more justification for being rebellious.

Another tactic of deescalation is befriending your "opponent" through *humor*. In one training program, a young man was arguing with most everything the trainer said, by asking questions like "But don't you think?; Aren't there exceptions?; How do you know?" At one point during a discussion of marital conflict, the man leaped from his chair and asked "How do you know? Are you married?", to which the trainer responded, "Why, would you like a date?"

A third way to deescalate is to use an *alter-ego* tactic. For example, several people in one group of businessmen looked increasingly wary of the ideas being presented by the trainer. They shook their heads, frowned a great deal, and turned their bodies away. One tendency is to try even harder to convince such people, but that response often increases counterdependence. The trainer instead alter-egoed the men by saying "And these people in front here don't believe a word I'm saying. Why, they can't believe that I think this stuff." That response, if accurate, usually lightens the interaction and allows for a straightforward discussion of ideas; it empowers the participants to reown their responses.

A fourth way to deescalate conflicts (see Watzlawick et al., 1967) is switching to *metacommunication*, open discussion of the interaction. For example, in the law enforcement training session, the trainers could honestly say that they were bothered by what was happening and request an open discussion of the participants' response to the training. Metacommunication during conflict

---

[1]These games, and ones similar in purpose, can be found in the Pfeiffer and Jones structured experience handbooks, published annually by University Associates, Inc., San Diego, California.

presupposes some basic goodwill. Trainers should gauge the group climate before giving and asking for direct, fairly risky, feedback.

A fifth approach to deescalation is *inquiry* (Hocker and Wilmot, 1978, p. 138). A participant, for example, says, "I don't agree with what you just said," to which the trainer responds, "Tell me more about the disagreement and your experiences with the idea." Again, the goal is for trainees to clarify their ideas and make conscious choices about what they will accept and reject. The trainer is attempting to facilitate the sorting of information and to move participants to a response independent of covert authority issues.

Another tactic which can be deescalatory is *cooptation*. Cooptation means putting the participants who are resisting authority into authority roles, such as giving instructions or observing a simulation. Dependent people may increase their responses and responsibility; counterdependents may change their energy from resisting the training to being a main force in the training. In both cases, participants are reempowered.

Three tactics which combine escalation and deescalation are *dissipation, diversion*, and *dramatization*. For example, if a participant is talking on and on, complaining about one thing and then another, it may be helpful to let the person keep talking and to give the person little or no response. Since counterdependence relies on the resistance of the authority, giving little resistance or energy will often *dissipate* the response. If, however, the person is intent on monopolizing the group's time, the trainer can refer or divert the matter to the entire group, asking other participants what they think about the remarks. When given a chance, other group members often will manage the conflict, and many of the issues may be clarified when the "authority" is not intervening. In other words, if there are "real" questions trainees have, but they cannot hear the trainers' responses because of the authority issues, it may be helpful to *divert* the conflict to the whole group.

Finally, *dramatization* means acting out, in a theatrical way, responses to certain interactions. For example, one man kept repeating his comments even after the trainer and several participants had acknowledged his remarks. Participants were becoming agitated: moving around a lot, frowning, and looking out the window. The trainer, after doing many listening behaviors—paraphrasing, saying she understood and that it was time to move on—finally dramatized her internal response by collapsing physically on the floor. The action escalated the conflict, made the exhausting quality of the interaction clear, and then deescalated it by opening up the responses for discussion.

Another means of dramatization involves the training group. Once, for example, some dependent participants talked about how awful it would be to act assertively. The trainer spontaneously led the entire group to respond in Greek chorus fashion with "Ohhhhh, NOooooo." The response dramatized the exaggerated scare and at the same time lightened it with humor. Participants then could sort out the real from the imagined threat in the situation.

A basic tactic that trainers often forget is *giving participants the interpersonal needs* for which they are asking covertly. If some need control, let them take charge for awhile. If some need affection and attention, give them positive reinforcement. If some do not feel included in activities, facilitate their involvement. Ironically, this tactic can either escalate or deescalate conflicts. Deescalation occurs when trainees' self-esteem permits positive need fulfillment. Escalation occurs when participants feel they do not deserve it. For example, a trainer may commend a participant on the excellent role play, only to find that the person argues vehemently with that perception. The participant may even indicate that the trainer must not know much about that role if he/she thought the enactment was good. Trainers need to be aware of this pattern and be prepared to fulfill needs, unconditionally, without expecting people to be gratified by their generosity.

A third overall strategy occasionally needed for dealing with conflict is avoidance. This strategy is useful with participants who disrupt the training continuously. This can occur in large groups when some people need to avoid feeling anonymous. One tactic is physical avoidance—refusing to make eye contact or otherwise recognize the speaker nonverbally. Another is to divide and control. If there are several disruptive people sitting together, the trainer could have participants number off for small-group formations. People sitting together, therefore, will be in different groups.

Conversely, if there are a number of "determined to be nonresponsive" participants, the trainer could put them all in one group and spend minimal time with that group. They then will not drain energy from the rest of the group and have to deal with their own boredom. It should be remembered that these tactics are not the first to be used, but *can* be if other responses to participants are not working.

The basic goal remains reempowering participants, having them take responsibility for their own responses. If the tactics are used as punishment, they will have the effect of increasing rebellion and/or dependence, thereby increasing the problem the trainer is trying to solve. The trainer also needs to remember that for some people rebellion or passivity may be a necessary stage in their personal development, not a reaction to this particular training situation. For example, for some people, being openly rebellious with authorities is new behavior and important for establishing their independence. The trainer, therefore, does not want to squelch the rebellion but rather, should facilitate the trainees' move from counterdependence to independence.

The trainer can facilitate this movement by asking for elaboration when trainees automatically reject an idea. When questions are asked, people usually have to think in order to respond, and thinking is a move to independence. For example, if a trainee responds to some idea with "That does not make sense," the trainer can ask "How does this idea not fit with your experience?" or "Can you modify the principle according to your experience?" The trainee not only must think to answer the questions, but also can be recognized for extending some idea that may be useful to others in similar circumstances.

Finally, a fourth strategy for dealing with conflicts in training is maintenance of the conflict, neither escalating or avoiding it (Hocker and Wilmot, 1978, p. 133). One tactic of maintenance is *agreeing on the rules of conflict*. For example, one common response from participants who do not want to own (or are not aware of) their own feelings and thoughts is to preface their statements with "*All* people here believe . . ." or "*This* group thinks . . ." Statements such as these could escalate the conflict from that person to the entire group. The conflict can be contained to that particular participant if the trainer suggests some rules for doing conflict: asking the participant to refer to him/herself when giving feedback by using "*I* believe . . ." or "*I* think . . ."

Another way to maintain conflict productively is to have the trainer and participants *voice* their *inner thoughts* so that the covert concerns of both can be addressed. For example, if participants (or a group) look fairly disinterested, the trainer might ask them to complete certain phrases, such as "If I were interested, I would . . ." or "If it weren't for . . . , I would participate." These are high-risk statements and, therefore, are often more functional when done in dyads or small groups which then report back to the large group. In this way participants are given permission for having their reservations and fears. They become aware of where they are and are encouraged to express their resistance rather than being punished for it.

Sex Differences

The kinds of conflicts described above centered around authority issues. Another kind of conflict, becoming more prevalent as women increase their professional visibility, has to do with male/female differences and expectations. Since most of these conflicts also revolve around power issues, many of the strategies discussed in the preceding section can be used to equalize power and enhance independent control responses. There are, however, additional ways for female and male trainers to respond, particularly to participants of the opposite sex. First, we will consider common female trainer conflicts and possible responses. Second, we will focus on male trainers and their potential conflicts with female participants.

The traditional cultural expectation, of course, is that in public arenas males are dominant and women, submissive. The role of the female trainer reverses those roles; therefore, women trainers can expect power conflicts to be accentuated on some occasions.

There are some predictable ways in which males and females (mostly unconsciously) diminish the credibility of female trainers. During the contracting phase, one typical way is to assume that women will work for less money than male trainers.

Male managers from organizations occasionally have contacted inexperienced female trainers and suggested that they might want to conduct a program to gain some valuable experience. No mention was made of pay. As with all the suggested responses in this section, righteous indignation does little good. A direct response giving information is better. For example, "I would be glad to talk with you further about training and my fee for planning is . . ."

During the training, male responses to female trainers include flirting and redefining the trainer-participant relationship as a sexual one; differential treatment of female and male cotrainers; stereotypic put-downs; and increased verbal and nonverbal dominant behaviors—patronizing voice tones, continuous interruptions, touching, violation of personal space, and so on (see Table 13–2).

Several suggestions may help female trainers cope with these responses and even use them to enhance training. As we have said, no one in the long run "wins" interpersonal battles to prove who is best, most competent, or the better sex. Increased self-responsibility, choices, and awareness of consequences for participants should be the aims of trainer responses.

A theme that has guided male/female relationships for time eternal is sexuality. Stereotypically, males have been the aggressors and females the pursued and conquered sex. Therefore, a tendency, when control roles have been reversed, is for males to increase their overt sexual advances to equalize the power. Training is no exception. Knowing this, women trainers need to be aware of the covert sexual signals they learned as young girls and which they may do almost automatically particularly under stress—high-pitched voices, tilted heads, excessive blinking, laughing to relieve tension, leaning forward seductively, or allowing undesired touching. If women are not aware of these signals, they could be encouraging, unknowingly, sexual overtures from males.

This is not to say, however, that women are responsible for the sexual advances they receive. Regardless of signals, male participants may flirt to redefine the training relationship. Trainers have many possible responses, some of which are ignoring them (verbally and nonverbally); saying they are complimented; recognizing and diverting the covert message through humor; or talking frankly about consistent sexual messages. The choice should be based on the trainer's skills and the intensity of the sexual overture. For example, a male participant may say in a seductive tone, "You sure are easy to look at—I mean, listen to," to which the female could respond, "I appreciate both compliments," and then move on with the training. Or someone could say, "How could a girl so cute know so much," to which the female trainer may respond, "I don't know— just guess we girls mature faster than you boys." If overtures continue and become disruptive, trainers also have the option of metacommunication, acknowledging the interplay and how they are reacting to it.

Women trainers and consultants may have difficulty assessing the intent of sexual messages anew in each situation. It is easy to carry "baggage" and resentment from one experience to another and overreact to a comment that may simply mean the participant has never interacted with a female "authority" and is looking for ways of making contact. As with other kinds of communication, the female trainer may want to wait for obvious patterns to emerge before she responds.

Another problematic response is differential treatment of female and male

TABLE 13-2 Asymmetrical Communication Behaviors

	DOMINANT	SUBMISSIVE
Nonverbal Cues		
Eye contact	Look or stare aggressively Look elsewhere at times while listening	Do not look into the other's eyes for long periods of time Lower, avert eyes part of the time Watch speaker while listening
Face	No smile or frown Impassive, not showing emotions	Smile Expressive facial gestures, showing emotions
Posture, bearing	Relaxed, more body lean Loose legs, freed arms	Tense, more erect Tight, legs together, arms close to body
Gestures	Larger, more sweeping, forceful, such as pointing	Smaller, more inhibited
Touch	Touches other	Does not touch other or reciprocate touch; yields to the touch
Use of space	Expands, uses more space	Condenses, contracts, takes as little space as possible
Distance	Determines distance by moving close or far away freely Cuts across other's path	Approaches more distant, slowly, cautiously Moves out of the way
Verbal Behaviors		
Interruptions	Interrupts frequently	Avoids interruptions, gives way when the other interrupts
Fluency	Fluent speech	Halting speech
Length of statements	Talks for longer at a time	Makes short comments; waits to be instructed to give more information
Content	Makes personal comments about other; asks personal questions Gives orders or directions	Makes personal comments about self, reveals personal information when asked Follows instructions
Expressiveness in language	Uses forceful expressions Stresses positive assertion, opinions	Uses diminuative words like "cute," "itsy-bitsy" Uses disclaiming qualifiers like "I was thinking," "Of course, I may be wrong," "possibly," etc. Uses tag questions at the end of assertions: "..., don't you think," etc.

Source: Adapted from Barbara Eakins and Gene Eakins, *Sex Differences in Human Communication* (Boston: Houghton Mifflin, Copyright © 1978). Adapted with permission.

cotrainers. One example, mentioned earlier, was attributing expertise to the male by calling him Dr., but calling the female trainer by her first name. Other examples involve asking questions of the male trainer, even when the question is about material covered by the female, and interrupting the presentation of the female but not that of the male. To handle this situation productively, the cotrainers should be clear about their relationship. They must model peer-level communication. For example, without commenting verbally, the male can look toward the female when being asked a question about her material. This nonverbal gesture often will direct the questioner's response to the woman. If the pattern persists, either trainer might describe it openly and request a change from participants. If there is open discussion, it is also important that the female trainer not be "rescued" by the male by letting him do all the confronting. Otherwise, they will be modeling the behavior they are trying to change.

A third response women trainers often get is sexist put-downs, from mild to extreme. Subtle ones include language use: using the generic "he" even when there are women involved. Trainers can model different language use in their own talk and even can call attention to participants' language after some rapport with them has been built. Put-downs also can be injected in little jokes, such as "How can a woman conduct a budget planning session—I thought women were not supposed to be good with numbers." To which the woman may respond, with humor, "I hope I can do as well as males have done with budgets, like the federal budget, but I may not be able to reach those heights."

Humor that mirrors the intent of the comment but reverses the roles can also be effective. For instance, one male participant said, "I'm impressed. You can teach just like a man," to which the female trainer responded, "Why, thank you; and you can give compliments just like a woman." Unless they are persistent, women also can ignore the comments.

Finally, there is a whole cadre of behaviors, both verbal and nonverbal, that reflect and help to maintain positions of dominance and power and positions of submission. Not surprisingly, men usually exhibit dominant behaviors, and women, submissive behaviors. These behaviors, in turn, accentuate the power differences of the sexes (see Eakins and Eakins, 1978). Dominant behaviors include taking up space, low-pitched voices, squarely facing others as they are addressed, and initiating touching. Submissive behaviors include taking up a small space (psychological as well as physical), high-pitched voices, tag questions such as "Don't you think?", looking down with a tilted head, and being touched. Inadvertently, some women act submissive even when they are competent trainers. Even when they are aware of these behaviors, many women are hesitant to modify them because they have been the source of their indirect power for a long time. If not assured of success with more direct forms of power, women do not want to lose what they have. In the public arena, however, most women eventually have to learn that strength through weakness goes only so far and does little for the enhancement of professional respect.

Conversely, women may find their credibility increased and put-downs less frequent if they become aware of and proficient in dominant behaviors. This does not mean that women should adopt an overcontrolling style of training; it does mean they may need to be aware of submissive behaviors and their effect on credibility.

We also have found it helpful, particularly in training related to sex roles, to adjust our goals. For example, a trainer in one such program judged herself as having succeeded only when the males changed their attitudes about the competency of women. She had, unknowingly, set up failure. In the first place, attitudes formed through a liftetime will not change in a day- or week-long training program. Furthermore, if she and the males are covertly locked into a power struggle, the men would "win" simply by "refusing to learn," thereby frustrating the trainer and maintaining power. It was suggested to the woman that she change her goals and, therefore, her teaching methods. Instead of trying to convince the male trainees of the "errors of their ways," she began having them generate situations they had difficulty handling and possible new ways of responding. She could then be a resource for them in terms of *their* problems, although their aims might not mesh with hers.

The discussion thus far has centered on the problems of female trainers. Conflicts of male trainers around sex differences also occur but are less frequent simply because males are in their expected roles of leadership and usually are training other men. A special case arises, however, when males lead or colead training for women professionals. Typical problematic reactions from women include "catching" the male in sexist behaviors (verbal and nonverbal), in-jokes concerning his ignorance of the problems of women, and accumulated anger directed at the male authority.

A male trainer must be highly skilled to deal productively with these reactions, most of which are born from a feeling of powerlessness. First, it helps to know how modern women perceive their professional roles. Second, the male should examine his masculine identity so that he will be aware of his overt and covert messages to women. For example, one man we witnessed recently was in his sixties, very supportive financially of women's efforts, and thought himself to be totally nonsexist. While addressing an audience of 300 women professionals, he was asked about hiring and promotion practices, to which he responded by saying that "girls," like all others, were promoted on merit. When asked who made the decision about merit and how women's salaries compared to men's in his company, he responded that men, of course, made the decisions and that women's salaries were lower because they had not been promoted. He attempted to assure them that women, nevertheless, had no need to worry because there were plenty of laws on the books to deal with discrimination. At this point, all 300 women arose in anger at the naivete of his assumptions. The point is that the male trainer who is conscious and candid about his viewpoints on feminist issues may be received better than one who is patronizing.

Finally, the male should remember that if the reactions he is getting arise from powerlessness, then the remedy is to reempower—having participants take more responsibility for the session, say what they prefer to hear about, and so on.

Male trainers, unlike female trainers, can avoid these situations altogether, and so may never have to examine these issues. However, because there will be increasing diversity of people (sexes and backgrounds) in the professional arena, trainers limit themselves—their markets and their value—if they draw the line at their current point of awareness and remain oblivious to emerging sex-role issues.

It is important to remember that for the responses suggested to be communicated congruently, we presuppose a fairly high level of self-awareness for male and female trainers. Without that awareness, confusing, mixed messages can arise from unresolved internal conflicts. For example, women trainers may want to be seen as competent *and* feminine, but think the two qualities are mutually exclusive. Therefore, they may respond to questions in a competent, straightforward manner followed by an inappropriate smile and submissive tilt of the head. The mixed message can seem manipulative and damaging to credibility.

Unresolved conflicts in male trainers may also lead to mixed messages. For example, men may want to be seen as nonsexist *and* macho. Therefore, they may be very careful in using nonsexist language, but if challenged by a female participant, immediately reinstate control. We noticed one particularly charismatic trainer, who effectively regained dominance by touching female participants lightly as he explained *his* point of view that was contrary to theirs. It is difficult for participants to talk as equals when the trainer is standing above and touching them, both of which are dominating gestures.

Male and female trainers need to *model* effective, congruent interaction. To do so, women typically need to work on their direct expressions of power and their tendencies to want to please *everyone*. Men, typically, need to enhance their nurturing skills and to temper their competition and control needs. Men and women, therefore, have things they can learn from each other.

We believe that trainers' flexibility and congruency are enhanced when they are more "androgynous" than strongly masculine- or feminine-typed. Androgyny applies to a person who embodies awareness and acceptance of both masculine and feminine characteristics and who expresses those qualities appropriately—someone, in other words, with a comprehensive sense of self (see Jongeward and Scott, 1976; Singer, 1976).

Communication Games

The third kind of conflict that presents special problems to trainers is characterized by communication games (in the Transactional Analysis sense). By definition, a game has three parts: a social or ostensible message (usually the spoken words); the psychological or ulterior message (usually nonverbal); and the payoff, which is always a "discount" or put-down to self, other, or both (Berne, 1964).

Games are problematic because they thwart the goals of training programs, such as information exchange or human relations development. We have stated that effective training is based on awareness and acceptance of self and others, congruent communication, and flexibility of choice and behavior. Games decrease all three since they are based on ulterior messages and their outcomes are put-downs. Trainers' responsibility is to intervene, directly or indirectly, to retard the games of participants and to stop any games they themselves are initiating. To do so, it may be helpful to discuss, briefly, the reasons games are played, some kinds of games, and means of stopping them.

Why Are Games Played?   First, most games are not conscious. People learn them by watching others and often assume that a "game" is the appropriate way to respond. It rarely helps to assume that participants are playing games intentionally. If this assumption is made, trainers can launch a game of their own—"Now I've Got You" and "I'll Straighten You Out."

Second, games emerge from, and maintain, three orientations to others: I'm OK—you're not OK; I'm not OK—you are OK; and I'm not OK—you're not OK. The fourth, I'm OK—you're OK, is the basis for congruent communication.

Third, games fill time and create predictable responses. People often do not know any alternative to game playing. They are not accustomed to, nor do they feel safe, communicating authentically.

Finally, games can lead to recognition, albeit negative. However, for some people, negative recognition is better than none. People who do not know how to get positive recognition usually will welcome any attention at all, even if it stems from being seen as annoying, intimidating, or helpless.

What Kinds of Games Are There?   Games usually are classified according to the life positions they foster (see Table 13–3). For example, some participants, coming from an "I'm OK—you're not OK" position, refuse responsibility by blaming *others* for their behavior. The pattern often is evident

TABLE 13–3   Games Organizations Play

THEME	NAME OF THE GAME	PURPOSE: TO PROVE:
	Discount others	
Blaming others	If It Weren't for You	You're not OK
Saving others	I'm Only Trying to Help You	You're not OK
Finding fault	Why Don't You—Yes, But	You're not OK
Getting even	Rapo	You're not OK
	Now I've Got You, You S.O.B.	
	Discount self	
Getting sympathy	Look How Hard I've Tried	I'm not OK
Provoking put-downs	Kick Me	I'm not OK
	Stupid	
Enjoying misery	Wooden Leg	I'm not OK

From Goldhaber, Gerald M., *Organizational Communication.* © 1974 Wm. C. Brown Publishers, Dubuque, Iowa. All rights reserved. Reprinted by permission.

when a workshop experience has evoked conflict. Participants will play "If it weren't for you, I wouldn't have done what I did," a game which includes the trainer since he/she is the one who ostensibly is "in charge" of the experience. Blaming in this way drains energy from the session.

To intervene in this game, trainers have several choices. One is to avoid buying into the argument, or beginning another one, by accusing participants of not taking responsibility for their behaviors. Instead, acknowledge part of what the person is saying and extend it. For example, "What other people have done does influence your choices. I also wonder how your behavior influences theirs." In this way, the trainer does not argue with the comment, but extends it to enhance self-examination.

Trainers also can give direct feedback to participants about the gamelike behaviors being observed. They can give positive recognition when people describe their own behavior. They also can recognize others who are willing to own their reactions. People intent on playing games can sidetrack the attention of the trainer and other participants, which may better be given to participants encountering the work productively.

A game emanating from "I'm not OK and others are" is "Poor Me." These participants remain passive since they are "not smart enough to know the answers" or "have so much on their minds, they can't pay attention to what is happening here." Trainer responses can include providing positive recognition for contributions when they *are* made and providing structure to guide the participant's observations. As with most games, it is tempting to become exasperated and participate in the game by overtly or covertly putting those participants down—through sarcasm or with irritated voice tones.

In sum, games can be defused by giving positive recognition (since games are based on negative recognition); by refusing to play the complementary hand in the game (such as pitying the person playing "Poor Me"); and by communicating congruently (since games are based on incongruent, ulterior communication). Readers not familiar with the structure and function of games may want to spend more time studying and observing games and ways to stop them (see James and Jongeward, 1971; Berne, 1964; Jongeward, 1973). A trap for trainers who are conscious of game playing, however, is to be the "catcher of those playing games." To decrease games it is essential to be "nongamey" oneself.

This chapter has dealt with a number of special problems in the areas of trainer credibility and conflicts during the training program. Numerous suggestions were given for handling these problems. The essence of them all is trainer flexibility, which, synergistically, is the goal for training participants, as well.

CHAPTER FOURTEEN
EVALUATING TRAINING

Evaluation often has little appeal for trainers. To those integrally involved in the instructional process measuring outcomes can seem just a tedious chore to complete. It extends the time that must be given to a training project; it feels dull and heavy with figures—not lively and social like interacting with learners; it surfaces participants' judgments, sometimes petty criticisms, and seems to reflect only a part of the learning that occurred. Evaluation need not have these qualities. Instead, it can be done parsimoniously, in interesting, humane, informative, valid ways, and it can prove a valuable asset to trainers as well as to their employers and students. In this chapter we discuss how evaluation can make a positive contribution to the training process.

WHO SHOULD PLAN AND CARRY OUT THE EVALUATION?

Since evaluation results can have a future impact on everyone involved in training, it is essential that it be planned and carried out appropriately and without bias. The more it is separated from the training process, the more it can become an irrelevant, distracting, suspected, even resented intrusion. Hence, we recommend that trainers be as actively involved as possible in designing the evaluation system to be used, so that it is in harmony with what they are trying to do and how they plan to do it.

The trainer's optimal contribution would be in assuring that the goals and methods of instruction are covered and are harmonious with the evaluation process. The means for measuring the variables identified and analyzing the data gathered can be a demanding process calling for additional help. For a precise evaluation of a comprehensive program, Stockard (1977) recommends using academic consultants. He offers these possible benefits of this policy:

> First, the parent organization is much more likely to gain an impartial assessment of T & D activities. Secondly, the importation and exportation of ideas and techniques, methods, and devices through the catalytic effect of the [consultants] is a constructive practice. Thirdly, the involvement of the academic community in the evaluation of an organization's T & D work can further its objectives by having in-service T & D programs recognized by colleges and universities, so that the employees can, if they wish, be awarded credits that further career advancement or qualify them as candidates for academic degrees. [P. 343]

One precaution must be kept in mind when using outsiders in this role. Watson (1979) refers to a distinction between an evaluation that is done as thoroughly as *possible* and one that is done as thoroughly as is *practical*. The former approach views as uppermost the internal consistency of the evaluation (does it validly assess achievement of all training objectives?). The latter seeks to find out what those using the evaluation want to know by the easiest, least costly, least intrusive measures. Watson described an evaluation plan for management training that called for pretests, posttests, and interviews with trainees, their superiors, and subordinates before and after the program. These procedures made participants feel like rats in a maze being observed by scientists or like small children whose parents watched their every move. They inferred that their company did not trust them to go away to a program and learn and that the measures and reports were to make sure they did learn what was intended. Hence, the evaluation had a detrimental effect on their attitudes and on the attitudes of others in their organization toward training. Evaluation can intimidate people, so it must be done cautiously and with the feelings of those who are being studied in mind.

WHAT IS EVALUATION FOR?

The term "evaluation" commonly implies a judgment of good versus bad. This connotation constricts its value. Instead, it is better viewed as a process of providing *information* to those involved in training regarding questions they genuinely want answered. The trainer labors to plan an effective program and then stands before a group facilitating learning goals both want to be achieved. In the context of a classroom it is difficult to know what exactly is going on within participants—what is working and what is not, how the trainer is being perceived, what difference the experience actually is making. Evaluation data can satisfy the trainer's curiosity. Sponsors of training programs are even further from the scene of the action and are likely to wonder if they made wise decisions in setting up the program, if they sent the right people to it, if it requires follow-up. They, too, need evaluation data. Trainees are curious about their own growth, about how their newly learned behaviors appear to coworkers, about their impact on the organization's output. Evaluation data can yield this information, as well.

Evaluation, therefore, is simply feedback. When done well, it can be used as a mirror in which everyone involved in the training process can see meaningful reflections of themselves. They can use that cybernetic information to give themselves a pat on the back, or it can be used to guide adjustments in their *modus operandi,* making them more likely to achieve desired results.

For example, the General Electric Company once carried out an evaluation of the effectiveness of a safety training program. Its purpose was to reduce the number of accidents and to increase the regularity with which all accidents, major and minor, were reported. The training program consisted of the usual presentations, discussions, and movies, which were very dramatic in describing accidents and their implications. Their evaluation indicated that the program did not adequately achieve its goals. Consequently, a new approach to training was adopted which was oriented to the job relationship between the foreman and each worker. Evaluation of this second approach revealed it to be much more effective. As a result, the information gained from evaluating this program proved welcome and useful to everyone involved in it (Kirkpatrick, 1976).

There generally are thought to be five areas of a training program which merit evaluation (Watson, 1979). These are:

1. *Reactions:* trainees' reactions to all facets of the learning experience itself
2. *Learning:* changes in attitudes, knowledge, and skills of the trainees
3. *Job behavior:* how and to what extent trainees behave differently because of the training, how they have applied what was taught on the job
4. *Organizational impact:* how trainee changes affect the functioning of their organization(s)
5. *Additional outcomes:* results or by-products of the training not identified or assessed by the other four areas, such as the social value of training, its effect on trainee self-concept, its relation to trainees' personal goals (for example, career development), and other such issues

Each aspect of evaluation is discussed in some detail in this chapter. The approach(es) taken to evaluation should be selected only after careful consideration of why evaluation is being done. This includes identifying *who* it is for, what that person intends to *do* or *decide* with the aid of that information, and what *questions* must be answered in order to make those decisions most appropriately.

For example, if trainers want to improve the degree to which future learners will perceive their program as useful or interesting, *reaction* data are needed; if developers of training materials want to know what learnings participants have retained from an audiovisual aid, *learning* data are obtained; if program coordinators want to know whether trainees are actually using what they have learned after returning to their work setting, *job behavior* data are sought; if a chief executive wants to know if his/her training department is a cost-effective operation, *organizational impact* data are vital; and if training seems to be touching participants in subtle ways beyond its overtly stated goals, measures of *additional outcomes* may be warranted.

By the evaluator asking, "What decisions will I (and/or others concerned with this training program) be making?" and "What do we need to know about it in order to make them?", the relevant areas for evaluation will emerge. Each area subsumes its own kind of information and means for obtaining it, which are discussed below.

HOW ARE REACTIONS TO TRAINING EVALUATED?

The most commonly used approach to evaluating a training program is assessing participants' reactions to their experience in the program itself. The leader(s) and the sponsor of the training want to know how its consumers felt about what they received and did during the session(s). Since participants often are adults with previous work and school experience, and they are dealing with a narrow subject area that they soon will put to use, they are apt judges of the value of the training. They can provide a relatively valid assessment of the degree to which the training experience has met its goals.

From such an evaluation, the trainer seeks to learn what "worked," that is, what ideas seemed most novel and useful, and what learning methods proved to be most stimulating and memorable. Ideally, the evaluation data will allow for comparison from one workshop to another. Thereby, poorly received approaches can be eliminated and a repertoire of optimally effective methods can be developed.

As trainers grow more experienced and sensitive to their audiences they usually know intuitively, as they proceed, which elements in their workshops are striking home and which are falling flat. However, a formal evaluation system can provide, in addition, objective, quantitative, written data to submit to the program's sponsor, or to potential future employers, validating the worth of their efforts.

Program coordinators often use evaluation data to decide whether a training effort merits continuance, whether (and/or what kind of) follow-up would be welcomed by the participants, which subgroups from among the participants gained substantially and which profited minimally from attending, and so on. Light can be shed on all these concerns when a carefully planned evaluation system is used.

No one method of evaluation is fully comprehensive. In fact, to obtain reliable evaluation data it is best to solicit information from as many sources as possible. The most commonly used method is administering a paper-and-pencil self-report questionnaire at the end of a training session. The findings obtained from this structured instrument ought to be supplemented by face-to-face contact and dialogue with participants. This can occur during workshop breaks, after the session is over, or back on the job.

A method sometimes used to promote trainer-learner dialogue is asking a few participants to volunteer to serve as a "steering committee." They meet with the trainer at the end of a day's session to share their views of how things have been going, to hear a preview of the next day's agenda, and to suggest ways for making the upcoming session maximally relevant and palatable to the trainees. Since those steering committee members are now familiar with the goals and methods for the next session, they can be helpful in an additional way by serving as small-group discussion leaders at that session, keeping group interaction on track and aimed toward the intended ends of the session.

Picking up evaluation information through interacting with participants usually occurs as an informal, spontaneous process, often improvised on-the-spot over coffee, lunch, or a cocktail. Written evaluations are more objective, systematic, and are planned in advance. Hence, they will be discussed here in detail.

It can be helpful to make two kinds of distinctions regarding the information to be gleaned from written surveys. One is dividing between the *content* (or *what* is to be learned) and the *process* (or *how* it is conveyed) at the workshop. Sometimes, the content is fixed and only the process is flexible (as in an initial job training session); in other instances, the content also can be changed to suit the participants' needs (as in a job-enrichment session). A second division is between *formative* evaluation (checking midstream to see how well the workshop is going and how it still can be improved) and *summative* evaluation (assessing at the end or even later how adequately the training goals have been met).

One can use standardized instruments to assess participants' reactions; or, questionnaires can be developed that are tailored to the aims, content, and methods of each specific workshop. Questionnaires that have been standardized (that is, demonstrated to be reliable and valid measures of variables that are prominent in the literature of organizational behavior, such as Theory X versus Theory Y orientation) have the advantage of previous use and modification, as well as the occasional availability of norm scores to which one's own group can be compared.

A limitation of published tests is that very few training programs aim directly or exclusively at achieving goals identical to those measured by these instruments. For the most part, therefore, evaluators devise their own forms. These are custom-designed to obtain the information needed to determine how their programs are working in their own unique context.

There are two essential issues to keep in mind when developing a questionnaire: (1) the specific questions it is intended to answer, and (2) the form in which those answers are to be provided. Several sample forms are offered at the end of this chapter to illustrate how questionnaires differ depending on what is to be learned from their use.

These forms provide general prototypes for instruments trainers can develop to suit themselves. In some instances, the form provided here may seem appropriate for use virtually as is. In others, the reader may find specific items that seem immediately usable or a format that fits but which requires some modification in wording to be directly relevant in a particular setting. View these forms as raw material to be used in cooking up evaluation systems that you can use.

Note that all the forms provided have two features in common:

1. They state explicitly, and in a somewhat personal way, the purpose of the form. This brief introduction orients respondents to how the form relates to them and to how it will be used by the trainer. Without this information trainees often feel apathetic or even suspicious about such forms and do not complete them conscientiously.
2. They do not call for the respondent's name. People generally respond more candidly when their replies remain anonymous.

Form 14–1 seeks a formative evaluation. It is intended for administration at a point midway in a workshop. That might be at the end of the first day, *after* the participants have had an introduction to its purposes and some exposure to the methods used to achieve them and *before* another major segment is to be presented. Of course, there must be time available to adjust some features of the upcoming segment to reflect what has been learned through the formative evaluation about how to make it optimally suited to that group.

Note that it distinguishes between the content and the process of the workshop. It gives the participants a chance to "unload" their personal reactions to the session and provides the leader with a sense of how the group is responding. It is useful for groups of modest size, in workshops where some fine tuning can be done as the program progresses.

Form 14–2 seeks a more detailed formative evaluation. It reminds participants of the steps covered in the workshop and yields a more precise comparison of their reactions to each aspect. It allows for a quantitative comparison between workshops, as well, should one want to compare how one method or topic is received relative to another used on a different occasion.

Form 14–3 is a summative evaluation measure that is intended to provide information of interest primarily to the *organization sponsoring the training program*. Part I stresses issues such as the cost/benefit ratio of the training program, its efficiency and practical utility, and the kind of follow-up that should be planned for it. Part II asks for several items of background information from the participants. These data can be used in two ways. The first is to answer the question, "What group of employees benefit most from this kind of training?" that is, "Who should be sent to this workshop the next time it is offered?" The second is to help explain results which indicate that the training had *mixed* benefits.

Negative reactions sometimes are isolated to a particular subgroup among the trainees. For example, the material might have been too difficult for new employees or "old hat" to more experienced people; those forced to attend might have been resistant to learning; the advertising for it might have been misleading; the workshop might have done its job as well as possible, but the assigned topic may have been inherently dull, unwelcome, or inappropriate for the trainees.

Form 14-4 also is to be administered at the end of the training program, and it provides information of interest primarily to the *trainer*. Part I lists some common elements involved in virtually every training program. Nevertheless, some might be deleted and others added to make it maximally appropriate for specific programs. Part II calls for filling in the training agenda in the left-hand column.

Form 14-5 is another variant on the end-of-workshop form (Fast, 1974). It can be used in addition to any of the others, or it can be administered after the second offering of a workshop that is being repeated. It provides information that helps to clarify the meaning of results obtained from other measures. Sometimes, the items participants rate especially low or high are of minor importance, yet those scores are given equal weight with others that are crucial to trainees. Also, trainees may not like a method used even though it achieves the objectives intended for it. This form takes into account and provides data about the *importance* and *achievement* of each training objective. If each amount in column A is multiplied by the corresponding amount in column B, and those results are tallied, the item scores and the total score provide a useful index of the training's effectiveness. The "Effectiveness Score" for the entire workshop is the total of the item scores divided by the maximum possible total (1000) or, in the example provided, .83.

Trainers should experiment with the design and use of these forms until they believe, in each situation, that the system used to assess learners' reactions provides the information they actually want.

HOW IS TRAINEE LEARNING EVALUATED?

Training programs are established so that participants will leave more competent than they were upon entering. Therefore, assessment of their competence in the target areas of training is the next step in evaluation. What is to be measured at this point depends upon the learning objectives for the program. These can be specified by identifying:

1. The facts they need to know
2. The concepts (principles, theories)
3. The techniques (skills, methods, procedures)

4. The processes involved in identifying where, when, how, with whom to apply appropriately the knowledge learned
5. The attitudes or values that underlie participant acceptance or enthusiasm for the training content

There are two major criteria that an evaluation of learning must satisfy. First, it must validly measure the identified competencies. In other words, it must yield accurate, useful, precise information regarding what the trainees actually know, feel, or can do in regard to the learning objectives.

Second, it should reveal the degree to which it actually was the training experience that affected those competencies. Trainees usually enter a program with some degree of competency already developed. The impact of training is the difference between their ability at the beginning and at the end of that program. There also are ways in which learners can improve without training, for example, simply by picking up information and procedures while on the job. Trainers sometimes want to learn whether or not their training program facilitated more learning than participants had upon entering it, than they would have gained without it, or than they would have gained from another form of training. In this section we explore ways to evaluate learning that meet these two criteria.

The first step is specifying the learning objectives for the program. (This was discussed in detail in Chapter 2.) The next step is obtaining means for measuring the achievement of those objectives. Again, the most expedient method is purchasing a commercially available standardized test, should one be available that addresses those learning objectives. If not, as is often the case, instruments can be developed that do the job for the specific situation at hand. Here the question of "validity" arises. A set of tasks must be identified that can be performed by someone who has the desired competencies and that cannot be done by someone without them.

To prepare such tasks is a two-phase project. The first is developing test items that appear to call for the desired knowledge, attitudes, and/or abilities. The second is administering those items to a "pilot" group, to determine whether people who have the required competencies can complete them successfully (which enables one to eliminate any that are too hard) and to determine whether those who do not have those competencies generally are unable to do them (which provides a means for eliminating any that are too easy). The pilot group, therefore, usually includes a handful of people, some with and some without the requisite expertise. The items that discriminate between these two groups are the ones to be retained for use in the evaluation measure.

Items on the measuring instrument are likely to differ depending on the nature of the learning objectives. The most basic form of learning, *factual knowledge*, can be measured by short-answer questions. There are essentially two kinds: ones that call for *recall* of knowledge (these are assessed by questions which require the respondent to fill in missing information) and ones that call for *recognition* of information (these are assessed by true/false or multiple-choice questions). The choice among these types of questions depends upon how those facts are to be used on the job (that is, must the learner memorize them or can they be looked up whenever they are needed?).

Conceptual knowledge can be tested by short essay questions. Each of these call for the learner to relate an aspect of what was to be learned that can be expressed in three to five lines. This permits a test to cover a fair number of points and enables pinpointing where gaps in knowledge exist. A way of scoring the answers given is to use a scale of 0 to 3.

0 = missed the question entirely
1 = was partially correct, but lacked real understanding
2 = was essentially correct, but omitted a necessary point or was slightly in error in some respect
3 = completely correct; fully answered the question

The ability to carry out the *techniques* or procedures taught need to be assessed in as active and pragmatic a way as possible. Sometimes, a performance test is obvious and simple to devise (for example, when the skill to be taught can be demonstrated readily, as in typing, driving a forklift truck, fixing a broken watch, role playing a preemployment interview, etc.).

Sometimes, more ingenuity has to be employed to devise a means for manifesting a skill. For example, the American Telephone and Telegraph Company wanted to assess their management trainees' sensitivity and empathy for others. They first asked them individually to rank, in order of importance, 10 items dealing with human relations. The trainees were then assigned to groups which worked 15 minutes at the task of arriving at a group ranking of the 10 statements. Following this hurried decision-making period, each person was asked to complete a short inventory, whch included the following questions:

1. a. Were you satisfied with the performance of the group?
      Yes _____ No _____
   b. How many will say that they were satisfied with the performance of the group?
2. a. Do you feel that the discussion was dominated by two or three members?
      Yes _____ No _____
   b. How many will say that they thought the discussion was dominated by two or three members?
3. a. Did you have any feelings about the items being ranked that, for some reason, you felt it wise not to express during the discussion?
      Yes _____ No _____
   b. How many will say that they had such feelings?
4. a. Did you talk as often as you wished to in the discussion?
      Yes _____ No _____
   b. How many will say that they spoke as often as they wished?

Thus, while still at the workshop, students were required to employ one of the empathy skills they had been taught and their accuracy at doing so could be assessed quantitatively (Kirkpatrick, 1976).

As learning goals become more complex, developing useful evaluation methods is increasingly difficult, for example, as we seek to assess whether trainees can *apply appropriately* processes, such as conflict management or problem-solving skills, that must be integrated in the ongoing flow of a committee meeting or at an intense crisis point on the job. One cannot measure validly learning goals that require judgment, timing, tact, patience, and so on, on a written test taken under conditions that are insulated from the pressures of interaction with others. Sometimes, more active evaluation experiences can be incorporated within the context of a training session. These could include simulations or role-playing episodes, such as those discussed in Chapters 7 and 8. The critical ingredient that expands these activities beyond being just practice or try-it-out sessions is the use of systematic feedback, that is, means for recording and comparing trainee behavior in relation to the learning objectives for that program. After each experiential evaluation procedure trainees can assess their own behavior; peers can observe and comment upon what they see; or the trainer can note what is being done and identify instances of competent functioning and approaches that could be improved.

The final domain requiring evaluation is the learner's *attitudes* or values about the training content. It usually is not enough for learners simply to know the ideas a program is intended to teach them; they also must *believe* that those ideas are worthwhile and be predisposed, or even enthusiastic, about putting those ideas into practice. The simplest way to evaluate the attitudes with which learners emerge from a workshop is to include in whatever measurement instrument is used items that call for this information. For example, an item that assesses trainees' *attitudes toward an idea* in management training might be:

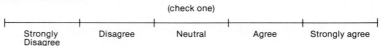

Managers should allow subordinates to decide how they will carry out their own jobs as much as possible.

(check one)

| Strongly Disagree | Disagree | Neutral | Agree | Strongly agree |

An item that assesses trainees' *predisposition to implement an idea* might be:

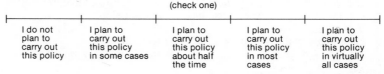

Managers should allow subordinates to decide how they will carry out their own jobs as much as possible.

(check one)

| I do not plan to carry out this policy | I plan to carry out this policy in some cases | I plan to carry out this policy about half the time | I plan to carry out this policy in most cases | I plan to carry out this policy in virtually all cases |

There are several difficulties that must be kept in mind when attempting to measure attitudes. These include:

1. People sometimes report attitudes to which they do *not* subscribe, but which appear in accordance with what they perceive either to be "correct" or what they believe the trainer wants them to say.

2. Many people hesitate to take an "extreme" position at either end of the scale, even if that reflects how they really feel.
3. At a training session, what people believe they will do in the future does not reflect what they actually will do when on the job.

To minimize the distorting effect of these tendencies, it is essential to eliminate any hint of coercion that might be misinterpreted by the trainees. This means doing such things as (1) making it evident that the attitude measure will remain anonymous; (2) making clear it will in no way be used to judge them; (3) assuring them that their honest responses are sought, regardless of whether they agree or disagree with the trainer's; (4) phrasing some items on the form in terms they are likely to check positively and others in ways they are likely to check negatively, so that a response "set" doesn't develop, and they are forced to give each item some thought before responding to it; (5) inserting "distraction" items on related topics, so that what is being measured is not so readily apparent; and (6) administering this form at some point after they have returned to their job setting and have had a chance to digest what the workshop had to offer.

After developing a means for assessing what trainees know, can do, and/or believe, the evaluator must consider how to determine the extent to which the training itself influenced the trainees' scores on those measures. There are several ways of doing this.

The simplest is administering the assessment instruments both before and after the training session. The difference between the pre- and post-training scores indicates how much impact the training had.

Even if this method is used, however, one still does not know whether spending the time given to training in other ways would have been as effective. To answer this question, one would have to split the group of potential trainees at least in half. (This split should be done randomly, so that the two groups essentially are equivalent.) One half is given the training, the other is not. Both groups then take the evaluation measure. To the extent that the group that had the training received significantly higher scores than those who did not, one can make inferences about the impact of training.

A still more definitive way of determining the value of a training program is to compare it to an alternative approach to dealing with its topic. Sometimes, people who have been given training do better simply because they know that something more or different is expected of them. (This is known as the "Hawthorne" effect.) To assess the effect of simply giving them more attention or just focusing on a given topic, the potential training group might be divided into thirds. One-third would receive the planned training program; one-third would receive some special attention, encouragement, or another form of training (for example, a more economical approach, such as reading about the topic) that consumes a comparable amount of time; and one-third would receive no training or special attention at all. The effect of the training would emerge still more clearly if the results of these three groups were compared.

Handbooks of measurement and evaluation provide far more information than can be offered here on design and data analysis for studies of program effectiveness. As these procedures become more controlled and complex they are less commonly included in the routine training plans of functioning practitioners. They are most useful when one is seeking to test the impact of an approach to training that is to be widely circulated to others in the field, by means of a journal article or book, or when an expensive, far-reaching program is to be launched and its value must be assured by pilot-testing sample workshops beforehand.

HOW IS ON-THE-JOB
BEHAVIOR EVALUATED?

Even if evaluation data indicate that trainees have fulfilled the program's learning objectives, one cannot be assured that they actually will transfer or apply those new competencies in their work roles. For example, Kirkpatrick (1976) describes a foreman he had in a workshop whose comments during case-study discussions indicated that he had an extraordinary grasp of human relations principles and techniques. Kirkpatrick then had a chance to speak with someone who happened to work for that man, and he was shocked to learn that on the job he actually was insensitive and dogmatic in dealing with subordinates. That was a revealing lesson about the remarkable discrepancy that can exist between the principles a trainee espouses and what that person really does in practice.

Of course, once the trainees have left the classroom and returned to their jobs, obtaining desired evaluation data becomes much more difficult. This is true for several reasons:

1. Trainees begin to have a greater vested interest in "looking good" to the evaluator. While at the workshop, trainees could ascribe their problems in learning the material to shortcomings in the training. Once back on the job, they themselves resume more responsibility for doing well. They are likely to fear that any inadequacies that are revealed will affect their status. Thus, although self-reports can still be helpful, they must be balanced by the opinions of others as to the competencies of the former trainee.

2. The training program is an environment especially created to encourage the use of new learnings. Sometimes, trainees are inhibited in using what they have learned when they reenter the social world of work. To make full use of training, they need to work in a permissive environment where they are free to try out the new ideas—even throughout the awkward period they may have to endure at the beginning stages. Furthermore, they may need occasional help from someone else who is enthusiastic and skilled in what they are trying to do. Since this kind of support is not always present, an evaluation of on-the-job behavior may require a reading not only of the trainees' behavior, but of the "environmental press" which influences them, as well.

There are several ways to overcome these problems and obtain valid, comprehensive information about how trainees are performing. To avoid the limits of self-report measures, the on-the-job measure should include behavioral indices. Some are obvious: increased sales volume, successful introduction and acceptance of new systems and equipment, reduction of customer complaints. Occasionally, however, such readily observable outcomes are not available.

In these instances, some creative preplanning of measures may provide unobtrusive indications of trainee behavior. For example, 15 supervisors from an insurance company took a course on democratic leadership. Eight were classified as primarily authoritarian on the basis of their behavior prior to the program. During the three-month period immediately following the program, the trainees' behavior was monitored through a study of their interview records. They used standard printed forms that made provision for recording the reason for the interview, attitude of the employee, comments of the supervisor, and action taken, if any. Each trainee was required to make a complete record of each interview. There were 376 interviews with 186 employees. For the evaluation each interview was classified as authoritarian or democratic. The quantity of each type provided useful information on the pragmatic impact of their training (Blocker, 1955).

It is important to note that the supervisors did not know that these records were to be used for an evaluation study. This practice increases the reliability of the data obtained, but it also raises an ethical question about the gathering and use of evaluation data. It would be essential in cases such as the one just described to follow at least two precautions: (1) Individuals' scores should be kept confidential; the results should be reported only as aggregate or group data—or anonymously if they must be tabulated by individuals; and (2) the trainees should be informed after the evaluation is completed about how and why the data were collected, how they were reported and used, and what the results were. These precautions protect the trainees' rights and prevent the training department from gaining a reputation within the organization as espionage agents for higher management.

A second way to get a reading on trainees on-the-job behavior, and simultaneously to learn about the environment in which they work, is to ask people whom they contact to report their observations and opinions of the trainees' behavior. This can include the trainees' superiors, their subordinates, their peers, and other coworkers who might have occasion to observe their use of skills taught in the training session. Tarnapol (1957) reports that five employees are a good minimum for measuring the behavior of their superior. The large number of people who might be involved in a really comprehensive evaluation suggests that a trade-off may be needed between the number of people to be polled for each trainee and the number of trainees to be followed up in an evaluation study. The decision depends on the people best qualified to provide the desired information. Sometimes, only a single supervisor needs to be asked to aid in the evaluation. At other times, the reactions of a full range of coworkers are required to measure trainees' job behavior. In the latter case, it may be expedient to evaluate outcomes for only a sample of the group that was trained. If the results of that study are to prove representative of the entire training group, the group of people selected are best chosen randomly from the large group (for example, every fifth name on the roster, pulling names out of a hat), or they should be chosen randomly from major subgroups within that population (for example, the people from private and public organizations, the people who scored at the high and low extremes on a pretest).

Coworkers' reactions may be elicited through a questionnaire or an interview. Each instrument ought to have two basic dimensions: (1) a checklist designed to record objective indications of the trainee's behavior, to minimize the influence of the observer's own biases; and (2) an opportunity for the observer to offer subjective or overall reactions to that person's behavior.

The first kind of observation may be elicited in a straightforward manner. Form 14–6, Part I, suggests a general format for listing in small "bits" or segments of the trainees' behaviors and for the observers to record how often or how well those behaviors have been used. The rating scales can contain as many subdivisions as needed and the divisions can be labeled in any way that is meaningful to the behavior being evaluated.

If the behaviors are all virtually self-evidently positive, the raters might be inclined to slant their scores in the trainees' favor. In that case, as mentioned before, it would be wise to include in that list several "distracting" items that will disguise somewhat the evaluator's intent. The less raters believe they know exactly what is a "good" and what is a "bad" behavior, the more likely they are to think, when filling out this form, of what the trainee actually does rather than what he/she is "supposed" to do.

Part II provides information that can aid in determining the extent to which the trainees' ratings can be attributed to the experiences provided by the training program. This question might be better answered if the raters would fill out Part I at two points in time; before and after the training program. Sometimes, however, this is not possible or is too time consuming. Their recalled ratings can provide a more convenient, if somewhat less accurate means of obtaining this information.

Part III asks for raters to fill in the degree to which they perceive that the target behaviors are important, their attitude toward the target behaviors, and how they overtly react to them. These scores help to provide a basis for understanding the context in which the trainees must apply what they learn. The results on this part of the observer rating form might be compared to those on the first part. People are unlikely to carry out learned behaviors if their coworkers generally do not perceive them to be important, do not like them, and/or do not encourage their use. At times, low transfer scores—from workshops that deal with sensitivity training, for example—are attributable to negative reactions from people in the back-home environment rather than from ineffective training programs.

HOW IS ORGANIZATIONAL IMPACT EVALUATED?

Most training programs are directly or indirectly financed by the organizations that employ the people who participate in them. Hence, a fundamental issue in evaluation is assessing the degree to which the functioning of the sponsoring organization has been affected by that training. When we shift from looking at the behavior of specific individuals to looking for evidence that quantifies their impact on the organization in which they work, we face an increasingly demanding challenge.

The most important step is identifying indices that reveal how effectively an organization is operating. For business the ultimate criterion is the "bottom line." Zemke (1977) proposes the following formula: the organization's earnings before taxes, less the actual cost of the training program, divided by the compensation and benefit costs for the portion of the work force that receives training. If this margin improves over time, the training process is paying off.

However, there is a major limitation of "bottom line" measurement that should be kept in mind when evaluating training impact: It is a lagging indicator of what is going on in the organization. Profit figures actually show the effects of organizational units and their personnel at an earlier time—sometimes six months, a year, or even two years behind the performance of the persons involved in a training program. Hence, the first step in measuring training results must be looking at short-term indicators.

Donaldson and Scannell (1978) offer a more detailed breakdown of the ways the outcomes of training can be manifested:

1.   Direct cost reductions
2.   Grievance reductions
3.   Productivity of trained versus untrained employees
4.   Productivity after versus before training
5.   Work quality
6.   Quantitative results
7.   Accident rates
8.   Absenteeism
9.   Employee suggestions
10. Supervisory ratings
11. Profits
12. Sales volumes
13. Turnover rates
14. Customer complaints
15. Worker efficiency
16. Training time required for proficiency
17. Cost per untrained employee
18. New product development
19. New customers
20. Public relations [Pp. 138–139]

The impact of training on a sponsoring organization differs depending on the purposes that the organization is intended to fulfill. For example, Glaser (1976, p. 279) suggests a number of criteria for outcome measures that are differentiated according to the needs of three common employers:

OUTCOME MEASURES

Manufacturing	Social Service	Local Government
Direct labor cost in relation to units produced (or percent of yield from so much input of raw material)	Volume of cases handled Percent of successful outcomes	Financial solvency Costs of labor and equipment for particular services Cost-of-living statistics and tax rate compared with other, similar cities
Reject rate or process losses Machine downtime due to equipment malfunction	Average time required for satisfactory closure of a case Cost of services per case	Periodic ratings by citizenry regarding quality of services to the community, broken down by categories such as crime statistics, compared with comparable cities Range and adequacy of services provided compared with those of similar cities
Number, type, and disposition of labor grievances per month	Number, type, and disposition of labor grievances per month	Number, type, and disposition of labor grievances per month
Employee absenteeism rate Employee turnover rate Tardiness rate Safety performance Ability to adhere to a schedule	Staff absentee-rate Staff turnover rate Tardiness rate Safety performance Ability to adhere to a schedule	Employee absenteeism rate Employee turnover rate Tardiness rate Safety performance Ability to adhere to a schedule
Index of employee satisfaction with the work situation	Index of staff satisfaction	Index of staff satisfaction

HOW ARE ADDITIONAL OUTCOMES EVALUATED?

The process of training itself can have effects that extend well beyond the learning objectives consciously intended for it. These include its impact on the learners, the trainer, the sponsoring organization, and people not directly associated with the training program at all.

Learners can gain increased satisfaction, stimulation, and pride in the work that they do. The experience of learning new ideas and methods can be an inherently gratifying event, which enhances one's morale and keeps a job feeling fresh and invigorating. In an era in which worker alienation and anomie reportedly are increasing, training experiences offer a countervailing force. They can give an employee a sense of being recognized, affirmed, and supported. Often, new learnings that are useful on the job also have relevance in situations elsewhere (for example, at home, with friends, and in the community). We have taught workshops dealing with a wide range of communication and problem-solving skills that trainees subsequently have reported to be extremely useful in their interactions with people in many other settings. Of course, the improved well-being that comes from a private life in which the learners are relating successfully with others carries over into their attitudes while at work. Their growth in skillfulness at effectively applying workshop principles—which comes from practicing dealing with people in the recommended ways after hours—also has residual benefits on the job. If the trainer should wish to measure these learner outcomes, a simple questionnaire can be drawn up that asks directly about the extra gains that he/she suspects are occurring.

Trainers can benefit from their own training experiences, as well. Learning events in which all parties feel stimulated, surprised, and/or personally expanded generally are the most successful. There is an inherent liveliness and an underlying validation of the trainees' self-worth when they sense that the workshop leaders are learning from their contact with them. The process of professional growth can continue at every training event if trainers consciously seek input from the people they face. This process is more likely to provide honest and thorough information if a systematic approach is taken. Form 14–7 is a sample of an instrument that can be used for this purpose.

Organizations also reap several "extracurricular" gains from the training programs that they sponsor. Recruitment of personnel, particularly those who perceive themselves to be upwardly mobile in technical and/or managerial positions, is facilitated for a company that has an outstanding training program. Appropriate career counseling can be provided by a trainer who has an opportunity to see what employees can do in tasks unrelated to their current positions. A training program also builds loyalty and productivity among personnel. As Watson (1979) states:

> The mere act of engaging in training goes a long way in conveying the message to members of the organization that on-going improvement and personal development are important matters and that the organization values good management. This helps to establish and strengthen desirable organizational norms, such as keeping members up to date in their own fields and encouraging them to remain mentally active. There is a tremendous difference in the climates and the levels of performance of organizations that have these kinds of norms and those that do not. [P. 310]

Finally, *society* at large is enriched by people who can do their jobs well and who enjoy them. These people contribute their skills to the professional, religious, political, and service groups they join; they are more mentally and physically healthy; and they carry out a share of their town and nation's economic performance. We are all interdependent and to that extent worthwhile training benefits everyone.

HOW ARE EVALUATION
RESULTS REPORTED?

Our emphasis throughout this chapter has been on designing evaluation systems that accurately answer questions people genuinely want answered. The same question-answer approach applies to report writing. It is tempting either to omit this final task before completing a training program or to use it as an opportunity to put out the whole story of a workshop, from its inception to everything the participants said about it afterward. Instead, trainers need to ask themselves: "What do the readers of this report really want to know?", "What would turn them off?", and "What do I want this report to accomplish for me?"

Most readers want the following:

1. A very brief initial orientation to what the report is about and what it contains (who it is intended for, who it is from, what can be learned from it, etc.)
2. A summary of what was done in the training, the evaluation process, and the major findings and conclusions obtained after analyzing the evaluation data. Generally, it would be wise to confine the summary of the training and evaluation to one paragraph each and to report the evaluation findings and conclusions in a series of one sentence bits of information (and/or in vivid tables or graphs). If appropriate, they can be divided into the five kinds of evaluation discussed in this chapter.
3. At this point, if the report is neat, concise, and informative, the readers' basic needs have been met and the major shortcomings of reports—sloppiness, burdensome length, and confusion or inaccessibility of information—have been avoided. The next concern is what the trainer wants to highlight in the report. This might be any message he/she wants to leave in the minds of its readers, such as the cost-effectiveness of the program, the need for follow-up sessions, the way unexpected results might be interpreted, and recommendations for future programs.
4. Finally, in subsequent sections, or in appendices, which are clearly headed and easily followed, there might be included for future reference by various readers material such as:
    a. A list of training objectives
    b. An outline of the training program
    c. A roster of participants
    d. A copy of evaluation instruments
    e. Tabulation of evaluation results
    f. A list of statements made on evaluation forms
    g. The budget for the program
    h. A narrative account of the whole program
    i. Any other material that would be informative for someone who wanted to know what happened in that program

A complete evaluation report can provide useful feedback not only to those who participated in the program, but also to those who will be involved with the same training topics, trainee population, or sponsoring organization in the years to come.

FORM 14–1 *MIDPOINT PARTICIPANT REACTION FORM*

Purpose: Thus far, you have gotten a sense of the goals and methods to be used in this workshop. In order to make it a maximally valuable experience for you, I would like to learn your reactions to what we have done thus far and whatever you have to suggest regarding the remainder of our time together. I will use the information compiled from these forms to make what is to come as relevant to your needs as I possibly can.

I.   The topic(s) or idea(s) (the content) that I valued *most* in today's session:

II. The topic(s) or idea(s) that I found *least* valuable in today's session:

III. The method(s) of presentation or activities (the instructional methods) I found *most* useful in today's session:

IV. The method(s) of presentation or activities that I found *least* useful in today's session:

V.   My message to you about how our next session can be most valuable to me:

VI. My message to you about what I'd like like to see minimized in our next session:

FORM 14–2 *MIDPOINT PARTICIPANT REACTION FORM*

Purpose: Thus far, you have gotten a sense of the goals and methods to be used in this workshop. In order to make it a maximally valuable experience for you, I would like to learn your reactions to what we have done thus far and to what is planned for the remainder of our time together. I will use the information compiled from these forms to make what is to come as relevant to your needs as I possibly can.

1. My evaluation of the goals pursued thus far have been:

(Check one)

Goals	Minimal Value				Great Value
	1	2	3	4	5
a. [To be filled in with	___	___	___	___	___
b. the topics, attitudes,	___	___	___	___	___
c. skills that were stressed	___	___	___	___	___
d. in the preceding	___	___	___	___	___
e. session(s)]	___	___	___	___	___

2. My tentative evaluations of the goals we plan to cover in the coming session are:

(Check one)

Goals	Minimal Value				Great Value
	1	2	3	4	5
a. (To be filled in with	___	___	___	___	___
b. the topics, attitudes,	___	___	___	___	___
c. and skills to be addressed	___	___	___	___	___
d. in upcoming sessions)	___	___	___	___	___
e.	___	___	___	___	___

3. My evaluation of the methods we have used thus far have been:

(Check one)

Methods (Examples are provided below)	Minimal Value				Great Value
	1	2	3	4	5
a. Lecture	___	___	___	___	___
b. Film	___	___	___	___	___
c. Case study	___	___	___	___	___
d. Role playing	___	___	___	___	___
e. Group problem solving	___	___	___	___	___
f. Large-group discussion	___	___	___	___	___
g. Working in pairs	___	___	___	___	___

4. Wherever you have evaluated a method of learning as 3 or below in the item above, would you explain what diminished its value for you and suggest what, if anything, would have to be done (by me, yourself, the other participants) to make this approach more useful to you in the upcoming session(s).

5. Please add any message to me about what you found worthwhile in our preceding session(s) and what you would like to see happen in our upcoming one(s):

PART I

Purpose: The items below assess the overall value of this training experience.

1. Did you find the quality of this program to be (select one):

   ____ ____ ____ ____ ____
   Poor   Fair   Average   Good   Outstanding

2. Do you feel that this program was worthwhile in terms of its cost and your time away from normal job duties?

   yes _____   no _____   undecided _____

3. Would you recommend this program to your peers?

   yes _____   no _____   undecided _____

4. Rate the program for the qualities listed below:

	Poor				*Outstanding*
	1	2	3	4	5
a. Practical value	____	____	____	____	____
b. Thoroughness	____	____	____	____	____
c. New ideas gained	____	____	____	____	____
d. Helpful to self-development	____	____	____	____	____
e. Relevance to your job	____	____	____	____	____
f. Efficient use of time	____	____	____	____	____
g. Maintaining your interest	____	____	____	____	____
h. Clear, understandable	____	____	____	____	____

   Comments:

5. Check the degree to which the kinds of follow-up to this workshop listed below would be useful:

	Necessary	*Desirable*	*Unnecessary*
a. Talking with some workshop members to share experiences in applying ideas	____	____	____
b. Opportunity to consult with trainer if a problem arises	____	____	____
c. Advanced workshop in this area	____	____	____
d. Briefing for my superiors on what I've learned here	____	____	____
e. Other	____	____	____

PART II

The following information is sought to determine whether specific groups of people respond differently to this training program. It will *not* be used to identify you, only to analyze the results in terms of *group* averages. Check one space for each question:

1. Sex: Male _____   Female _____

2. Years in present job: 0–1 _____   1–2 _____   2–5 _____   5+ _____

3. Age: 20–30 _____   30–40 _____   40–50 _____   50–60 _____   60+ _____

4. Previous training experience:
   None on this topic _____
   One other on this topic _____
   Two on this topic _____
   Three or more _____

5. I volunteered _____ was told _____ to take this workshop.

6. This workshop provided what I expected it to _____, what I did not expect _____.

7. I believe _____, I do not believe _____ I needed training on this topic.
   (If you checked "I believe," answer the next item.)

8. This workshop met my needs as well as possible. _____
   This workshop would have met my needs better if taught differently. _____

FORM 14–4   *WORKSHOP EVALUATION FORM*

Purpose: We will be continuing to offer workshops on this topic in the future. For those to be of greatest possible value, we would appreciate your reactions to the experiences provided in this one. Would you rate each aspect of the workshop listed in the left-hand column below and add your comments on how any aspect can be improved.

PART I

		POOR 1	2	3	EXCELLENT 4	5
1.	The information you received beforehand Comments:	___	___	___	___	___
2.	The match between how this was advertised and what it was Comments:	___	___	___	___	___
3.	The general setting, your accommodations Comments:	___	___	___	___	___
4.	The arrangement of the room Comments:	___	___	___	___	___
5.	The refreshments and food Comments:	___	___	___	___	___
6.	The materials you received Comments:	___	___	___	___	___
7.	The overall topic Comments:	___	___	___	___	___
8.	The value of the ideas that were presented Comments:	___	___	___	___	___
9.	The opportunities provided to apply them Comments:	___	___	___	___	___
10.	The likelihood that you will use them in your job Comments:	___	___	___	___	___
11.	The thoroughness, the breadth of our coverage of the topic Comments:	___	___	___	___	___

FORM 14–4 (*Continued*)

12. The specificity, the depth of our coverage
    of the topic   ___ ___ ___ ___ ___
    Comments:

13. The length of the workshop   ___ ___ ___ ___ ___
    Comments:

14. The timing of segments, of breaks   ___ ___ ___ ___ ___
    Comments:

15. The sequence, the organization of the material ___ ___ ___ ___ ___
    Comments:

16. The use of visual aids   ___ ___ ___ ___ ___
    Comments:

17. Your ability to hear and see presentations   ___ ___ ___ ___ ___
    Comments:

18. The discussion of specific examples   ___ ___ ___ ___ ___
    Comments:

19. The friendliness, the frankness of the class
    interaction   ___ ___ ___ ___ ___
    Comments:

20. The organization and coordination of the
    program   ___ ___ ___ ___ ___
    Comments:

PART II

For each specific topic and activity listed below, please check one of the reactions provided:

	OK as is	Expand it	Shorten or eliminate it	Change it
1. [List here	___	___	___	___
2. each topic covered	___	___	___	___
3. and every method used	___	___	___	___
4. to deal with it	___	___	___	___
5. (lecture, case study,	___	___	___	___
6. question-answer session,	___	___	___	___
7. etc.)]	___	___	___	___

FORM 14-5 *EVALUATING ACHIEVEMENT OF OBJECTIVES*

Purpose: Our workshop was designed to achieve the objectives listed in the left-hand column below. We want to know how well we realized those aims, especially in regard to their importance to you. Please read the instructions below, and allocate points to each objective as described under columns A and B.

Objectives:	*A:* Degree of Importance	*B:* Degree of Satisfaction
Read the list of workshop objectives below. Put a check next to those that are important to you. (Ignore those that are not.) For those you have checked, fill in columns A and B.	Weight each checked objective for its importance to you, allocating exactly 100 points among all of those checked. A total of 100 points must be assigned. If you checked only one objective, assign all 100 points to it; if you checked two or more objectives, spread the 100 points among them.	Rate each checked objective from 0 to 10 to indicate how well it was fulfilled. 0 = unsatisfactory 10 = excellent

(Sample objectives and ratings for a workshop on conflict management)	*A*	*B*	
1. Understand how conflict can have a positive effect on honest, creative work relationships.	*10*	*10*	*(100)*
2. Distinguish between win/ lose and win/win definitions of a disagreement	*20*	*9*	*(180)*
3. Express dissatisfaction with the status quo, without blaming the other person	*30*	*8*	*(240)*
4. Understand when cooperation is more appropriate than competition	—	—	
5. Defend a point of view that opposes one they currently hold	*25*	*7*	*(175)*
6. Identify several points on a continuum extending from their own opinion to an opponent's viewpoint	*15*	*9*	*(135)*

(Effectiveness score = .83)

FORM 14–6 *BEHAVIOR RATING FORM*

Purpose: We are asking your help to learn the long-range effect of our recent training program. The person listed below was a participant. Your report of his behavior in regard to the items in the left-hand column will be kept strictly confidential, will not affect his/her job status in any way, and will help us to improve the usefulness of the training that we provide.

Person being evaluated _____

Date _____ Course _____

Observer _____

PART I

Essential aspects of skill being measured	Rating scale [Place a check (✓) at the appropriate point]
Essential aspect 1	
Essential aspect 2	
Essential aspect 3	
•	
•	
•	
Essential aspect 7	
Overall rating of skill	

PART II

This part will help us to determine the extent to which the training program affected this participant's behavior. Would you go back over the rating scales now and put an "✕" at the points which best represent how you would have rated the person *before* the training took place. If it would have been no different than you rated him/her now, put your "✕" on top of the " ✓ " you made before (" ✕ ").

PART III

In this part we would like to learn how you yourself react to each of the behaviors listed on the preceding page, that is, how you *feel* about it and the extent to which you *express* that opinion. Would you rate them according to which point on the following scales best applies to you:

	Relative importance (expressed as a percentage)	5 = always like it 4 = usually like it 3 = neutral 2 = dislike it 1 = always dislike it	5 = often encourage it 4 = occasionally encourage it 3 = express no opinion 2 = occasionally discourage it 1 = often discourage it
Essential aspects of the skill being measured:			
Essential aspect 1	_____	1 2 3 4 5	1 2 3 4 5
Essential aspect 2	_____	___ ___ ___ ___ ___	___ ___ ___ ___ ___
Essential aspect 3	_____	___ ___ ___ ___ ___	___ ___ ___ ___ ___
•			
•			
•			
Essential aspect 7	_____	___ ___ ___ ___ ___	___ ___ ___ ___ ___
Overall reaction	100% Total	___ ___ ___ ___ ___	___ ___ ___ ___ ___

FORM 14–7   *INSTRUCTION EVALUATION FORM*

Purpose: I would appreciate your reactions to the instruction I have provided in this workshop. Your candid responses will be helpful in my self-awareness and growth as a trainer. Please write in a specific comment beneath any item rated "poor" or "fair." Thank you for taking the time to complete this for me.

		Poor	Fair	Good	Excellent
A.	Provided reasons for what was done				
B.	Ideas were clear, understandable				
C.	Ideas were novel, informative				
D.	Pace of presentations (slow, appropriate, fast)				
E.	Interrelated ideas				
F.	Examples to illustrate ideas				
G.	Related ideas to my job concerns				
H.	Receptivity to alternative views				
I.	Responses to questions				
J.	Use of visual aids				
K.	Sticking to important topics versus dealing with side issues				
L.	Summarizing of ideas				
M.	Use of language in presentations				
N.	Body language in presentations (gestures, position in room, eye contact)				
O.	Overall sequence of program				
P.	Leadership of active learning methods (those used can be listed here)				

    1.

    2.

    3.

Q.	Value of handouts				
R.	Control of group				

BIBLIOGRAPHY

ADAMS, JOHN. "The Use of Syndicates in Management Training," in *Training and Development Handbook*, 2nd ed., Robert Craig (ed.). New York: McGraw-Hill, 1976.

ARGYRIS, CHRIS. *Intervention Theory and Method: A Behavioral Science Method*. Reading, Mass.: Addison-Wesley, 1970.

BACH, RICHARD, and P. GOLDBERG. *Creative Aggression*. New York: Avon Books, 1974.

BANDLER, RICHARD, and JOHN GRINDER. *Frogs into Princes: Neuro-linguistic Programming*, John O. Stevens (ed.). Moab, Utah: Real People Press, 1979.

BECKHARD, RICHARD. "The Confrontational Meeting," *Harvard Business Review*, 45 (March–April 1967), 149–155.

BEISSER, ARNOLD R. "The Paradoxical Theory of Change," in *Gestalt Therapy Now*, Joen Fagan and Irma Lee Shepherd (eds.). New York: Harper & Row, 1970.

BENNIS, WARREN, and HERBERT A. SHEPARD. "A Theory of Group Development," in *Sensitivity Training and the Laboratory Approach*, Robert Golembiewski and Arthur Blumberg, (eds.). Itasca, Ill. F. E. Peacock, 1970, pp. 91–115.

BERNE, ERIC. *Games People Play*. New York: Grove Press, 1964.

BLAKE, R. R., and J. S. MOUTON. *The Managerial Gird*. Houston, Tex.: Gulf, 1964.

BLOCKER, C. E. "Evaluation of a Human Relations Training Course, *Journal of the ASTD*, May–June 1955.

BOSS, WAYNE R., and MARK L. McCONKIE. "An Autopsy of an Intended OD Project," *Group and Organization Studies*. 4, no. 2 (June 1979), 183–200.

BOULDING, ELISE. *Women in the Twentieth-Century World.* New York: Halstead Press, 1977.

CAPELLE, RONALD G. *Changing Human Systems.* Toronto: International Human Systems Institute, 1979.

CAPRA, FRITJOF. *The Tao of Physics: An Exploration of the Parallels Between Modern Physics and Eastern Mysticism.* Boulder, Colo.: Shambhala, 1975.

CASEY, DAVID, and DAVID PEARCE (eds.). *More Than Management Development: Action Learning at GEC.* New York: American Management Associations, 1977.

CHIN, ROBERT, and KENNETH BENNE. "General Strategies for Effecting Changes in Human Systems," in *The Planning of Change,* Warren Bennis, Kenneth Benne, and Robert Chin (eds.). New York: Holt, Rinehart and Winston, 1969.

DAVIS, LARRY NOLAN. *Planning, Coinducting and Evaluating Workshops.* Austin, Tex: Learning Concepts, 1974.

DEIKMAN, ARTHUR. "Bimodal Consciousness," in *The Nature of Human Consciousness,* Robert Ornstein (ed.). San Francisco: W. H. Freeman, 1968.

DONALDSON, LES, and EDWARD SCANNELL. *Human Resource Development.* Reading, Mass.: Addison-Wesley, 1978.

EAKINS, BARBARA, and GENE EAKINS. *Sex Differences in Human Communication.* Boston: Houghton Mifflin, 1978.

EGAN, GERARD. "Model A: The Logic of Systems as OD Instrument," in *The Cutting Edge: Current Theory and Practice in Organization Development,* Warner Burke (ed.). San Diego, Calif.: University Associates, 1978, pp. 105–110.

ENGEL, HERBERT M. *Handbook of Creative Learning Exercises.* Houston, Tex.: Gulf, 1973.

FAST, DOROTHY. "A New Approach to Quantifying Training Program Effectiveness," *Training and Development Journal,* September 1974.

FIEDLER, FRED. *Leadership.* New York: American Management Association, 1977.

FRENCH, WENDELL L., and CECIL H. BELL. *Organization Development: Behavioral Science Interventions for Organization Improvement.* Englewood Cliffs, N.J.: Prentice-Hall, 1973.

FRIEDMAN, PAUL. *Interpersonal Communication: Innovations in Instruction.* Washington D.C.: National Education Association, 1978.

HOCKER, JOYCE, and WILLIAM W. WILMOT. *Interpersonal Conflict.* Dubuque, Iowa: Wm. C. Brown, 1978.

GIBB, JACK. "Defensive Communication," *The Journal of Communication,* 11, no. 3 (September 1961), 141–148.

GIBB, JACK. *Trust: A New View of Personal and Organizational Development.* Los Angeles: The Guild of Tutors Press, 1978.

GLASER, EDWARD M. *Productivity Gains Through Worklife Improvements.* New York: Harcourt Brace Jovanovich, 1976.

HASTORF, ALBERT H., DAVID J. SCHNEIDER, and JUDITH POLEFKA. *Person Perception.* Reading, Mass.: Addison-Wesley, 1970.

HERSEY, PAUL, KENNETH BLANCHARD, and RONALD HAMBLETON. "Contracting for Leadership Style: A Process and Instrumentation of Building Effective Work Relationships," in *The Cutting Edge: Current Theory and Practice in Organizational Development,* Warren Burke (ed.). San Diego, Calif.: University Associates, 1978, pp. 214–238.

HINRICHS, JOHN R. "Personnel Training," in *Handbook of Industrial and Organizational Psychology.* Chicago: Rand McNally, 1976, pp. 829–860.

HORNEY, KAREN. *Our Inner Conflicts.* New York: W.W. Norton, 1945.

HOVLAND, C. I., and W. WEISS. "The Influence of Source Credibility on Communication Effectiveness," *Public Opinion Quarterly*, 15 (1951), 635–650.

JAMES, MURIEL, and DOROTHY JONGEWARD. *Born to Win: Transactional Analysis with Gestalt Experiments.* Reading, Mass.: Addison-Wesley, 1971.

JONGEWARD, DOROTHY. *Everybody Wins: Transactional Analysis Applied to Organizations.* Reading, Mass.: Addison-Wesley, 1973.

JONGEWARD, DOROTHY, and DRU SCOTT. *Women as Winners: Transactional Analysis for Personal Growth.* Reading, Mass.: Addison-Wesley, 1976.

KIESLER, C. A. *The Psychology of Commitment: Experiments Linking Behavior to Belief.* New York: Academic Press, 1971.

KILMANN, RALPH, and KENNETH THOMAS. "Interpersonal Conflict—Handling Behavior as Reflections of Jungian Personality Dimensions," *Psychological Reports,* 37 (1975), 971–980.

KING, STEPHEN. *Communication and Social Influence.* Reading, Mass.: Addison-Wesley, 1975.

KIRKPATRICK, DONALD L. "Evaluation of Training," in *Training and Development Handbook,* 2nd ed., Roger Craig (ed.). New York: McGraw-Hill, 1976.

LAIRD, DUGAN. "Learner Controlled Instruction," in *Training and Development Handbook,* 2nd ed., Robert Craig (ed.). New York: McGraw-Hill, 1976.

LEE, IRVING J. *Customs and Crises in Communication: Cases for the Study of Some Barriers and Breakdowns.* New York: Harper & Brothers, 1954.

LEWIN, KURT. *Field Theory in Social Science.* New York: Harper & Brothers, 1951.

LIEBERMAN, MORTON A. "Behavior and Impact of Leaders," in *New Perspectives on Encounter Groups,* Lawrence Solomon and Betty Berzon (eds.). San Francisco: Jossey-Bass, 1972, pp. 135–170.

LIPPITT, GORDON. *Visualizing Change: Model Building and the Change Process.* La Jolla, Calif.: University Associates, 1973.

LIPPITT, GORDON, and RONALD LIPPITT. *The Consulting Process in Action.* San Diego, Calif.: University Associates, 1978.

LOVELUCK, CLIVE. "The Construction, Operation, and Evaluation of Management Games," in *Training and Development Handbook,* 2nd ed., Roger Craig (ed.). New York: McGraw-Hill, 1976.

LOWEN, ALEXANDER. *Bioenergetics.* New York: Penguin Books, 1976.

MAGER, ROBERT, and PETER PIPE. *Analyzing Performance Problems.* Belmont, Ca.: Fearon Publishers, 1970.

MASLOW, ABRAHAM. *The Psychology of Science.* Chicago: Henry Regnery Company, 1966.

McGREGOR, D. *Human Side of Enterprise.* New York: McGraw-Hill, 1960.

MONGE, PETER R. "The Systems Perspective as a Theoretical Basis for the Study of Human Communication," *Communication Quarterly,* 25, no. 1, (Winter 1977), 19–29.

PALAZZOLI, MARA, LUIGI BOSCOLO, GIANFRANCO CECCHIN, and GIULIANA PRATA. *Paradox and Counterparadox: A New Model in the Therapy of the Family in Schizophrenic Transaction.* New York: Jason Aronson, 1978.

PETERS, THOMAS J., and ROBERT H. WATERMAN, JR. *In Search of Excellence.* New York: Harper & Row, 1982.

PFEIFFER, J. WILLIAM, and RICHARD HESLIN. *Instrumentation in Human Relations Training.* San Diego, Calif.: University Associates, 1973.

PIGORS, PAUL. "Case Method," in *Training and Development Handbook,* 2nd ed., Robert Craig (ed.). New York: McGraw-Hill, 1976.

POLSTER, ERVING, and MIRIAM POLSTER. *Gestalt Therapy Integrated.* New York: Vantage Books, 1973.

PREZIOSI, ROBERT C. "Organizational Diagnosis Questionnaire," in *The 1980 Annual Handbook for Group Facilitators*, J. W. Pfeiffer and John Jones (eds.). San Diego, Calif.: University Associates, 1980.

REICH, WILHELM. *Character Analysis,* 3rd ed. New York: Orgone Press, 1949.

ROGERS, CARL R. *Freedom to Learn.* Columbus, Ohio: Charles E. Merrill, 1969.

ROSSITER, CHARLES M., and W. BARNETT PEARCE. *Communicating Personally: A Theory of Interpersonal Communication and Human Relationships.* Indianapolis, Ind.: Bobbs-Merrill, 1975.

RUBEN, BRENT D. "General Systems Theory: An Approach to Human Communication," in *Approaches to Human Communication*, Richard Budd and Brent Ruben (eds.). New York: Spartan Books, 1972.

RUBEN, BRENT. "Communication and Conflict: A System-Theoretic Perspective," *Quarterly Journal of Speech*, 64 (1978), 202–210.

SATIR, VIRGINIA. *Peoplemaking.* Palo Alto, Calif.: Science and Behavior Books, 1972.

SCHEIN, EDGAR H. *Process Consultation: Its Role in Organization Development.* Reading, Mass.: Addison-Wesley 1969a.

SCHEIN, EDGAR H. "The Mechanisms of Change," in *The Planning of Change*, 2nd ed., Warren Bennis, Kenneth Benne, and Robert Chin (eds.). New York: Holt, Rhinehart and Winston, 1969b, pp. 98–108.

SCHUTZ, WILLIAM. *FIRO: A Three-Dimensional Theory of Interpersonal Behavior.* New York: Holt, Rhinehart and Winston, 1958.

SIMMONS, DONALD D. "The Case Method in Management Training" in *Training and Development Handbook*, 2nd ed., Roger Craig (ed.). New York: McGraw-Hill, 1976.

SINGER, JUNE. *Androgyny: Toward a New Theory of Sexuality.* Garden City, N.Y.: Anchor Press, 1976.

STANLEY, CHARLTON S., and PHILIP G. COOKER. "Gestalt Therapy and the Core Conditions of Communication Facilitation: A Synergistic Approach," in *The Growing Edge of Gestalt Therapy*, Edward W. L. Smith, (ed.). New York: Brunner/Mazel, 1976, pp. 160–178.

STEINER, CLAUDE. *Scripts People Live: Transactional Analysis of Life Scripts.* New York: Grove Press, 1974.

STOCKARD, JAMES G. *Career Development and Job Training.* New York: AMACOM, 1977.

TARNAPOL, LESTER. "Evaluating Your Training Program," *Journal of the ASTD*, March–April 1957.

TRUNGPA, CHOGYAM. *The Myth of Freedom and the Way of Meditation*, John Baker and Marvin Casper (eds.). Boulder, Colo.: Shambhala, 1976.

WALTON, RICHARD. "Two Strategies of Social Change and Their Dilemmas," *The Journal of Applied Behavioral Science*, 1, no. 2 (1965), 167–179.

WARREN, MALCOLM W. *Training for Results*, 2nd ed. Reading, Mass.: Addison-Wesley, 1979.

WATSON, CHARLES E. *Management Development Through Training.* Reading, Mass.: Addison-Wesley, 1979.

WATTS, ALAN. *Tao: The Watercourse Way.* New York: Pantheon Books, 1975.

WATZLAWICK, PAUL, JANEL BEAVIN, and DON JACKSON. *Pragmatics of Human Communication.* New York: W. W. Norton, 1967.

WATZLAWICK, PAUL, JOHN WEAKLAND, and RICHARD FISCH. *Change: Principles of Problem Formation and Problem Resolution.* New York: W. W. Norton, 1974.

WEISBORD, MARVIN R.   "Organizational Diagnosis: Six Places to look for Trouble with or Without a Theory," *Group and Organizational Studies*, 1, no. 4 (December 1976), 430–447.

WIGHT, ALBERT R.   "Participative Education and the Inevitable Revolution," *Journal of Creative Behavior*, 4 (Fall 1970).

WILMOT, WILLIAM W.   *Dyadic Communication: A Transactional Perspective*, 2nd ed. Reading, Mass.: Addison-Wesley, 1980.

YARBROUGH, ELAINE.   "A Collaborative Perspective of Social Influence," paper presented to the Western Speech Communication Association, Los Angeles, February 1979.

YARBROUGH, A. ELAINE.   "Intrapersonal Conflict: A Neglected and Necessary Level of Interpersonal Conflict Analysis," in *Public Communication: Perception, Criticism, Performance*, A. Goldman (ed.). Melbourne, Fla.: Robert E. Krieger, 1983, pp. 361–375.

ZEMKE, RON.   "Measuring the Impact of T & D," *Training*, October 1977.

INDEX